SELLING
THROUGH
SOMEONE ELSE

HOW TO USE **AGILE SALES NETWORKS AND PARTNERS** TO SELL MORE

ROBERT WOLLAN • NAVEEN JAIN
MICHAEL HEALD

WILEY

John Wiley & Sons, Inc.

Published by John Wiley & Sons, Inc., Hoboken, New Jersey.
Published simultaneously in Canada.

For general information about our other products and services, please contact our Customer Care Department within the United States at (800) 762-2974, outside the United States at (317) 572-3993 or fax (317) 572-4002.

Wiley publishes in a variety of print and electronic formats and by print-on-demand. Some material included with standard print versions of this book may not be included in e-books or in print-on-demand. If this book refers to media such as a CD or DVD that is not included in the version you purchased, you may download this material at http://booksupport.wiley.com. For more information about Wiley products, visit www.wiley.com.

ISBN 978-1-118-49638-1 (cloth); ISBN 978-1-118-52622-4 (ebk);
ISBN 978-1-118-52630-9 (ebk); ISBN 978-1-118-52652-1 (ebk)

Printed in the United States of America

10 9 8 7 6 5 4 3 2 1

Contents

Section II
THE NEW AGILE SELLING MODEL AND STRATEGY   91

Section III
BUILDING THE BETTER NETWORK—POSITIONING FOR SUCCESS AND EFFECTIVENESS   201

Preface

As Accenture has worked to help organizations of various shapes, sizes, and industries improve their growth and operational performance, one tenet has become abundantly clear to us: The selling (getting it sold) and service (keeping it sold) agenda for most companies is increasingly complex and, as such, delivering growth is a massive challenge for virtually every organization—large and small, in all regions of the world.

With sales models that have experienced, at best, incremental change in the past several decades (despite sweeping changes in technology and customer behaviors) it is not hard to imagine why companies can't keep up. Yet there are organizations that are succeeding in navigating their way through the complex web of vendors, competitors, service providers, distributors, resellers, and customers that play a part in their ultimate growth. Many of these organizations share a common trait: They have adapted their sales models with the times. They have embraced what we call *Agile Selling* models that are based, at least in part, on selling through someone else—that is, a broader mix of intermediaries, other channel partners, and even customers that extend companies' reach and growth. Agile Selling is the model of choice among the leaders in industries that have the most complex distribution channels and that thrive even with a highly independent partner network. Other companies have much to learn from these leaders' experiences.

In studying and working with companies around the world, we've identified the layers of "baggage" built up in sales operations that would become obvious, and could be corrected, if each step in the process acted as if they had to earn the right to serve their downstream business partner. Think about it: If you didn't own your sales force, how much more important would it be to optimize every step of your incentive compensation, your lead generation, your pricing, or your talent management? If every function and person in your organization had to justify—and continually improve—their performance in order to keep providing their services to you, how might that affect the performance of your overall sales organization? The path to selling through someone else is not a general theory; rather, it's a model based on the best practices—and the deepest, richest capabilities—gleaned from the companies that deal with the greatest market and channel complexity, face ongoing and heightened market volatility, and often operate with the tightest margins: those that sell through someone else.

The time is right—and the need is imminent—to realign, redefine, and refocus the selling model and fundamentally transform the principles that guide it. That's why we've written this book.

This book is different from most selling theory or methodology books you see cluttering bookshelves. It's based on our collective experience working with companies all over the world to dramatically transform their selling model, and it gets very specific about which elements of the sales model need updating and which specific areas you can change to infuse new growth and profitability. The book also brings in guidance from numerous other Accenture professionals with deep knowledge and experience in each of the underlying capabilities required to support the new Agile Selling model. And it shares the specific experiences of leading companies that have transformed the way they sell and the way they support their selling ecosystem.

In the opening section of the book, we explore why companies must embrace the elements of an Agile Selling model that makes greater use of sales resources not employed or owned by the sales function. We also describe what the Agile Selling model looks like in practice. From there we look at the experiences of companies in four industries that already rely heavily on the Agile Selling model—consumer goods manufacturing, electronics and high-tech, pharmaceuticals, and insurance—and highlight what other firms can learn from leaders in those industries.

We then dig more deeply in Section II into the core capabilities companies need within their organization to bring the Agile Selling model to life—including lead generation, incentives, pricing, and analytics. In Section III, we turn to what it takes to "build a better network" that extends far outside the walls of the organization and capitalizes on new market opportunities. Section IV explores the core infrastructure needed to sustain the relationships with customers, channel partners, and other entities that are critical to Agile Selling. Then, in the final section of our book, we devote our attention to the dimension that's arguably most critical to the success of the Agile Selling model: people.

If you're reading this book, you likely share some responsibility for driving growth in your organization—whether you're the CEO, Chief Sales Officer, Chief Customer Service Officer, CIO, head of human resources, or maybe all of those as a small or medium-size business owner. Regardless of your specific area of focus, we're glad you're joining us on this journey and hope that you find the insights on the following pages valuable and helpful to you as you consider how you can better position your sales organization to capitalize on the abundant growth opportunities before you.

SECTION

I

The Rising Impact of Sales and Distribution: Why "Good Enough" Isn't Enough Anymore

The amount of change the world has undergone in the past 10 years is truly astounding. The Internet has become virtually the center of life and commerce for people all over the world, serving as the main platform on which we entertain and educate ourselves, purchase goods and services, and stay in touch with friends, family, and companies with which we do business. Increasingly powerful, pervasive, and connected mobile devices are providing access to the Internet's content as never before while redefining the computing model—and, in the process, dramatically altering how and when customers buy. And the market for companies' offerings truly has become global, with emerging markets now taking center stage as not only the loci of growth but also the source of innovations that are making their way back to developed markets.

These momentous developments also have wreaked havoc with most companies' growth plans. Organizations used to the status quo have had a difficult time keeping up with the pace of change in the markets they serve. Most are struggling to fully digest these shifts, determine the implications of these shifts for their business, and make the changes to their organizations that will enable them to compete effectively in today's world. One of their biggest obstacles to change are the sales models they have relied on for far too long. Models that have not been updated in the past decade (or even longer)—even if they have served sales organizations well in the past—are likely flawed and not up to the challenge of delivering what sales needs, to be both effective *and* efficient today. In the opening section of the book, we explore in more detail the challenges companies—and their sales leaders—face in meeting their growth goals in a rapidly changing world, and why those challenges signal a need for companies to embrace a shift toward a sales approach that makes greater use of sales resources not employed or "owned" by the sales function. We also discuss in detail the core elements of this new approach—which we call *Agile Selling*—and outline how existing sales strategies must change to support such a shift.

We end this section by exploring how the Agile Selling model has proven highly effective for companies in the consumer goods, pharmaceutical, insurance, and high-tech industries, and what companies in other industries that are increasingly complex, global, and volatile can learn from these Agile Selling pioneers.

1

Why It's Time to Change Selling

Your Sales Model Is Broken

Robert Wollan

Chapter Summary

- Four powerful forces are driving sales improvement programs today—and they affect virtually every company in mature and developing markets.
- Uncertainty, complexity, and operational complications are blocking most ambitious growth plans, but companies can't put off dealing with them any longer.
- Companies are struggling with profitable growth, often because they are using outdated and ineffective sales channel models, which do not reflect recent major changes in markets.

Butch Cassidy: What's the matter with you?

Sundance Kid: I can't swim.

Butch Cassidy: Are you crazy? The fall will probably kill you.
         —*Butch Cassidy & the Sundance Kid*, Universal Studios, 1969

Forced to the edge of a cliff by forces out of their control, Butch Cassidy and the Sundance Kid utter these classic lines when facing the reality that they will need to jump for a chance to survive. It also illustrates the challenge facing sales leaders today. Forced to the edge of a cliff by market forces beyond *their* control—low-cost competitors, rising costs, and declining margins—today's sales leaders find themselves focused on areas where their capabilities are not strong (Figure 1.1).

The problem, like Butch Cassidy and the Sundance Kid, is that they are worried about drowning when the fall might actually kill them. Sales leaders might drown if they don't improve their sales execution, but the "fall" that might kill them (and that they should be even more worried about) is hidden in the foundational flaws of their sales model. Companies, big and small, are facing the reality that the complexity that has built up in their systems has left them without the agility needed to seize new growth.

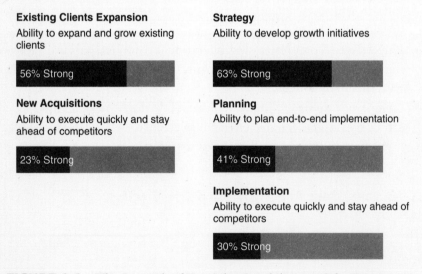

Existing Clients Expansion
Ability to expand and grow existing clients

56% Strong

New Acquisitions
Ability to execute quickly and stay ahead of competitors

23% Strong

Strategy
Ability to develop growth initiatives

63% Strong

Planning
Ability to plan end-to-end implementation

41% Strong

Implementation
Ability to execute quickly and stay ahead of competitors

30% Strong

FIGURE 1.1   The Strength of Key Sales Capabilities in Sales Executives' Minds

Source: Innovation & Growth Survey, March 2006; The Economist Intelligence Unit.

Even worse, today's sales leaders are in the unenviable position of driving growth in a volatile global marketplace, where growth opportunities are not as abundant or apparent as they used to be, even just a few years ago. In fact, in a recent survey of CEOs and chief sales and operations officers, only a small percentage think it is much easier today than two years ago to expand to new markets (16 percent), increase sales to existing customers (21 percent), and acquire new customers (17 percent).[1]

To compete at a high level and drive sustainable growth, today's sales leaders must make both sales execution and operations improvements *and* face a potential major structural problem of their current sales model—the need to become more agile and respond faster to new opportunities. The question is: Are they ready to leap?

Four Challenges Sales Leaders Face

In many ways, these sobering realities come with the top sales job. They are intractable issues that increase the blood pressure of every sales leader. But to make matters worse, a newer set of dynamics is making life even tougher for sales leaders. In particular, there are four distinct challenges to business growth and performance that every sales leader must confront. We call them the *A-B-C-Ds* of the new selling environment:

1. **A**—**A**nomalies
2. **B**—**B**lind spots
3. **C**—**C**onsumerism
4. **D**—**D**iversions

A—Anomalies: Are Your Sure-Fire Tactics Still Working?

As baseball fans know, every great pitcher has his "go-to" pitch—the fastball, slider, curve, or knuckleball he can count on when he absolutely has to get a batter out. Like that go-to pitch, sales executives always have relied on a few important tactics to drive sales and revenues. However, just like the pitcher who suddenly discovers batters have made the necessary adjustments to be able to consistently hit his go-to pitch, sales leaders are finding that those traditional levers are not delivering the results they used to.

Three levers, in particular, we see falling short in today's markets: "More, More, More" strategies; new product introductions; and price cutting and promotions.

When growth stalled in the past, sales leaders typically responded by "doing more"—adding *more* field salespeople, *more* marketing campaigns, or *more* channel partners. Unfortunately, in many industries, the efficacy of these practices has been eroding for quite some time. Simply adding more of the same no longer delivers the kind of returns companies need.

The second lever that doesn't work as well as it used to is new product introductions. Increasing the number of new products under development is a tried-and-true approach to spurring growth. The most successful product innovators in the past outperformed their less-innovative competitors across business cycles not just by coming up with better new products, but also by bringing to market *many more* new products. In one study, 30 percent of companies surveyed more than doubled their number of offerings in five years while only 1 percent decreased offerings in the same period.[2] These companies could count on new offerings to lift sales, market share, and profits. But more recently, many companies' new product pipelines produce far fewer predictable results. Respondents to the same study indicated that the breadth of product portfolio complexity had numerous negative impacts on their organization, from pressures on cost competitiveness to longer lead times, lower product quality, and reduced customer satisfaction. When it comes to direct sales impact, 29 percent reported portfolio complexity had a negative impact on sales effectiveness.[3]

Price cutting and promotions is the third lever whose effectiveness has declined. In the past, companies could count on gaining customers and revenues by lowering prices. But price promotions no longer deliver a durable lift in sales because they are so easily matched by competitors. For example, the mobile phone industry saw the price drop dramatically for phone service (voice) for commercial customers and consumers after phone numbers could travel with the customer from one provider to another. In the race to attract customers and the popularity of online/e-mail offers, prices became more visible and the time it took to be replicated by a competitor dropped. Price-cutting episodes are especially debilitating for companies whose competitors have lower cost structures. These competitors can more readily fight a price war, knowing the company that started the war time and again is the one that eventually will lose it. Instead of being forced into a competitive price reduction strategy, what is needed today to gain customers is a way to bring additional value to them through enhanced products and services.

The failures of "doing more," underwhelming product introductions, and price promotions that fizzle make it even more difficult for sales executives to hit their targets.

B—Blind Spots: Can You "See" the Changes in the Market and Translate Data into Insights into Actions?

You've invested in sales technology, and maybe even have given some new tools to your channel partners. So why aren't sales rising? Chances are you've got "blind spots" in your sales vision. You may be lacking the ability to do something with the huge volumes of information that are rushing in daily in today's increasingly digital and mobile world. Many organizations aren't proficient at sensing, evaluating, and responding to the data that's coursing through their sales systems. This sales analytics and insights problem is common even in companies that are using analytics in other parts of the business, and can obscure important industry trends that will affect sales results.

In many cases, the analytics problem stems from a paucity of the right data or the completeness and quality of the data they do get. In a business-to-business setting, this often results from a lack of access to a channel partner's relevant data regarding end customers. For instance, in the high-tech industry, it's common for manufacturers to sell their equipment through a vast and varied network of resellers, distributors, and other partners. A reseller based in Dallas may have a stable of 200 customers to which it sells the manufacturer's products. But if the manufacturer lacks access to data on who is buying the products, this becomes a blind spot. The manufacturer won't be able to fully understand its market share and opportunities in that market: exactly what kinds of companies are buying its equipment, how they are using and benefiting from the gear, and what other needs the manufacturer could fill. Add to this multiple partners that sell in overlapping markets, and the data holes become even more troubling.

Yet even if such companies had most or all of the data their sales organizations need, most wouldn't be able to use it to its full potential. This is because they lack a strong in-house analytics capability. They can't analyze the entire sales value chain—the sequence of events that begins when a salesperson or channel partner contacts a potential customer and ends when something is sold, delivered, and used. Without a strong analytics capability, they can't accurately understand how well their sales approaches, sales teams, and salespeople are performing. They also can't incisively determine how well their channel partners are doing. This, in turn, prevents companies from becoming highly proficient in a number of important sales domains: determining the optimal number of reps to allocate to a product line; understanding whether to organize sales teams by geography or customer segment; determining how to attract, develop, and keep strong salespeople; and deciding on the best channel to market for each customer segment. (We explore the topic of analytics in detail in Chapter 9.)

Without the fact base and analytics capabilities we describe earlier, salespeople have to rely solely on judgment and instincts. These are great qualities—especially when they are grounded in deep experience. They can be indispensable. Many premier salespeople become top performers because of their unusual ability to read a situation and instinctively "know" what to do. But competing on gut instincts, even those perfected over many years, has become hazardous to sales in just about every industry. The reason is that the business world is far more complex today.

The game is playing out among the sales organizations of large companies today. Those with the (a) best data on customers, competitors, salespeople's performance, and other key aspects of getting and keeping customers; and (b) best capabilities for analyzing that data are pulling ahead of rivals with poor data and old ways of analyzing it.

C—Consumerism: Are You Ready for New Consumer Demands, and Is Your Sales Channel Agile Enough to Respond Faster Than Your Competitors?

Consumers have become less patient, more informed, and more demanding. Two decades ago, companies shipped products at their convenience. Remember the typical message you received before or after placing an order: "Please allow six to eight weeks for delivery"? Tell that to a consumer today for many products and you're likely to lose her business. A built-to-order laptop computer in two months? Now it takes just a few days. Razor blade refills that aren't easy to find in stores and will take a week to replenish? You can get them online overnight.

If you sell consumer products or services through wholesalers and retailers, you'll easily relate to these consumer dynamics. But even if you focus on business-to-business products farther upstream, these consumer dynamics will affect you, too. Sales leaders are confronted with changing consumer dynamics that require companies to take a fresh look at how to provide greater value to all the parties that bring their products and services to market. Four such dynamics stand as the gaps to fill first:

1. *Consumers' expectations are rising*. Since 2007, Accenture has surveyed tens of thousands of consumers from around the world on what they expect of the companies they buy from. In 2007, only one-third said that their expectations were higher than they were the year before. In late 2011, 44 percent of more than 10,000 consumers surveyed told us their expectations had risen over the prior 12 months (Figure 1.2). This trend is especially evident in emerging markets: 59 percent of consumers surveyed in emerging markets (compared with 31 percent of those in mature markets) said their expectations had increased in the past year. Rising expectations are wreaking havoc on companies' efforts to develop long-term plans, and are requiring organizations to be much more agile in their planning and the executing of programs—whether such programs involve their own sales forces or channel partners.

   Are you and your sales channels aligned to today's expectations or are you always playing catch-up?

Change in Expectations—Global Sample

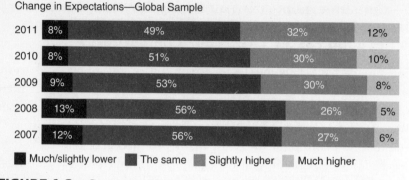

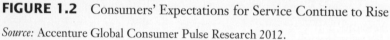

FIGURE 1.2 Consumers' Expectations for Service Continue to Rise

Source: Accenture Global Consumer Pulse Research 2012.

2. *Consumers are going digital.* The rapid adoption of the Internet, smartphones and tablets has put incredible shopping power in the hands of consumers. It's like a wave crashing onto the desk of the sales leader. One survey found that 80 percent of consumers around the world use the Internet to research their purchases of electronics, computers, books, music, and movies before they buy them in a store.[4] An Accenture survey on buyers of wireless communications products found 75 percent of consumers surveyed used the web to research products before they bought them in stores.[5] In other words, consumers can easily compare your products to your competitors' products on price, value, and availability. In fact, in addition to all this great buying information, consumers who use social media can also get their friends' opinions before the store clerk has a chance to say, "How can I help you?"

Many smart consumers are taking this an extra step. They are going to stores to see, touch, and try out a product, then are ordering it online from another company—a practice known as "showrooming." Showrooming has become even easier with the advent of powerful smartphones and price-comparison apps such as the Find®. These apps enable consumers to scan a product's barcode and immediately see which other nearby retailers and online merchants have the item and at what price. Showrooming is particularly prevalent in consumer shopping for electronics products, and has taken a big chunk of revenue from the stores of consumer electronics retailers. Attempting to stem the tide, Target Corp.® has asked suppliers for help by creating products that would be sold only through its more than 1,760[6] stores, hoping to minimize price comparisons.[7]

Although the Internet and the mobile devices connected to it have been a boon to consumers, they have become a major source of anxiety to many sales leaders of large companies. The largest channel partners are expecting their suppliers to help them deal with the digital wave. You can expect the margins of such suppliers to be pinched as they comply with the mandates of their largest channel partners, especially big retailers. Will digital capabilities enhance your ability to attract new customers, or will your competitors beat you to the punch?

3. *Consumers are less loyal, but want more recognition for staying with a company*. Given everything we've stated thus far, it should be no surprise that Accenture's Global Consumer Pulse research found consumers to be less loyal than they used to be. Our 2011 study[8] found only one in four consumers surveyed felt "very loyal" to the companies from which they bought products and services. Just as many professed no loyalty at all.

Consumers increasingly expect to be rewarded for being good customers. It's one reason why participation has been rising in loyalty programs across most of the industries we surveyed (Figure 1.3). For example, 53 percent of consumers in this Accenture study were part of at least one retailer's loyalty program in 2011, compared with only 45 percent in 2009. And 31 percent of bank customers were part of at least one loyalty program in 2011 versus 18 percent in 2009. But this isn't enough; consumers want more than rewards and recognition. They want companies to know more about them, their needs, and their history with their products. Between 2009 and 2011, our research saw a 14-point increase in the percentage of consumers surveyed who expected customer service representatives to be more knowledgeable about them. All this means consumer loyalty is diminishing, but consumers remain interested in loyalty programs and recognition—programs that place a strain on the entire supply chain and further erode the profitability of each

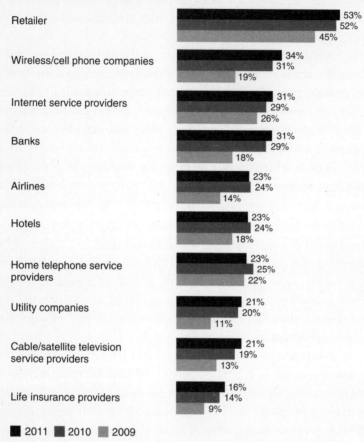

Loyalty program participation
(at least one program)

Retailer — 53%, 52%, 45%

Wireless/cell phone companies — 34%, 31%, 19%

Internet service providers — 31%, 29%, 26%

Banks — 31%, 29%, 18%

Airlines — 23%, 24%, 14%

Hotels — 23%, 24%, 18%

Home telephone service providers — 23%, 25%, 22%

Utility companies — 21%, 20%, 11%

Cable/satellite television service providers — 21%, 19%, 13%

Life insurance providers — 16%, 14%, 9%

■ 2011   ■ 2010   ■ 2009

FIGURE 1.3   Consumer Participation in Loyalty Programs Has Been Rising across Most Industries

Source: Accenture Global Consumer Pulse Research 2012.

sale. It begs the question: Did you even evaluate your channel partners' loyalty programs when you chose them?

4. *Consumers will switch faster than ever before.* We don't mean to paint most consumers as overly fickle, as willing to drop a provider instantly for another that offers a better deal. In fact, one of the biggest findings from our 2012 Global Consumer Pulse Research is that consumers reported higher satisfaction with their providers

in all 10 of the service dimensions of the sale (or postsale) that we asked them about. In fact, satisfaction levels on three service characteristics—being able to resolve questions/issues on their own without speaking to a service agent, the amount of time it takes to completely resolve their issue or problem, and the amount of time they have to wait to be served—jumped more than five percentage points in 2011. But companies shouldn't get too comfortable. Despite being more satisfied, two-thirds of consumers switched providers in at least one industry in 2011 because of poor customer service.[9]

Which of your salespeople and which of your channel partners can best capitalize on consumers/customers looking for something new, or thinking about taking their business elsewhere?

D—Diversions: Did All Those New Tools Deliver, or Were They Diversions with Not-So-New Results?

For many years, successive technology innovations helped continually boost the sales organization's ability to grow the business more efficiently or more effectively. However, in the past decade, such support has stalled. In some cases, technology has undermined sales performance. The last great leap in technology-enabled sales force productivity was the sales force automation/effectiveness (SFA/SFE) of 10 to 20 years ago. Companies outfitted their salespeople with laptop computers and more advanced tools for tracking leads and managing their contacts. But since the exciting early days of SFA/SFE, technology advancements have mostly failed to deliver substantial results for the sales organization. According to the 2012 CSO Insights® Study, fewer than 15 percent of organizations achieved improved win rates from implementing sales tools—mobile or otherwise.[10] To make matters worse, more than 85 percent of organizations surveyed did not increase revenue from technology deployments and more than 90 percent did not reduce the time it takes to close a sale.

The culprit: the "dueling complexities" faced by the chief sales officer and chief information officer. The main complexities for CSOs are proliferating channels to market, new and more nimble competitors, more geographically dispersed and diverse customers, and an explosion in the number and types of products and services the typical company provides.

The complexities for CIOs include heightened *internal* data and technology complexity in the form of rigid legacy systems created over several decades (Figure 1.4). These complexities clash today: CSOs need tools that can make them more agile and better equipped to respond to *external* changes in the marketplace, while CIOs have to integrate and streamline their existing infrastructure to support the needs of today's modern business.

Even when their sales organization has effective technology, many companies don't arm their channel partners with the same capabilities. They thus starve their channel partners of information that's become crucial to winning over customers. Companies may grant channel partners access to some data, but they don't fully give the partners what they need to maximize their effectiveness. The mind-set of parceling

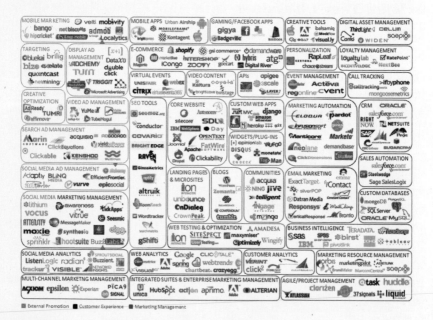

FIGURE 1.4 The Complex Sales and Marketing Technology Landscape

Source: Scott Brinker @chiefmartec, www.chiefmartec.com.

out the technology capabilities and information that can make the sale runs counter to the principles of an efficient ecosystem of partners.

Stumbling Blocks to Change

Although a wide variety of challenges exist for the sales leader today, by far the biggest impediment to change is that companies have been relying on the same basic sales models for decades. Your sales model may not have kept up with other change and is not equipped to support the kind of sales operation necessary to thrive in today's global marketplace. In fact, we argue that companies that are looking for sustainable, profitable growth should start by fixing this fundamental problem.

Today, many companies use some combination of three principal channel models (Figure 1.5). Although each has its strengths and weaknesses, many models remain inherently flawed in their current state due to what they try to optimize and their lack of evolution as the market has changed.

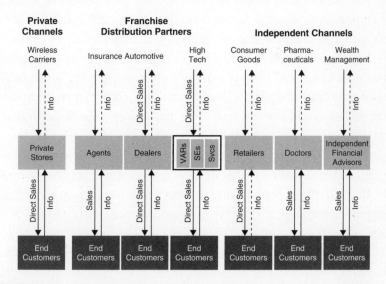

FIGURE 1.5   The Three Basic Sales Models Most Companies Rely on Today

Private Channels

The most traditional sales model is organized around the "owned" sales force (which today also includes an online direct channel). A private sales force is likely to be found in many, if not most, companies, especially those in the pharmaceutical, telecommunications, commercial banking, and real estate industries.

The private sales force model has many strengths, all of which relate to the issue of control: As all members of a private sales force are employees of the company, a firm can more easily exert its influence over them and their work. For instance, a company has direct control over the entire talent management process—from recruiting and hiring to performance management—which enables it to bring on board salespeople with the skills the company needs (or develop those skills, if necessary, through training programs). With this model, the company has the greatest flexibility in sales coverage, campaign execution, and opportunity management (especially with cross-product line sales). It also has full access to market data, the sales pipeline, and performance data, which allows the firm to craft more effective strategies and responses to changes in market conditions. And it has direct visibility into and management of pricing.

For all its strengths, the private sales force model also has substantial weaknesses. It can be very expensive, as the company is responsible for not only line salespeople, but also the associated layers of management and operations resources. The sales force's reach is limited by fixed capacity in fixed locations, and can't penetrate closed markets (i.e., those that are owned by product integrators). And owned sales forces are expensive and difficult to scale rapidly to capture emerging demand.

Beyond these limitations, private sales forces also suffer most from enterprise responses to economic downturns, as broad headcount freezes slow the adoption of new sales models. Furthermore, in most companies, a lack of reliable demand and individual sales performance data makes fear the biggest obstacle to action, as companies have strong concerns over cutting the wrong areas and putting current sales revenues at risk. And because many companies use a standardized one-size-fits-all compensation model for their own sales forces, their ability to accommodate more specialized selling resources is significantly constrained.

Franchise Distribution Partners

The franchise distribution "partner" model is common in industries such as insurance (agents), electronics and high technology (value-added resellers and integrators), automotive (dealers), industrial machinery (dealers), and restaurants and bars (franchises). With this model, a company benefits from its partners that are "on the ground" in desired markets—and, thus, are highly aware of local competitive changes and customer needs—as well as from partners that are entrepreneurs and typically motivated to perform at a high level. In addition, the franchise distribution partner model provides some semblance of consistency in how the company is represented by partners through the use of standardized processes, technologies, and marketing programs. And, with such a model, a company has access to external or private capital, which enables it to diversify its risk and require less of its own capital to expand.

On the other hand, companies using such a model often find they have less control in reality than expected due to product exclusivity requirements and contractual obligations. For example, an automotive manufacturer cannot unilaterally close during its own restructuring. Furthermore, such models can suffer from inconsistent talent quality and management, as the company has much less visibility into and control over how individual partners hire, fire, and direct salespeople. Similarly, inconsistent local execution can be a problem, as partners have considerable discretion in how they run their business.

Several other factors make the franchise distribution partner model an impediment to change. For one, channels are themselves struggling with adapting to the change—often distributors don't have any better access to data than the companies they represent. Additionally, consolidation over time has changed the landscape from a single, autonomous channel network to one that has significant differences between "large" and "small" partners, including gaps in scale, maturity, industry specialty, and selling tools. And an adversarial relationship can develop between partners and the company: Inherent distrust of "corporate" can lead to gaps in customer, product usage, and marketing effectiveness data, while partners may push back on requirements to invest in marketing programs, systemwide technology, or other capital improvements (which subsequently can slow, fragment, or dilute the ambition of change programs).

Independent Channels

At the opposite end of the spectrum from private sales forces is the independent distribution "partner" model. This model is typified by companies such as independent insurance agents who can sell policies from any insurance company they choose; third-party aggregators such as Sysco® or U.S. Foodservice®, which sell a wide variety of branded food and food-service items to cafeterias, bars, restaurants, and customers that are likely too small for manufacturers to serve directly; and retailers, which carry brands and products from dozens or hundreds of manufacturers. The common thread is that independent partners are free to carry and promote what they can sell, regardless of who produces it.

For companies upstream, independent agents enable simplified distribution and operations: The network provides the operational horsepower. Such agents also can help companies extend their reach into untapped markets (because of agents' lower cost of entry) or access closed markets (for instance, by having exclusive contracts with government agencies). And there are lower barriers to switching: If a company finds another agent that appears to be better aligned with its value proposition, there's generally nothing preventing the company from signing up that new agent.

The downsides of the independent distribution model are virtually the inverse of the strengths of the private sales force: very little control over partners' operations (unless the company makes a substantial investment, such as a wireless company paying to have its own reps on the floor of a retailer partner); and little to no visibility into customer data (and inherent disincentives for the partner to share such data). Additionally, there's nothing to prevent the partner from pushing competing products if it thinks they will sell better. Thus, a company is constantly jockeying with other providers for a more favorable position with the partner.

There are two other reasons the independent distribution model is inherently inefficient. The first one is unclear acquisition, selling, and support practices of the independent channels. Independent operators may acquire unprofitable or unqualified customers, given the lack of control a company has over their selling process. The financial service mortgage crisis exposed this risk for banks, which took over loans generated by independents. More often, the risks are less extreme—for example, retailers that don't understand or explain the full range of a provider's products to shoppers—but they nonetheless undermine the provider's marketing and sales investments.

The second reason is exposure to the operational risk of downstream partners. The varying degree of operational and technical maturity of downstream partners can undermine any operational savings from using an independent network, because offering improvements can prove to be much costlier—or even prohibitive—than the benefit they'd generate.

Conclusion

There's never been a more important time for sales leaders to step up and lead. They and the overall sales channels they lead are the key to predictable, sustainable, and profitable growth in today's volatile marketplace. But doing so requires overcoming obstacles, many of which are significant and entrenched.

In the next chapter, we explore some of the opportunities sales leaders have to change their selling model, and we introduce an approach that leading companies are using to capture those opportunities.

The Solution—Agile Selling

Growth Can Come from Investing in Your "Selling Force," Not Just Your "Sales Force"

Robert Wollan

Chapter Summary

- Sales organizations have not shown sustainable improvements in core sales metrics (overall conversion, quota attainment, retention) in the past five years. It is time to try something different.

- Most companies look at their competitors for innovation ideas, and miss the opportunity to adopt better ideas from other industries. Start by looking at industries with more complex markets and selling environments than your own. What are their secrets to success in driving profitability?

- Agile Selling—the next evolution of the selling model—builds on your current distribution strengths, but recognizes the role that customers, social media, employees, and other key influencers have on the sales process.

- Well-performing sales organizations get seven things right that can be applied across industries and around the world.

Given the challenges discussed in Chapter 1, business as usual is virtually guaranteed to be a recipe for sales teams that will be either too slow, too poorly armed, in the wrong place (or all of the above) to compete in changing markets. On the other hand, leaders who adapt quickly can grab market share and expand faster. Today's market is very much about the shift from "the big eating the small" to "the fast eating the slow."

As we've studied and worked with a vast array of B2B companies around the world, we've recognized there are organizations already employing new approaches to selling that are helping them address the market challenges we laid out in the previous chapter. This new sales model will help separate the winners from the losers in the coming years. We call this new model *Agile Selling*. The core tenet of the Agile Selling model is making greater use of selling forces not "owned" by the company. This can be accomplished by combining next-generation sales analytics, significant changes to the internal sales team/operations, creative extensions of the selling ecosystem with new partners, and empowering the entire ecosystem with new tools.

Agile Selling is not entirely new, in that it incorporates the most important and effective elements from the franchise and fully independent sales models long employed by leading companies in the consumer goods manufacturing, pharmaceutical, high-tech, and insurance industries. Indeed, for years, the companies in these industries have had to build and sustain high-value relationships with channel partners outside of their own sales forces—whether it be retailers and distributors for consumer goods companies, physicians for pharmaceutical firms, agents for insurance companies, and integrators and resellers for high-tech organizations. In fact, these companies' very success has hinged on how well they can identify the right channel partners to go to market with and through; create the right relationship with those partners that benefits all parties involved; and deploy the right processes, systems, and other resources to help partners sell successfully.

The experiences of these industries, which we explore in more detail in Chapter 5, illustrate how Agile Selling can provide the flexibility, accountability, and responsiveness necessary to capitalize on growth opportunities in today's new economic environment. Making greater use of the Agile Selling model, companies can:

- Increase sales: Develop a wider and deeper network of selling partners by becoming their "partner of choice."
- Increase profitability: Leads are converted at higher rates via channel optimization.
- Increase reach: Access closed markets by engaging channel partners with established relationships.
- Increase accuracy and insights: Channel partners trust and share critical sales and planning information, because it is in their best interests to do so. In the process, their insights become yours.
- Improve individual sales performance: Using better tools, training, and execution that is analytically based and technology-powered via mobility, the cloud, and digital waves.
- Reduce sales operations costs: Value-added steps are taken better and faster, while wasted steps are eliminated.
- Reduce complexity: Increased network complexity (where it adds value) is offset by widespread decreases in operating and technology complexity that slows response and overall sales cycle time.

In many ways, *Moneyball*® is analogous to Agile Selling. As Michael Lewis's 2003 book so eloquently laid out, the front-office personnel and field scouts running major league baseball teams operated for years on their instincts about how to evaluate players.[1] (Imagine these individuals as the sales force.) The "old-timers" believed their experience was the best tool for predicting which "customers" to acquire—that is, the players who would be the most productive team members.

But by the early 2000s, a new breed of baseball front-office executives entered the field, including Oakland A's General Manager Billy Beane, the protagonist of *Moneyball*. Armed with uncommon data and the analytics capabilities to understand it, these executives complemented the gut instincts of the old-timers with far more rigorous, fact-based approaches to evaluating talent. One of the most important findings was to uncover players who got on base (through hits and walks) at a much higher rate than those who didn't, especially those who struck out often. Such analytics capabilities enabled Oakland, a team with very low payroll, to consistently make the playoffs. The As outsmarted their much bigger competitors (teams with much greater revenue and payrolls) by having better data about the game of baseball and far better insights (supported by that data) about what led to wins.

Although the As did benefit from Beane's new thinking—they were able to make the playoffs consistently for several years with a payroll a fraction of the big-market teams—the real winners were the Boston Red Sox. The Red Sox front office looked for insights they could glean from the desperate moves by a margin-strapped team such as Oakland, adapted the insights to its own team, and then optimized the results: the team's first World Series championship in more than 80 years (which was followed by another championship three years later).

In effect, the *Moneyball* approach was the catalyst for baseball executives, a guiding principle that helped teams break free of the limitations of the model that was built and refined over a century, but that was losing relevance and effectiveness as the market changed around them. The Agile Selling model serves a similar function for B2B executives. And like the Boston Red Sox front office, innovative B2B sales leaders today will look at winners in industries that have effectively used such an execution model and take steps to move closer to that approach.

What Leading Companies Get Right

We explore the specific elements of the Agile Selling model in greater detail in the next chapter. But for now, let's take a look at what the companies that use this model most effectively get right.

They Redefine the Boundaries of Their Business

Many companies today still draw fairly sharp distinctions between themselves, their customers, their suppliers and other channel partners, and their competitors. Companies that are leaders in using the

FIGURE 2.1   Redefining the Business Boundaries: Who "Sells"

Agile Selling model have no such distinctions—instead, recognizing and accepting that the "dynamic ecosystem" is a permanent way of doing business (Figure 2.1).

Agile Selling companies define their "enterprise" not solely as their own company, but rather the amalgamation of key suppliers, channel partners, and others that are vital to developing, producing, and bringing to market their products. High-tech companies are great examples. A typical computer, for instance, is the product of a tightly integrated ecosystem: contributions from myriad partners all along the high-tech value chain in strategic locations around the world, including those that make the chips, the hard drives, the keyboards, and the display screens, as well as those that assemble the finished machine. Without embracing a broader definition of "enterprise," no single company could effectively satisfy its customers' demands for the latest in computing technology.

Leaders also have a different way of defining their "sales force." They recognize that many other entities beyond their "official" salespeople can and do influence the sales of their products. Inside the company, that includes sales support functions and call center employees, as well as other enterprise employees who can be mobilized to spot and feed new opportunities to the sales team. For example, while companies can encourage their employees to always be on the lookout for potential new business possibilities, leaders have formal ways to gather and process what employees uncover—such as an internal leads website through which employees can enter promising opportunities. PepsiCo® encourages its employees to spot new opportunities—like a restaurant opening or new building construction—and enter them on their leads site (www.iwanttoservepepsi.com) as employee referrals (see Figure 2.2). This not only generates more qualified leads, it builds an "always selling" culture.

FIGURE 2.2 PepsiCo Customer and Employee Lead Generation

Source: www.iwanttoservepepsi.com.

Outside the company, the sales force includes consumers and customers who can be instrumental in "talking up" the products—something that is especially important now that consumers have the powerful megaphone known as social media. One example of the importance that word of mouth still has on sales: In Accenture's 2012 Global Consumer Pulse Research, 79 percent of consumers globally said that "information from people I know" influenced their purchase decisions.[2] The point is, Agile Selling leaders understand the power and importance of these "other sales people" and make sure they include them as such in their sales strategies and programs.

Finally, Agile Selling leaders have an equally fluid definition of "competitors." In an Agile Selling model, companies that are competitors in one market often can be close allies in another. This view is a departure from the notion of "co-opetition" to a recognition that everybody has an opportunity to collaborate with everybody else for mutual benefit. That's a radically new definition of what constitutes "competition." (We discuss how to create such a collaborative selling relationship, which we call a "joint initiative," in Chapter 11.)

Agile Selling Companies Create a "Faster Front Office"

The pace of change in today's markets means that companies must dramatically increase how quickly they can respond to customer demands and competitor actions. Agile Selling companies have done so by decreasing the cycle time of processes that span sales, marketing, and service (Figure 2.3).

In most companies, response to market changes is often hampered by the silos among the traditional functions of sales, marketing, and service. Such silos slow campaign development and execution, impede the flow of customer data and insights, and result in inconsistencies across the myriad touch points companies use to interact with customers.

Agile Selling Leaders, on the other hand, have succeeded in forging a tighter relationship among these three front-office functions and, as a result, get a much stronger return on their investment through demand generation and fulfillment. One of the ways they've been able to create a tighter relationship is by identifying specific processes in which they could reduce complexity and cycle time to create a more efficient and agile organization.

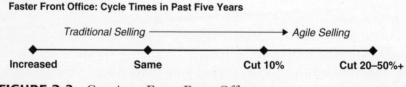

Faster Front Office: Cycle Times in Past Five Years

Traditional Selling ——————————→ Agile Selling

| Increased | Same | Cut 10% | Cut 20–50%+ |

FIGURE 2.3   Creating a Faster Front Office

To get a sense of the "speed" of your business today, track how long it takes from the time an idea or new sales opportunity is proposed to the time it rolls out as available to customers. When we ran this analysis for a mid-size communications company, decision makers there were shocked to find that it took an average of 19 weeks from idea to sale; most assumed it was much shorter. After focusing on this critical measure of agility and streamlining the "speed bumps" in their processes across marketing, sales, and service teams, the company decreased its cycle time to just five weeks—a drop of almost 75 percent. That is what we mean by operating "at speed."

This is an even more significant challenge and opportunity for much larger companies. Consider the experience of one $100 billion communications company. This firm faced a strong challenge from cable providers and new Internet Protocol (IP) businesses in competition for business among small- and medium-size business (SMB) customers. Complexity in the company's sales and marketing processes was hampering the company's ability to pursue opportunities in a timely way; thus, it was losing out to more nimble competitors. By overhauling its sales and marketing programs—integrating them within a single system—the company was able to more quickly identify the most promising prospects and get in front of them with a tailored offer of the right products and services. The new approach to sales and marketing enabled the company to boost revenue, run significantly more campaigns each year, devise campaigns much more quickly (i.e., in a day instead of a month), and boost overall sales close rates by more than 250 percent. We discuss this communications firm's experience in more detail in Chapter 12.

They Rethink their Sales Channel Mix by Investing in the "Selling Force," Not Just the "Sales Force"

The core tenet of the Agile Selling model is making greater use of sales forces not "owned" by the company (Figure 2.4). However, that doesn't mean a company has no salespeople employed by the organization. One of the keys to the effectiveness of the model is to determine the best proportion of *sales* force (i.e., the company's professional salespeople) and *selling* force (everyone inside and outside the organization,

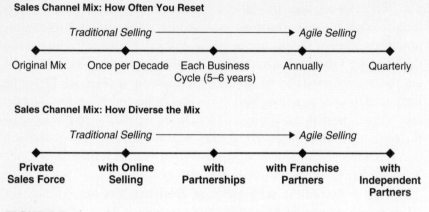

FIGURE 2.4   Adding Agility and Reach to the Sales Force

including channel partners, who can convince people to buy the company's products). The terms may sound like we're splitting hairs. On the contrary, leading companies get this mix of investments and activities right—especially by putting more resources into the *selling* force bucket—and are rewarded with uncommon sales agility as well as a greatly broadened reach into the marketplace. By making better use of their selling force, leaders create tens of thousands (sometimes hundreds of thousands, or millions) of people who, in effect, are selling their products.

This is especially important for companies pursuing opportunities in emerging markets, where the cost of entry is large and ever increasing. One of the Accenture studies we discussed earlier in this chapter found that 40 percent of executives don't believe their companies are up to the task of tapping into emerging markets. They believe they don't have the strategic or operational capabilities to do so. Another 40 percent worry that they don't fully understand the competitive dynamics that they will face in those markets.[3]

To compete in established and new markets, sales leaders must carefully examine the crucial ratio of "sales force" to "selling force" and find the mix that works best for them. In doing so, they likely will find that just as their company's products and services—and how they are delivered—have evolved over time, so, too, should the way their company sells them. One of the most globally diverse companies in the world, PepsiCo, offers important insights in the power of evaluating and updating the mix of its sales channel with regular review of channel mix. In the past few years, PepsiCo looked at its mix of private sales force and its channel partners and saw opportunity in changing the mix. PepsiCo made strategic acquisitions of certain independent bottlers in its networks, bolstering its national accounts sales teams in key markets while maintaining flexibility of independent franchises in North America. Similar approaches have been applied as PepsiCo looked to other markets like Mexico and Russia.

They Are the First to Embrace Digital Tools

Agile Selling leaders know that customers and salespeople want better information. They can take advantage of that interest by using technology (especially mobile) to redesign sales processes (Figure 2.5). The "pull" from customers and salespeople enables leading companies to change the selling experience at a much faster pace.

Consider Nationwide Insurance®. The company created an iPhone® app to help customers deal with the aftermath of a traffic accident. Customers can use the app to quickly contact a tow truck, take photos of the crash (and organize the photos), record the location of the accident, and start the claims process on the spot.[4] The app not only strengthens customer loyalty, it cuts costs for Nationwide's agent channel by reducing the number of emergency calls to agents.

Companies also should use mobile technology not only to provide better post-sale service, but to sell better. Sales leaders should continually think about how to exploit these new channels to customers but without creating channel conflict. For some companies, this might require creating different products for its digital channels than the products it sells through partners. For others, it may mean

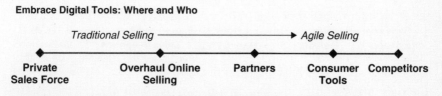

Embrace Digital Tools: Where and Who

Traditional Selling ────────────→ *Agile Selling*

| Private Sales Force | Overhaul Online Selling | Partners | Consumer Tools | Competitors |

FIGURE 2.5 Where and Who Uses Digital Tools for Selling

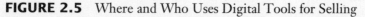

developing mobile apps that make life easier for consumers and channel partners alike, as Nationwide Insurance did.

In using mobile channels, sales executives must ensure that they are working well with other channels. Our experience tells us that customer-facing digital channels should all report to the same leader. This is not the case in many organizations, which have separate heads for online, digital, and social media channels. These silos inevitably produce channel conflict and confusion, and by extension, can greatly undermine initiatives for exploiting the channels.

They Become the Best Option for the Leading Distributors/Channel Partners in Their Markets by Treating Channel Partners Like Extensions of Their Business

Distributors and channel partners have many options for products to sell. Depending on the relationship structure, a partner could carry multiple competing lines of products, which creates a significant challenge for the producer of those products: how to convince the partner that your products are the ones the partner should put its resources and investments behind. In essence, the provider must make a compelling business case for its partners to prefer its products over those of competitors (Figure 2.6).

One of the ways to do this is to develop capabilities for partners that make it as easy as possible for them to sell your products. Historically, this has involved providing the partner with extensive training on the products so they fully understand what they do and how they can bring value to the end customer. It also has included some sharing of leads and customer insights, providing partners limited access to the

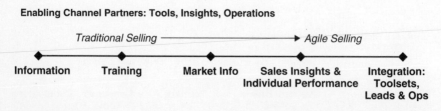

Enabling Channel Partners: Tools, Insights, Operations

Traditional Selling ⟶ Agile Selling

| Information | Training | Market Info | Sales Insights & Individual Performance | Integration: Toolsets, Leads & Ops |

FIGURE 2.6 Becoming the Best Option for Channel Partners

provider's systems to facilitate collaboration, and giving partners useful tools that help them build their business.

Increasingly, however, leaders are going far beyond such traditional "empowerment" methods. They are capitalizing on new technologies—especially cloud-based software-as-a-service solutions —that enable a partner and provider to collaborate as never before.

American Express®, for instance, has rolled out a new program based on FourSquare®, the mobile check-in service that is designed to give holders of the American Express card discount offers on certain products when they use FourSquare to check in at American Express merchant partners' locations. On checking in, cardholders automatically get the discount if they buy the item with their card. By accepting the American Express card, merchant partners benefit from location-based marketing without having to invest in the capabilities themselves. In addition, by using the built-in metrics on American Express' network, merchants can at a glance see how effective the program is in driving sales in their establishments.[5]

Another early leader in this space leveraged learning across the channel network to drive improved performance. When Avaya®—a global leader in business communications software, systems, and services—embarked on a plan to grow and improve market share with an aggressive schedule of new product launches, a critical success factor was ensuring that its workforce and channel partners were ready to sell and service those products through its "Avaya University." In six months, end-to-end learning services were available to more than 50,000 learners across the globe, including employees, business partners, and customers. Over the course of the first 12 months, as Avaya deployed the most new products in its history, the sales, service, and channel workforces were prepared to help the company drive toward high performance. In some cases, time to proficiency has been accelerated by 60 percent for customers, channel partners, and employees, returning 35,000 workdays to the corporation and channel partners. To support revenue growth in the IP telephony space, Avaya University also created a "Fast Track" learning program in the Caribbean and Latin Americas region to support the rapid development of a select group of presales and systems engineers. The program helped these individuals produce a 35 percent increase in revenues in six months.

They Use Analytics Surgically, to Run a More Profitable Business, instead of "Analytics Everywhere"

Just about every large company today uses analytics software to make decisions. However, the most sophisticated sales organizations are surgical in how they apply analytics technology (Figure 2.7). Realizing they could "boil the ocean" to uncover insights about their customers, sales force, channel partners, and competitors—an approach we refer to as *analytics everywhere*—these companies instead are far more focused. They determine the most important business decisions they must make and use that to decide on the analytics that would help them make better and faster decisions. It's a reverse engineering of sorts. Those areas could include customer targeting (to improve lead management and demand creation), sales operations (to foster faster and better decisions), and sales performance (to boost the internal and external sales force). We explore these types of analytics applications in more detail in Chapter 9.

A more targeted approach to analytics sometimes requires gathering and analyzing data that spans more than one department or function. This will be a change from the way many companies have used analytics in the business. Typically, each function uses analytics to optimize its own activities. Supply chain analysts, for example, use analytics tools to solve problems in production, inventory, and transportation. Marketing uses analytics tools in customer segmentation, pricing, and campaign effectiveness. Comparatively, most sales organizations have not made as extensive use of analytics.

On the other hand, leaders in employing the independent sales model are highly adept at using analytics to fuel and, when necessary, transform their sales organizations. They use such tools to help them account for how every dollar is spent—for instance, on incentive

Applied Analytics

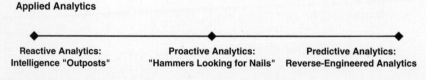

| Reactive Analytics: | Proactive Analytics: | Predictive Analytics: |
| Intelligence "Outposts" | "Hammers Looking for Nails" | Reverse-Engineered Analytics |

FIGURE 2.7 Applying Analytics in a Focused Way

compensation, trade promotion, and sales territory coverage—and know what each dollar returns to the organization in revenue and profit. Using analytics, they're able to segment their channel partners by each partner's value to the company—both in terms of volume of revenue generated and profitability—so they can determine which partners to put more of their weight behind. And with analytics, leaders can excel in what we call "contextual pricing"—that is, pricing that includes consideration of the context in which a sale is made so a company can tailor its value proposition in a way that will increase the likelihood of a purchase by customers (something we discuss in more detail in Chapter 8).

Procter & Gamble was an early leader in analytics and continues to grow its business globally through an applied analytics model. Consider the following passage from an *Informationweek* article that illustrates P&G's continued analytics push:

> [Procter & Gamble CIO Filippo Passerini] is investing in analytics expertise because the model for using data to run a company is changing. The old IT model was to figure out which reports people wanted, capture the data, and deliver it to the key people weeks or days after the fact. "That model is an obsolete model," [Passerini] says. The new model Passerini envisions is something of a virtual, instant-on war room, where people huddle in person or by video around the needed data, pulling in the right experts to fix a problem the moment it arises.[6]

P&G's approach highlights the bias toward real actions when it comes to sales and marketing leaders' daily jobs:

> [They focus on delivering analysis] in real time on screens that all the executives see. Is a sales dip in detergent in France because of one retailer, so that's where to focus? Is that retailer buying less only in France, or across Europe? Did P&G cut promotions or raise prices, letting a rival grab share, or is the category overall losing sales?[7]

In each case, P&G puts a premium for its analytics on targeting (i.e., where in the system does the challenge or opportunity exist?) and a bias to action (i.e., what changes now?).

They Look for Growth in Some of the Most Difficult, Untapped Growth Areas

More and more B2B companies are pursuing the small- and medium-size business segment. The reason: This segment has substantial buying power. According to research firm IDC, worldwide SMB spending on information technology alone is expected to top US$610 billion by 2014.[8] But many B2B companies have long overlooked the SMB market, in part because it is extremely fragmented. This means selling to any one SMB won't generate nearly what one could book when calling on a Fortune 500 company. Furthermore, SMBs tend to act more like consumers than large enterprises. That means the big-company marketing and selling programs aren't likely to be as effective with the SMB market. See Figure 2.8.

Leading companies are leveraging the inherent strengths in the Agile Selling model to help them more effectively—and profitably—target and mine the SMB segment. As we discuss in Chapter 12, these companies develop a plan for market segmentation to be able to create micro-segments of the market and perform predictive modeling. They also build an offering strategy that articulates the SMB segment needs and their implications for the firm's product/service offering and pricing, with offerings tailored to the needs of that segment. They create a multichannel SMB customer engagement model that incorporates a variety of approaches, including direct sales, channel partners, inside sales, indirect channels, teleweb, and others. They consider the new or enhanced capabilities required to execute the SMB strategy and synchronize their marketing and sales organizations by creating globally standardized operating procedures. And to boost their capabilities, they

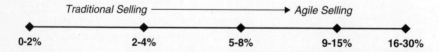

FIGURE 2.8   New Growth Mix: Percent Revenue from "Core Business" in Five Years

invest in a customer data management and analytics function that gives the marketing and sales functions a common data set and customer models.

In addition to the SMB market, emerging economies outside of companies' traditional geographic markets (particularly in Asia-Pacific) offer substantial growth opportunities—but also corresponding complexity. An Accenture survey of nearly 600 business leaders around the world found that 80 percent are now focused primarily on high-growth markets in emerging economies.[9] There's good reason for this. Household incomes in emerging economies are predicted to jump by more than US$8.5 trillion in real terms from 2010 to 2020, accounting for almost 60 percent of the global increase this decade.[10] As household incomes rise, so does consumption of products and services. But that doesn't mean these opportunities are easy to exploit. In fact, a number of Western companies have been discouraged by their slow progress in generating profits from emerging economies.

Many companies are pinning their hopes on China, the world's most populous nation (1.34 billion people in 2011, according to the World Bank). China has also become one of the largest and fastest-growing economies. By 2020, only three countries are expected to have a greater number of households earning at least US$30,000 (the United States, Japan, and Germany).[11] By all measures, the Chinese market provides immense opportunities for companies around the world.

Yet China isn't the only place where sales leaders of large B2B and business-to-business-to-consumer (B2B2C) companies should be panning for gold. In fact, 27 other countries—including those that have never been economic powerhouses (Poland, Colombia, and Turkey)—have a greater number of households with annual income of US$30,000 or above than does China.[12] Mexican households in this income band are expected to boost their incomes by US$340 billion by 2020.[13] That's a higher increase than is expected for Germany. Turkish households with an annual income of more than US$50,000 are expected to rise by US$380 billion, the highest of any emerging economy.[14] And Africa is considered by many to be an even more promising market than China, with its growing consumer wealth, rising per-capita gross domestic product, and improving infrastructure.

Although many companies in general have charted a path to such global markets, those that are using the Agile Selling model to support their expansion into such markets are finding greater success. As we explore in Chapter 14, these companies are building strong relationships with partners—whether they are government agencies, other businesses, or even groups run by influential families—to gain access to capabilities needed to tailor their offerings to local customers and rapidly scale their presence in those markets more effectively and with substantially less risk.

Conclusion

As we highlighted in the previous chapter, the world has become an increasingly difficult place in which to do business. Sales leaders, in particular, face many challenges as they seek ways for their company to generate sustainable, profitable growth. The simple fact is that, for most companies, the answer is an obvious, albeit far from simple, one: They must make a substantial change in the way they sell and go to market.

Based on our experience, that means adopting elements of what has proven to be a more efficient and effective sales model, one that's much better suited to the complexity and volatility of today's economic environment. That is the Agile Selling model.

We're not saying that every company necessarily has to fully embrace Agile Selling. To the contrary, such a complete and dramatic shift may not be the right one for every company and, in fact, may be impossible to make. What we are saying is that every company can benefit from taking steps toward that model or, at the very least, adopting some of the practices that companies excelling in the use of the Agile Selling model employ.

A shift toward the Agile Selling model will necessarily challenge a company's incumbent position every step of the way. And in today's environment, companies should welcome such a conversation, as it will illuminate where they have opportunities to substantially improve their sales effectiveness and, ultimately, their ability to compete and thrive in their chosen markets.

In the next chapter, we delve more deeply into what the Agile Selling model looks like, the implications of this model for the current ways of working, how to prioritize the changes companies should make to move toward this model, and pitfalls to watch out for along the journey.

The Agile Sales and Distribution Ecosystem

Mike Heald and Paul Neumann

Chapter Summary

- The new sales ecosystem contains many of the old elements, but with dramatically different execution speed, measurements, and especially, collaboration with partners outside the traditional sales force.
- Sales leaders need to first understand where they are with respect to having the sales capabilities for Agile Selling and then focus on three key areas to begin the transformation.

Manufacturers, distributors, resellers, competitors, service providers, and customers—the new B2B ecosystem has many different players that operate in anything but a static environment. Customers are now actively involved with their providers in coproduction and delivery of products and services; vendors and partners are embracing new forms of B2B collaboration; and companies that are competitors in certain areas are teaming together in other, well-defined areas that can drive mutual growth—these are only a few examples of how the world of selling and distribution is changing. The

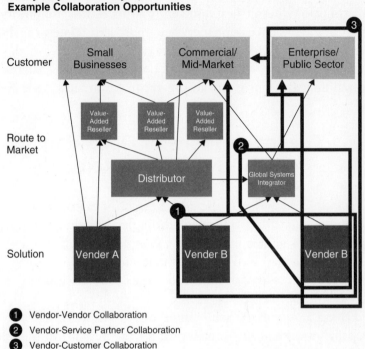

**Today's Dynamic Ecosystem
Example Collaboration Opportunities**

FIGURE 3.1   The New Sales and Distribution Ecosystem

boundaries of markets, competition, and value chains are all fluid, and relationships are constantly being redefined (Figure 3.1).

With this changing dynamic, companies are finding ways to collaborate with ecosystem partners they never imagined before. For example, Accenture® has created a joint initiative with multiple companies that several years ago would likely not have considered working together. These companies are competitors in some product lines. But, in this new "best of breed" ecosystem, they have formed a joint initiative with product lines that are complementary rather than competing and that form a highly valuable collaboration for clients, producing solutions which the participants couldn't have created on their own. The relationship at a first glance does not seem intuitive, but it is a realistic example of the dynamic way in which companies are now working together to expand relationships with existing customers and attract new ones.

However, in most companies, a traditional approach to B2B sales and distribution doesn't flex sufficiently to meet the complexity and volatility of today's environment. A new approach and new capabilities are needed. In this chapter we discuss the implications of the new selling and distribution ecosystem and how to prioritize changes your organization may need to make the move toward an Agile Selling model.

The Implications of Operating in This New Ecosystem

As discussed in Chapter 2, the new normal is global, agile, digital, collaborative, and data-informed through analytics. Competitive advantage is now gained by designing complexity "out" of the system with globally standardized processes that should be iterative and can be revised, if necessary, in days and weeks, not months, to remain market-relevant.

Table 3.1 provides a useful framework for determining how ready a company's sales and distribution are for the new world in which it operates.

If your company does not possess the characteristics that define leading practices for the Agile Selling model, you are likely a lot like your peers. Moving to this new model requires transformation and a longer-term commitment, but instead of making the necessary overhaul, most companies have focused on making incremental improvements to sales activities.

Getting to the Details: Changes to Sales Processes

Although the blueprint for Agile Selling includes many of the traditional processes and activities that CSOs have managed for decades, it requires companies to operate at dramatically different execution speeds, and collaborate on a much deeper, more open level, with new partners. The sales processes we all understand—sales strategy, sales management, sales execution, sales operations, and sales talent management—still hold, but best practices in each have changed, in some cases radically (Figure 3.2).

TABLE 3.1 How Well Can You Operate in the New Sales and Distribution Model?

	Leading Practices: Traditional Model	Leading Practices: Agile Selling Model
Structure and Processes	• Standard processes for direct and indirect selling motions • High process automation with integration to internal back-end systems, releases in months • Discrete operating structures for the direct and indirect channel, established metrics by channel • Automated workflows enable key escalations and decision authorization • Capabilities built by vendor and offered to channel; emerging use of cloud technologies and agile deployment approaches	• Selling processes mapped to targeted buying experience and segmented by customer type • Processes enabled with cloud technology, internal and external integrations, releases in weeks • Unified operating structure, collaboration natively embedded into processes, structures, and metrics • Dynamic workflows in place to fluidly manage internal and external approvals • Joint capabilities built, connected, and deployed via the cloud; iterative deployment is the standard
Access to Information	• Clear data definitions, standards, and stewards established and shared internally	• Close collaboration with partners on data definitions, standards, and governance

(continued)

TABLE 3.1 (*Continued*)

	Leading Practices: Traditional Model	Leading Practices: Agile Selling Model
	• Data flow specified and agreed to and from partners to support transactional flows • Static information stores exposed to partners to pull collateral as needed	• Information contextually available to partners in real-time via collaboration platforms • Dynamic information exchanges can be enriched at point of access by partners, customers, and vendors and pushed to partners based on contextual need
Collaboration and Boundaries	• Defined rules of engagement with programs in place to protect channel partners' ability to pursue work (such as deal registration programs) • Formal programs existing to stimulate partner activity via market development funds, trade promotion, and lead and opportunity sharing • Specified operations teams tasked with ensuring compliance of partners to program guidelines	• Boundaries of company are redefined to include top ecosystem partners in a "virtual enterprise" that is vertically integrated • Holistic view of total return on investment in individual partners is one input of a transparent performance dashboard • 360 feedback loops are embedded into collaboration model; joint operations teams established to orchestrate operating the "virtual enterprise"

TABLE 3.1 *(Continued)*

	Leading Practices: Traditional Model	Leading Practices: Agile Selling Model
Analytics	• Defined sales analytics used periodically to inform sales management, for example, channel mix optimization, pipeline health • Dedicated analytics team formed to support needs of internal business • Data warehouses, analytics, and ad hoc capabilities enabled with prepackaged analytics routines, oriented on an aggregation of transactional information (reactive analytics).	• Sales analytics embedded into regular sales disciplines and execution • Analytics available "on demand" for internal, select partners and customer audiences for real-time decision support • Focus on proactive and predictive analytic routines, using targeted information to generate dynamic insights. Examples: Am I placing my investments in the right places? What aspects of my selling model are translating into solution selling the best? How do I correlate the attributes of my teams to propensity to sell a certain type of solution? Where is the biggest bang for the buck when investing in channel enablement?

Operating Model Blueprint
Old Capabilities; New Measure of Success

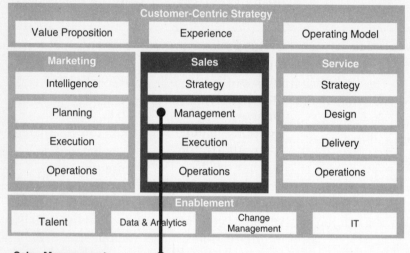

Sales Management:

What most look to address
- Refreshing internal sales methodology
- Aligning pipeline and forecast
- Managing direct, channel, overlay territories
- Monitoring internal incentive compensation

What leaders are addressing
- Aligning sales methodology with partners
- Collaborating on joint pipeline
- Analyzing multichannel market coverage
- Optimizing spend and ROI across channels

FIGURE 3.2   Blueprint of Sales Processes and Subprocesses

Sales Strategy

In Agile Selling, the sales strategy has to be quick and fluid to respond to the dynamic ecosystem, which is moving at an ever-increasing velocity. Traditional sales strategies that were built on fixed routes to market and static rules of engagement are replaced by a continuous monitoring, evaluation, and refinement of strategy. For example, when a technology company launched an online sales channel, its largest distribution partner responded by dramatically reducing focus on the manufacturer's product. Because the manufacturer was able to quickly adapt its sales strategy, it preserved its channel relationships by focusing its online channel on selling products that minimized conflict with partner strategies. Its responsiveness resulted in its ability to preserve its existing distribution channel revenue streams and generate net new revenue through a new sales channel.

Leading-edge strategies in the Agile Selling model include letting the ecosystem define new value chains, push the collaboration boundaries farther, and make them more dynamic. Leading sales strategies also tailor the customer experience and the associated value proposition based on the specific type of customer. We will discuss this in more detail in Chapter 4.

Sales Management

While companies have increasingly learned how to sell through someone else, and interacted with more partners or "nodes" in their selling ecosystem, their sales management process has not evolved. Traditional pipeline management is not at all sufficient.

Sales management in an Agile Selling model requires significant focus and commitment, including more frequent communication and collaboration with partners outside the sales force who play a role in the sales pipeline. This includes jointly assembling and managing the pipeline of all opportunities being pursued across the different nodes in the ecosystem and capturing updates to the pipeline from multiple sources, internal and external to the company. In this sense, information sharing across the ecosystem is critical to enable Agile Selling. Leaders use joint incentive structures and integrated territory management processes to encourage collaborative information sharing.

Sales Execution

Just as your company is looking for ways to optimize, drive costs out, and accelerate its sales cycles, your partners may be doing the same—and they might want and need your help. Emerging leaders in Agile Selling work with partners in their ecosystem and use cloud technology and other tools to enable advanced collaboration and to upgrade the sales processes. Cloud applications such as Salesforce.com® bring the promise of faster rollouts and improved ease of use. However, leaders are careful not to focus too much on the technology and not enough on managing the rollout, and the changes that come with it.

While building efficient processes, partners must also deliver against higher customer expectations for the buying experience. Customers' expectations are rapidly shifting and, across industries, customers are playing a more active role in shaping the buying experience—whether you harness their input explicitly or not. Everyone knows the change Apple® has driven into the retail experience. What they may not realize is how this has also changed the expectations of companies, including those buying and selling B2B.

Sales Operations

In the Agile Selling model, leaders continue to push collaborative boundaries outward by creating next-generation sales operations and, in some cases, creating dedicated joint operations teams with selling partners. Operations teams are launching value-creation offices as a way to continually define and prioritize actions of highest joint value, sustain focus on adopting new behaviors, and create new value opportunities. In a Joint Initiative, for instance, building a shared Program Strategy and Solutions Office (PSSO) is a critical enabler of success. This group functions in practice as an operations team dedicated to supporting the sales execution and performance of the Joint Initiative partners. Embedding analytics into joint operations is another way to drive science into the selling process, such as using propensity-to-buy and precision targeting models to more effectively direct finite sales resources. We explore the PSSO in more detail in Chapter 11.

Sales Talent Management

Historically, recruiting of sales talent has been based on finding people with an established track record in sales, and developing people through sales training. Yet most CSOs would agree that these practices are no longer effective. The world has changed. Recent CSO Insights research shows that almost 40 percent of sales representatives surveyed do not succeed, and the average annual voluntary and involuntary turnover of sales representatives is one in five (21 percent).[1]

Leaders in talent management today have a more analytical and attribute-based approach to sales talent recruiting and development, and they are deploying that capability with their partners throughout their sales and distribution ecosystem. According to Accenture analysis, talent hiring and retention approaches impact as much as 10 percent of top line revenue each year. Analytical profiling can reduce attrition rates, as well as the time it takes for sales representatives to become proficient and fully productive.

If the company wants to enable channel partners, it has to figure out the best practices of its own sales force, and how to build that into its partner ecosystem. It also needs to fully understand how the requirements would be different for a partner's force versus a direct force—again through analytics. Companies are making big steps to take an active role in shaping the selling talent they don't ultimately control. The extent to which these partners are skilled and have measurement criteria in place to be successful influences the company's success. We discuss talent development more specifically in Chapter 18.

Where to Begin

Where do you start, if you want to move your organization toward an Agile Selling model? Of the number of things that have to change, how does an organization identify which areas are the most important to "move the needle"? Fortunately, not everything has to be done at once, and not everything is equally important. There is a short list of changes to consider first, because the decisions made in these areas can help to build the momentum required to sustain long-term transformation.

Start Your Move toward Agile Selling with Two Things

Effective Agile Selling generally starts with marketing analytics and customer segmentation. The key change in customer segmentation in an Agile Selling model is that customers now need to be segmented through two different lenses: the one for the organization and the one for its ecosystem partners. This segmentation is supported by deeper analytics on target markets and customers, possible product and service offerings for each segment, and analysis of which partners would best help develop the right offerings to reach target customers. The new segmentation is critical as it unlocks new opportunities for the ecosystem not previously seen by any one company.

Analytics and segmentation enable an organization to better define its sales strategy, routes to market, product portfolio, and coverage model. The sales strategy can be the unifying mechanism for the organization to execute new sales models, through new channels and with new partners and products to satisfy customer segments.

Build the Territory Coverage Model

The territory coverage model is the foundation for driving efficiency in Agile Selling as it directs how multiple account teams across various channel partners will interact and overlap in the field. Companies should start by reviewing the direct and indirect territory structure; understanding existing sales overlay teams; and defining rules of engagement within each channel. This will enable a fact-based analysis of the return on investment for each channel and sales coverage model. A key step is to explicitly check potential coverage variance by region, customer type, and partner type. Furthermore, using the sales strategy as a guide, companies should model different territory scenarios and use predictive models to inform the right sales coverage approaches. For instance, by analyzing prior purchase behaviors a company can do predictive modeling of the propensity for customers to buy through a given channel and adjust territory coverage accordingly. In a segment as fragmented as small- and medium-size businesses (SMB), a number of techniques can be used to inform the best coverage approach by industry or region. We discuss more about targeting the SMB market in Chapter 12.

Design for the Customer Experience, Including the Role of Partners

A critical principle in enabling the Agile Selling model is designing processes "outside in" from the customer perspective, and clearly defining the role of partners in delivering the customer experience. This involves creating a detailed inventory of the possible selling scenarios across all routes to market. As part of the inventory, companies should think through how often that scenario occurs, analyze whether execution categories exist (e.g., high- versus low-touch), and prioritize the scenarios based on expected impact and complexity. For those high-priority (high-profit) scenarios, the next step is to define the desired experience, articulate the guidelines for collaborating with partners, and use analytics that inform offers to specific customers via specific channels. If a company already uses cloud-based technology to enable its sales processes, it should look at how it can accelerate key processes, collaboration with partners, and performance.

Companies should also think about how to streamline the execution of sales that involve partners and, more specifically, how to engage partners to deliver a great customer experience. Even in the core business, partners are playing a role. How do the sales teams collaborate and what do partners need to be successful on the company's behalf? These are key questions to answer with your partners.

Conclusion

Every company has unique characteristics that will ultimately determine the right Agile Selling road map for them. To get started, sales executives must first understand what it means to adopt an Agile Selling approach and how to design the sales processes to build the capabilities they need. Then there is a short list of changes to make to begin the transformation, including new customer segmentation and territory coverage models supported by analytics and role definitions and processes designed for the customer experience.

Change can be extremely difficult, and the effort is far from simple. It requires an ongoing effort that combines "quick wins" with a strategic and long-term focus—all of which are tightly aligned among ecosystem partners. In the following chapters, we provide more detail about how to develop Agile Selling strategy, capabilities, and technologies. Moving toward Agile Selling requires a comprehensive strategy and a strong governance model to execute the transformation. Leading companies are making progress, and it begins with crafting the new sales strategy, which we discuss in Chapter 4.

Time for a Refresh

The Updated Sales Strategy

Naveen Jain and Varun Ratta

Chapter Summary

- The Marketing Age is stalled; the chief sales officer must drive the next wave of growth strategy and execution.
- Weak sales strategies can cripple growth. They must be both actionable and understandable across the organization.
- The center of gravity for the sales strategy has to move from the boardroom to the field—centered around deeper and continuous customer understanding, clear optimization direction, and a premium on the field's ability to operationalize it.

As we described in Chapter 3, today's new multichannel environment requires companies to more fully engage other entities beyond their traditional direct sales force—including distributors, wholesalers, and value-added resellers, as well as the social and digital networks where companies' customers increasingly congregate. In this complex environment, chief sales officers have an opportunity to be the conductor of a "symphony" that is played across the ecosystem. Just as the conductor helps the various instruments in the symphony play in rhythm and harmony to entertain the audience, the CSO can articulate how the various functions of the organization and its channel partners work together to execute the company's go-to-market plan to delight the customer. And just as the conductor relies on his baton to communicate his directions to the orchestra's musicians, the CSO must have a powerful sales strategy that articulates the company's intentions and guides the actions of all the internal and ecosystem players.

In our experience, however, most chief sales officers today do not approach their sales strategy with a "conductor of the symphony" mind-set. They, instead, have focused their sales strategy more tactically on aligning the sales function internally around macro-level market and customer dynamics, and broad, nonspecific volume targets. This focus, perhaps not surprisingly, has led to little more than incremental gains and has left a significant opportunity on the table.

But there are rays of hope. Recognizing the opportunities before them, leading companies are beginning to use new tools, channels, and technologies as the impetus to reorient their sales strategy around the customer experience, and do so with an eye on improving margin performance. Enabling this reorientation requires a dramatic transformation of all aspects of the company's sales model (Figure 4.1). The customer-centric sales model, while modular in components, must be fully integrated from end to end to drive results. The model takes the most important aspects of the franchise and fully independent sales models being employed by leading companies in the consumer goods manufacturing, pharmaceutical, high-tech and insurance industries, and ties them together to achieve the agility and flexibility to scale in the multichannel environment.

One has only to look at pharmaceutical companies to see how this reorientation can pay off. As we discuss in more detail in Chapter 5, these companies were forced, out of necessity, to rethink their sales strategy. And they've responded. In the past two to three years, they have been at the forefront of integrating digital, mobility, and other levers to fundamentally transform the physician interaction model.

Indeed, the companies that will truly shine in the Agile Selling model are those that build and sustain high-value relationships with channel partners outside of their own sales forces—whether it be

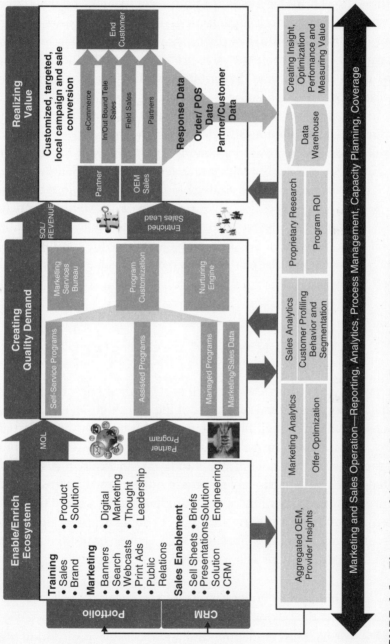

FIGURE 4.1 Elements of the Sales Strategy to Create the "Symphony"

53

retailers and distributors for consumer goods companies, physicians for pharmaceutical firms, agents for insurance companies, and integrators and resellers for high-tech organizations—and build the sales strategy to optimize the capabilities of the ecosystem. The modular nature of the symphony must enable the value propositions of the various players in the ecosystem to create the harmony with agility to drive value to the customer.

In this chapter, we aim to help Chief Sales Officers position themselves as the conductors of the symphony that guides and unifies the selling ecosystem toward a common goal. We will highlight the new guiding principles for sales strategies in the Agile Selling model, clarify what an effective sales strategy looks like, and explore the right questions to ask to assess the maturity of the sales strategy in place today. Most importantly, we share practical ideas on how to mobilize the organization around the sales strategy to drive the transformation of the selling engine that can help the company achieve its profitable growth goals.

Do You Have a Sales Strategy?

Often when we ask sales leaders to tell us about their sales strategy, they begin (and sometimes end) with describing their high-level tiered customer segmentation, their financial goals and targets, or their coverage model. As we start to probe a little more deeply, we quickly conclude that the sales strategy documents of today are tactically focused, have limited ability to be actionable, and are not integrated across strategies articulated by other functions. More specifically, we find that most companies fall short in some critical areas of their sales strategies. CSOs today are using several key questions such as these to test the maturity and effectiveness of their sales strategy:

- Do we have a clear understanding of the customer needs and what matters in the buying process?
- Do we have a compelling and unique value proposition that creates a differentiated customer experience? And what are the

implications internally for us to deliver the desired customer experience?

- Do we fully understand what our customers want to buy as commercial constructs change? And can our supply chain deliver what we intend to sell?
- Have we clearly articulated how our sales strategy enables us to drive growth from both the existing customer base and new customers and markets?
- Do we have a clear understanding of what level of selling productivity is required to meaningfully drive the sales strategy?
- Does our sales strategy outline the specific tactical and strategic actions that are required to maximize the value from our channels?
- Do we fully understand the pressures to reduce cost to serve that must be considered as we create our sales strategy?
- Do we explicitly address how the sales strategy will improve customer retention and increase share of wallet?
- Are we certain of what sales and channel incentive strategy will manage the talent and motivate the right culture and behaviors?

Meeting the customer's expectations for how they want to interact with the enterprise—how they want to learn from the organization, how they want to buy, how they want to be supported over time—also demands integration and coordination beyond the sales function to vendors, partners, and other enterprise functions such as marketing, supply chain, and service. Thus, a sales strategy also should articulate how every "instrument in the symphony" has to play together to meet the customer's expectations. It is the method to drive change within the sales function *and* with the rest of the organization impacted by the selling transformation.

Transforming the Sales Strategy with New Guiding Principles

A superior sales strategy includes actionable terms, and it clearly connects the strategy to executional implications. Furthermore, it guides changes in the process, people, and technology dimensions. Therefore, we begin the discussion on how to create an actionable sales strategy, with five guiding principles on which the sales strategy must be grounded to excel in an Agile Selling model.

Principle 1: Becoming "Customer Smart": Connecting Deep Customer Understanding and Value Proposition Implications

It is the "outside in" focus on the customer experience that anchors all aspects of the sales strategy in the Agile Selling model. The sales strategy reflects a clear articulation of the customer value proposition and buying experience for a manageable number of customer segments and includes practical and tailored approaches for interacting with each. This requires a clear understanding of two dimensions of the puzzle: determining the principal buying orientation of the customer and creating a shared view of the customer's strategic value.

Determining the principal buying orientation of the customer has been practiced in a variety of ways in the past decade. What is more exciting—and effective—are the collaborative and analytical approaches being used by leading companies to augment traditional approaches. These companies are more accurately understanding customer buying orientations by using conjoint analysis to do real-time preference modeling while collecting insights directly from customers.

Here's one example: A large computer manufacturer used a leading real-time preference analytics tool called TrueChoice® to understand distinct customer buying orientations and then subsequently utilized them to define the necessary customer experiences (see Figure 4.2). Knowledge gained from this exercise was used globally to construct distinct selling strategies for specific customer segments. This exercise also enabled the company to understand what needed to change in its internal value chain, what could be standardized or consolidated. As a result, the company was able to improve the customer experience, and the standardization and consolidation of many areas helped it reduce costs and improve margins. Another outcome of this exercise was that it allowed the company to simplify parts of its operations and reduce unnecessary business complexity.

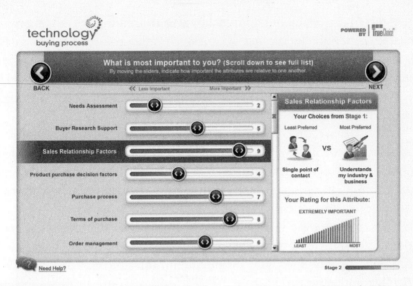

FIGURE 4.2   Leveraging Sales Dialogues to Extract Analytics that Drive Understanding of Customer Behavior

Such analytical platforms are being increasingly used on an ongoing basis to collect relevant data from the field, and serve as an open and collaborative mechanism to converse with customers during sales calls. In addition, simple tools can be developed that can facilitate a more active dialogue between the sales management and frontline sales resources to assist in precall planning and prepare for account planning for key accounts.

Principle 2: Managing Variability in Selling Approaches and Processes: Clearly Articulating the Sales Models That Can Capture Variations across Segments, Geographies, and Product/Service Bundles

Many companies that address the sales productivity challenge must consider multiple geographies in which they do business, as well as multiple businesses each with their own orientation toward go-to-market models and sales processes. Not only are the models different, but the sales methods used across different parts of the business are different as well. With high variability in selling approaches, unique customized processes and approaches mushroom in parts of the organization, thereby increasing business complexity. Traditional sales productivity tools are not often sufficient to manage this variability. Furthermore, these companies often have difficulty determining how to most efficiently integrate the sales resources of their channel partners and utilize them more effectively.

We believe that being customer smart implies that sales leadership fundamentally aligns around a small number of distinct sales models based on the defining variables described in our first principle. For example, in our experience with a global computer manufacturer and a large global chemical company, we found that between five and six sales models were sufficient in accommodating the variability and complexity these companies had to manage across their vast customer segments, geographies, and product/solution bundles. Imagine how effective and efficient go-to-market activities would be if we could articulate the sales models, build a common terminology around them, have a defined customer experience blueprint, defined go-to-market approaches and, most importantly, build an operating model that creates the "customer smart symphony."

Principle 3: Grounded in Insight-Driven Beliefs and Thesis: The Evolution from "Gut Feel" to "Gut Plus"

The transformation to the new selling model, as described in Chapter 3, requires a strong orientation toward scientific and repeatable analytics. There are four key areas in which sales analytics can be a critical component of making the sales strategy actionable (see Chapter 9 for more on the sales analytics topic).

1. Customer analytics—New channels such as social media and new analytical tools provide huge steps forward in an organization's ability to establish a deep understanding of customers and to provide insights along several steps of the sales process. For example, customer analytics are the foundation of creating the right customer buying experience (see Chapter 7) and provide critical insight in demand generation strategies (see Chapter 6).

In addition, the network analysis approach to coverage optimization can be used not only to determine network coverage but to focus precious selling resources on the "decision and influence points."

2. Base compensation and incentive spending analytics—Two of the largest areas of spending in the sales budget are sales force salaries and incentives (both sales incentive compensation and marketing incentives such as channel incentives and trade promotion). The use of analytics to optimize these categories of spending presents significant opportunity and is further discussed in Chapter 10.

3. Sales performance analytics—A dashboard of sales performance provides the means to monitor and "course correct" the execution of the sales strategy, highlight short-term successes, and maintain focus on the longer-term sales transformation. The usefulness of the dashboard is dependent on knowing which metrics are the most important and having access to quality data from which to build them.

4. Descriptive to predictive opportunity and pipeline management and analytics—The sales strategy provides the bridge from demand generation to customer acquisition and retention and, as such, connects to other parts of the organization including marketing and service. By applying analytics to the end-to-end process, a company can address the cause and effect between activities that may span discrete processes and functional silos.

Importantly, organizations that are creating more analytics-based sales strategies have had to do a tremendous amount of work making sure they have the right data. Because selling has historically been treated as an art not a science, the data to support sales decision making is not always reliable enough for analytics purposes. One company we worked with spent a full year of their transformation journey (along with significant budget) to clean data and build a data foundation before implementing further change. Thus the data strategy is an important component to consider as part of enabling an analytics-based sales organization.

Principle 4: Building an Agile Operating Model—Balancing Decentralized versus Centralized Decision Making with the Goal of Reducing Variability

Sales leadership has struggled to balance the need for control with developing "scalable expertise." Many schools of thought exist around the operating model issues of decentralization and centralization and what dimensions of the capability blueprint are true differentiators.

An agile operating model means that the company can structure parts of its enterprise and its various capabilities in a manner that allows it to respond faster and more reliably to changes in its marketplace. Our experience suggests that as companies get customer smart and reduce variability through sales models, it presents a perfect opportunity to build such agile operating models. Once the company has defined distinct sales models, it must further define the various sales capabilities that are key to its success.

For example, if forecasting is identified as a key capability, then the company should define the design elements for this capability that specify what the primary value drivers for this capability are, who performs and manages the tasks associated with this capability, where this capability should be performed, how some parts of this should be standardized or automated, and how the roles and handoffs should be structured. Only by working on the right operating model design elements can the company create a forecasting capability that helps its overall enterprise respond to the marketplace with more certainty and speed. Leading companies are also creating centers of excellence and shared front-office business services to rapidly scale access to precious skills while dramatically changing the cost to serve.

Principle 5: Rethinking the Incentive Strategy across the Ecosystem: Typically a Very Large Spend That Provides Accelerated Dividends If Addressed in a Targeted Way

Incentive spending comes in a variety of forms depending on the industry and product/services orientation. In B2B companies, it tends to bulge in the area of sales force incentives; in other models it takes the form of trade or channel incentives. Regardless, it is always a very large spend category. Leading companies are realizing the power of this spend category and the opportunity it offers to unleash capacity and investments to drive growth. Although Chapter 10 explores the topic of incentives in detail, we want to stress here that the sales strategy should explicitly address how and what type of incentives will be used (and for whom), as well as what metrics will be used to gauge incentives' effectiveness.

What Does the Good Sales Strategy Look Like?

We've found that the most effective sales strategy excels in identifying the explicit linkage between four things: a company's vision and objectives; sales goals and targets; the operational execution initiatives that can help a company achieve the preceding; and the dashboard of metrics that enable a company to monitor its performance. A great sales strategy that builds differentiated advantage typically contains eight sections:

1. The market dynamics and competitive environment
2. The customer experience and proposition
3. Customer segmentation and hot spot evaluator
4. Sales and distribution models and key sales processes
5. Resource and coverage optimization
6. Pricing strategy
7. Enterprise mobilization
8. Productivity drivers: capability and enablement roadmap

An Example of an Actionable Sales Strategy

As an example, a large global manufacturing company utilizes customer segmentation as a basis to construct sales strategies and calibrate the level of effort and detail required to create these strategies. For large key accounts that represent the majority of the margin, customer-specific sales strategies are constructed. However, for other smaller accounts, segment-specific strategies are constructed and deployed across the individual accounts. The process for constructing strategies for key accounts is disciplined, established, and well practiced over years. The expectations and roles are very clearly defined in the sales strategy development process.

The process starts by first building a shared understanding of the customer's business, trends in the customer's industry, and the customer's growth ambition. In our experience, this basic understanding of customers' businesses is often missing from sales strategy development (however, not at this company). The company recognizes how the customer competes in the marketplace, its competitive advantage, and even the key attributes that go into its customers' buying decision process. It builds these insights not just by collecting external information, but by also leveraging historical knowledge of having worked with similar customers and by integrating the knowledge from the various divisions that sell to the customer globally. After the company has developed such a customer insight foundation, it evaluates the profitability performance at the customer. The company evaluates volume trends from the past three years, its variable and pocket margin, and its own share of wallet. It performs this exercise at a business/product line level, as large differences may exist across product lines, thereby necessitating different strategies to improve performance. The company also collates information on its most significant competitor and other emerging competitors.

The second step is documenting the customer's demonstrated purchasing philosophy, and how the customer's historical buying behavior demonstrates the relative importance placed on price, service, technology, innovation, and cost-reduction initiatives. The company goes to great lengths to identify key decision makers and understand their role in the buying process, and assess its current relationships with those key decision makers. In this way it creates a targeted relationship action plan that aims to improve or maintain the required relationships.

The company next places itself in the customer's position and evaluates the compelling reasons that this account should buy from them versus the next best alternative. Detailed knowledge of the customer, its business, its growth ambitions, and its challenges is key raw material to making such decisions. The next step is the typical opportunity management process where major opportunities and related measures of success are documented—this being a continuous process throughout the year. Goals are laid out at a very granular level by product line, and then a short action plan is created for every goal with a clear understanding of accountabilities and roles within the customer. In this way, granular and pragmatic sales strategies are devised for all key accounts.

The same strategy is followed for a large number of other customers, albeit this is done at a customer segment level, collecting a number of these customers into specific segments and performing the above exercise for the segment as a whole. For companies that do this well, good sales strategy development is hard work, and it relies on a deep understanding of the customer.

Building an Actionable Sales Strategy—What Leading Companies Get Right

In our experience, many of the companies we have worked with have great vision, ideas, and strategies. So what stands in the way of making these resonate across the ecosystem and making them actionable? We believe that three factors are critical to making sales strategies actionable and responsive to competitive and market dynamics:

1. Having the right approach.
2. Engaging the right ecosystem stakeholders.
3. Relentlessly focusing on change management.

The Approach

First, the sales strategy must connect the dots. In other words, it must have a clear line of sight from vision to objectives, strategies, actions, targets, and goals. Although this sounds simple, in our experience we find that either all these components of the connected chain do not exist, or if they do, they are not connected because different stakeholders have different pieces.

Consider, for example, if we are speaking to a company about cross-sell and up-sell strategies. Interestingly, the specific strategies for these fall across sales, service, and marketing. When we ask, "What is the collective belief on the key strategies?" we get different answers from different stakeholders. No wonder the ability to specifically measure and refine strategies becomes difficult. Executing the right approach requires a clear alignment of the key short-term and long-term objectives and how they will be measured, which then should clearly link to the three or four strategies that the leadership believes will achieve the objectives. Then each of the functional groups can have specific executable elements, but all are tied to the strategies that represent the collective belief.

Second, the approach should clearly position for this to be a dynamic and living orchestra. Many companies realize that in today's rapidly changing world, with access to social media and mobility mechanisms, much can be achieved by integrating "test and learn" approaches into sales strategies. As such, as a company aligns on some beliefs on its strategies, it should clearly define how it will quickly test these strategies and continuously refine its approach. The companies that execute with agility not only have aligned strategies but very clear metrics that are aligned to their strategies and an ongoing mind-set to review and test these strategies. The value case around this can be significant as it enables sales leaders to test strategies in an agile manner before making decisions to make large investments in capabilities that may not pay dividends.

The Engagement

Although we have alluded to this before, it is too important not to emphasize it here. The very thesis of this chapter is that sales strategy creates the orchestra that aligns and tunes the various instruments in the symphony. Not surprisingly, this has the challenge of engaging and aligning key stakeholders not only within the organizational firewall but across the ecosystem. Engaging so many stakeholders and aligning them can be an overwhelming exercise. Companies that are successful in this endeavor make it simple. They (1) focus on aligning the stakeholders on the key objectives, strategies, and how they will measure them; (2) focus on three or four things to get right; and (3) ensure each stakeholder takes ownership of targeted metrics with a clear linkage to incentives.

In summary, engagement goes beyond the meeting to share plans. It requires clear leadership agreement on the key strategic objectives and strategies to achieve those objectives, and then clear assignment of specific targets and incentives for each stakeholder.

Relentless Focus on Change Management

Achieving this high-performing orchestra through the sales strategy is difficult. In fact, one of the most overlooked pieces of making the sales strategy actionable is an explicit focus on changing behavior. Although there is no predefined answer to this puzzle, what we do know is that companies that excel in change management do a few things right.

First, they embed the sales strategy in the operating rhythm. For instance, one company we have worked with clearly defined how the leadership meetings should flow—that is, what the various leaders in the symphony should report out on the "review cycle." If we believe in the approach, then each instrument in the symphony should have the specific questions they should review in every meeting. In other words, we play the sales strategy symphony in every meeting.

Leading companies also focus not on the lagging indicator but on the leading indicator. Here's a common example: Companies often set ambitious goals such as, "We will increase sales productivity of our people by 20 percent." Measuring progress against that goal is difficult and takes considerable time. And even when a company measures whether the goal is achieved, it's too late to change anything if it has fallen short. Instead, a company should measure some leading indicators such as: Are the sales people using the tools they have been given? What percent of sales people engage in preplanning? These represent the specific components that will impact productivity. If a company can identify these leading indicators, measure them, and have change management interactions around them if needed, the lagging indicators are more likely to come to fruition.

Conclusion

The sales strategy provides a practical route for companies to increase the effectiveness of their sales forces and invigorate their commercial strategies. It requires organizational discipline to both develop and execute and, because it has implications that span changes beyond the sales organization, requires extensive collaboration. But the prize is worthy. Suppliers that are able to optimally allocate resources to serve customers and end markets can boost customer value through tailored end-to-end customer experiences and outperform their peers for the short and long term.

Looking for Channel-Selling Innovation?

Four Industries That Stand Out

*Robert Wollan, Anne O'Riordan,
Jean-Laurent Poitou, Fabio Vacirca,
and John L. DelSanto*

Chapter Summary

- Regardless of how close a company is to the end consumer, companies all along the sales chain are feeling the impact of changing consumer behaviors.

- Although many regional, regulatory, and purchasing differences exist across industries and countries, four industries stand out from the rest.

- These four—consumer goods, insurance, electronics and high technology, and pharmaceuticals—have developed world-class capabilities in parts of their selling organization to survive and thrive. In those capabilities are lessons that can quickly make a difference in other companies' businesses.

- The power comes from understanding not just what has worked, but what hasn't—avoiding the potholes in the road based on their early trials with new approaches.

Companies in virtually all industries are feeling the impact of consumers' evolving preferences, behaviors, and financial wherewithal. And those shifts—along with a variety of regional and regulatory differences—are changing how companies sell. However, one thing has not changed: the opportunity to learn from the successes and setbacks of others—to apply "lessons learned" to an organization's own business.

To this end, most businesses scrutinize their competitors. However, there is an equal and potentially greater benefit to emulating companies in other industries—to discover what "outsiders" have done to maintain and enhance profitability.

Generally speaking, the best industries to observe are those that are particularly bedeviled by frenzied competition and mounting global complexities. With a specific focus on selling and sales channels, we profile four such industries in this chapter:

1. Consumer goods manufacturing
2. Pharmaceuticals
3. Insurance
4. Electronics and high-tech

Each of these fields is populated by numerous companies that have reinvented key selling approaches and capabilities in response to significant industry change. Out of necessity, these organizations have become adept at structuring channels and partner relationships in ways that maximize reach and profitability. In essence, they are models for how to develop and sustain a powerful Agile Selling approach.

Common Ground

Why have we chosen to use these four industries as models of contemporary selling behavior? As we mentioned, companies in each of the four areas are frequently beset by compromised margins and shifting global markets. But another relevant trait is that they depend heavily on their indirect channels: Consumer goods companies sell through retailers and distributors. Pharmaceutical companies work with doctors and health-care providers. Insurance companies rely on independent agents and brokers. Electronic and high tech (EHT) companies use technology integrators, value-added resellers (VARs), retailers, and telecom operators. Model companies in each of these groups also share a number of practices that are indicative of a highly effective Agile Selling approach.

They Leverage Analytics

Companies in each of the four industries often excel at applying analytics to understand the effectiveness of specific channels and routes to market, and to ensure that each step and partner in the sales process contributes materially to return on investment (ROI). Consumer goods companies, for example, use analytics to learn more about distribution coverage and cost to serve; and they use those insights to devise new channel strategies for supporting their sales efforts. Insurers—especially those competing at the high end of the market—recognize that analytics can help them segment customers more precisely and develop customized treatments using various channels. Channel-management analytics and segmentation capabilities also help electronics and high-tech companies reward the right partners (whether it means they sell more, they sell more profitable products, they service the enterprise customers most effectively, or are most willing to provide valuable end-customer information). Pharmaceutical companies traditionally measure the effectiveness of their sales forces by tracking sales data in a territory. Most recently many are expanding into analyzing multiple channels of communication to assess the best way to get messages to physicians and patients.

They Provide Salespeople with the Resources They Need

Many companies in these industries recognize the importance of giving channel partners access to what they need to grow their own business—better tools, data, training, and insights—thus helping educate and create a sustainable reason for those partners that prefer to sell that company's products over a competitor's products. At the same time, these entities focus tightly on returns because empowerment can be costly.

Pharmaceutical companies increasingly are equipping their field sales forces with iPads® that put valuable content at reps' fingertips, while consumer goods companies provide their salespeople with in-depth data on in-store activities and performance, as well as general category, market, and shopper trends, so they can have more fruitful discussions with retailers.

For their part, insurers use extensive product training and easy access to product information to help agents become more conversant, as well as sophisticated customer-needs analysis tools to accelerate the sale. Many insurance companies also provide agents (employees and independents) with leading-edge collaboration tools and mobile time- and prospect-management applications.

And many EHT companies provide sales reps with "product configurators," which allow a sales rep to directly configure the often complex set of options and features of the product/solution they sell. In the more advanced situations, the sales reps are equipped with "solutions design aids": software on their tablets or laptops that allow them to provide a combination of products, software, and services using the customers' business requirements as input parameters (rather than just technical parameters) to determine the right configuration.

They Build Digital Channels

With more and more end customers embracing digital channels, many companies in our model industries excel at creating compelling online experiences. A good example are consumer goods businesses, which spend more each year on digital channels and less on traditional media. Other examples include high-tech companies, which increasingly use social media channels as "listening posts" to understand what end customers are looking for. Insurers have made significant inroads in property and casualty markets by selling insurance via the Internet.

They Involve Intermediaries and Customers

Consumer goods companies use crowd sourcing—loosely defined as "outsourcing information-gathering tasks to an undefined public rather than a specific group"—to support product launches, perform simulations, and deploy field-based personnel to gather data in stores. High-tech companies often work with partners in special facilities to co-develop customer-focused solutions. Pharmaceutical companies leverage their relationships with experts in specific diseases, therapies, and technologies to enhance product development, improve clinical trials, and market more effectively.

They Exercise Channel Versatility

Many companies in these model industries recognize that business goals are reached through "dynamic ecosystems." As a result, they're continuously looking for ways to redefine channel boundaries and develop relationships with new partners. Many consumer goods companies use multiple channels, such as in-house (field sales, direct store delivery, van selling) and third parties (exclusive and multiparty distributors and wholesalers). To keep pace with customer needs, some high-tech companies have embraced a culture of channel segmentation and rapid evolution of business models. Pharmaceutical companies are developing interlinked channels (e.g., between websites and call centers) that align with physicians' and patients' needs.

In the remainder of this chapter, we explore each of these four model industries in more detail, highlighting along the way some specific practices other industries can learn from as they look to restructure their channel relationships.

Insights from Consumer Goods Manufacturing

Consumer goods manufacturing is an interesting mix of the old and the new, introducing innovative items at a brisk rate while continuing to market generations-old brands. Colgate-Palmolive's Colgate©

toothpaste was first marketed in a tube in 1896. Kimberly-Clark created Kleenex© facial tissues in 1924. Procter & Gamble's Tide© was introduced in its present form in 1949. Yet the same industry orchestrates thousands of new product introductions every year, with more and more of these items focused on less-mature markets and specific niches.

Given this dichotomy, it isn't surprising that consumer goods companies face a variety of common and uncommon challenges. One is a changing consumer base. Demographics are shifting rapidly, with the rapid growth in the sheer number of consumers globally and the rise of a strong middle class in emerging markets. Another challenge is the fact that consumers have unprecedented levels of power and influence. These factors naturally contribute to rapid changes in purchasing behavior and in the stimuli that prompt people's purchase decisions. Similarly, consumer goods manufacturers must be acutely mindful of emerging markets' robust growth and the concurrent saturation of mature markets. They're thus compelled to manage an expensive and uncomfortably diverse global product portfolio. For example, sales organizations in developed markets generally need to emphasize maintenance of share and profitability. In emerging markets, the name of the game is *gaining* share and aligning product attributes with localized tastes and an ever-shifting variety of consumer needs.

It isn't a reach to say that the consumer goods sales function is being revolutionized by mobile sales processes and their ability to capture data at the point of sale. Companies that only recently relied on paper to support third-party and in-store negotiations are now equipping their field forces with up-to-date, mobile-enabled information. Mobile technologies also are behind the rise of social media, which is changing how consumer goods companies communicate with, and receive feedback from, consumers. In an increasingly connected, always-on world, consumer commentary on brands and companies can affect buying trends within hours.

Looking upstream, volatile commodity prices are a major influencer of consumer goods manufacturers' behaviors. But it isn't always possible for low-margin companies to pass higher material costs on to customers. New efficiencies and smarter, more-aggressive selling strategies are often a better bet. Another reason pass-through costs aren't always possible is today's tough economic climate and its effect on retail purchasing behavior. Times are hard. Consumers are pickier. Generics have greater appeal as do private-label brands, which are flourishing. Private-label growth is an ongoing fact of life in the consumer goods industry, as retailers continue to increase the amount of private-label categories and shelf space. This makes it harder for branded products to compete for consumers based on traditional metrics.

How Are Consumer Goods Companies Responding?

New forms and levels of collaboration are helping consumer goods companies deal with many of these challenges. By working more closely with distributors, some are developing better demand forecasts and subsequently improving the focus and expertise of both groups' sales forces. In one sense, this makes the entire selling process more consultative—positioning salespeople as advisors by leveraging better information (e.g., on category, marketing, and shopper trends) from a wider range of sources.

In a slightly abstract sense, manufacturers are even collaborating with consumers. Although retailers and distributors remain the dominant path to developed markets (and part of the channel mix in emerging markets), consumer goods businesses are also extending their reach and influence through crowd sourcing. In this context, "input from everywhere" can help with product development and product launches, and even create informal networks of field-based personnel who conduct in-store activities and data gathering.

Technology adoption is equally important in the consumer goods industry. Perhaps the best example is leveraging analytics to understand distribution coverage and the cost to serve, and using the analytically derived insights to develop new channel strategies to support sales. Portable technology is another highlight. Take the use of smartphones as point-of-sale (POS) devices. Insiders expect this to become a mainstream capability—replacing many of the more expensive, less-efficient, and increasingly anachronistic cash register stations. Apple is the retail model here; but the same mobile-technology efficiencies that Apple enjoys at its stores can also apply to consumer goods sales personnel in the field—improving order-taking, data-capture, and presentation capabilities.

Last, changing consumers and markets are driving a shift in trade spend toward new consumer-centric channels. The consumer goods industry is a leader in shifting trade spend toward digital channels—directly targeting and selling to consumers online and providing targeted promotions that are redeemable in stores.

What Sales-Related Innovations Are Working in Consumer Goods and How Can Other Industries Benefit?

Companies in the consumer goods industry have responded to today's challenges in a variety of ways. Following are some of the most successful behaviors that many have adopted. Each represents a potential learning opportunity for companies in other industries. Interweaved through every practice (and thus not broken out as a specific "lesson-learned") is the smart, aggressive use of technologies such as analytics and digital communications.

Build multiple routes to market. Many consumer goods manufacturers have become leaders at selling through various types of distribution. Retail consolidation in developed markets often means that these companies' sales efforts are becoming more concentrated. In emerging markets, top manufacturers are more likely to use numerous channels, some of which have been orchestrated in-house (field sales, direct store delivery, van selling) and others through third parties or multiple parties (distributors, wholesalers, independents).

Constantly measure sales effectiveness. Many manufacturers now have processes and systems that provide accurate windows into what is happening at the point of sale. On the process side, teams of merchandisers assess product/shelf compliance in larger retail outlets. On the technology side, new POS-analysis capabilities help companies refine product mixes, devise better sales forecasts, enhance supply chain execution, assess promotional effectiveness, and improve overall category management.

Maximize availability. Better data captured in the field or supplied by a distributor is helping manufacturers make significant improvements in product availability. More often than not, companies that excel at rapidly and accurately interpreting retail sales trends, quantifying the impact of a particular trade promotion, and understanding when (and under what conditions) out-of-stocks occur also are leaders at determining and adjusting inventory and replenishment levels. The net effect is often higher availability without higher costs.

Manage and optimize trade spend. Below-the-line promotional spend represents a significant amount of the industry's net sales value. In fact, a one percent improvement in trade spend effectiveness can create millions of dollars in bottom-line benefit for a typical manufacturer. Small wonder that many consumer goods companies have enhanced the visibility and management of their trade spending by using advanced analytics tools instead of relying solely on their instincts and past practices. Manufacturers also are using more sophisticated tools to collaborate more tightly with channel partners, formulate promotional activities, justify expenditures, and identify optimal spend levels within categories.

Support innovation. Sales organizations at many consumer goods companies have become key contributors to product and process innovations. Sales people are encouraged to suggest new products, debate the merits of others' suggestions, offer rationale and data points, and even recommend shelf-utilization and pricing strategies.

Increase direct-to-consumer communication. Consumer goods manufacturers often lead the way when it comes to embracing new communication channels with shoppers and consumers. Raising digital visibility and interaction has been imperative; consumer goods was one of the first industries to apply digital couponing and vouchers that are redeemable in-store. In addition, the growth of companies such as Groupon® has increased the popularity of "voucherization"—the selection and redemption of vouchers that provide shoppers with benefits and discounts.

Insights from the Pharmaceutical Industry

Globally, health-care costs are rising faster than many GDPs. This unsustainable situation is driving pressures on pharmaceutical pricing as governments, payer groups, and patients tighten their spend on pharmaceuticals and shift to generic equivalents. In addition, many large global brands are facing patent expiration in major markets resulting in both top- and bottom-line pressures.

Emerging economies are also playing their part: Seismic growth in emerging markets like China and Latin America means that pharmaceutical companies must rapidly establish alternative cost and channel structures, often using volume-based models with lower price points and creative options for reaching rural and under-served populations. Take China, as an example, which has roughly 2 million doctors. With a 3,000-person sales force, a typical pharmaceutical company can only expect to reach 150,000 to 200,000 doctors per year. So, does a pharmaceutical company increase its staff tenfold (i.e., replicate the Western market sales model) or find a different way to educate and influence buyers and distribute products? The price point in these vast markets makes that classic Western-model scaling very uncompetitive and too slow for the pace of change; thus, companies are forced to develop new models for these new markets.

It is not enough to simply reach more people. Every health-care-related change—growth in new markets, more governmental controls, changing priorities in product development—alters *how* and *to whom* the industry sells. Pharmaceutical companies should look at both more channels *and* additional buyer/influencer populations. Education, promotion, and sales are fundamentally different. The sole target is no longer the physician writing prescriptions, but also the payers, hospitals, caregivers, health-care authorities, governments, and patients (where permitted by law).

How Are Pharmaceutical Companies Responding?

The past three to four years have seen a significant rise in the number of channels pharmaceutical companies use to reach, educate, and sell to customers. Call centers, staffed by medically trained professionals, now do both outbound calling and response to queries from doctors or patients. More pharmaceutical websites are appearing. Pharmaceutical companies also are becoming sophisticated users of iPads, which allows them to put large amounts of information at a sales reps' fingertips and to work in extremely tight time frames with doctors. "Walking presentations" are becoming an iPad specialty in the pharmaceutical business. Both digital content management and analytics are underpinning these trends.

Pharmaceutical companies are getting good at circulating content by "multichanneling." Suppose a physician needs to supply a patient with instructions for using an injectable drug. Such information may be proffered with a specialized app, phone-based audio instruction, e-mail attachment for computer use, or a DVD. Digitized content that is easily tracked and modified can move around the world in near real time—reaching sales and training venues, public health agencies, regulatory bodies, retailers, physicians' offices, and education venues via websites, iPads, mobile phones, audio/video formats, and apps.

Channel mastery goes hand in hand with new opportunities to create and distribute content; the industry is using digital technology to centralize key marketing, training, patient adherence, and support and selling messages, thus engendering new levels of economy and consistency. In effect, content is more of a digital asset than ever. Akin to the music industry's shift to digital asset management, the pharmaceutical industry is moving toward managing digital content in an insight-driven way to ensure the quality, reliability, and traceability of medical content to the physician and the patient.

Pharmaceutical companies are beginning to leverage analytics to help them gauge the effectiveness of multiple channels, messages, and selling approaches, and using that information to raise patient satisfaction, hone branding strategies, and reapportion time and resources across different channels. This is not a luxury: It's increasingly necessary given the amount of information and the speed that it's replicated across digital devices.

What Sales-Related Innovations Are Working in Pharmaceuticals and How Can Other Industries Benefit?

Innovative and effective channel management is clearly a sales-related linchpin in pharmaceuticals. Call centers, websites, and mobile technologies help companies reach more customers, make reps more productive, and optimize their marketing/channel spend. New digital mechanisms improve both reach and compliance—helping people take medications in the right quantity at the right times and for the right duration. The rise of additional channels opens up new health-improvement opportunities, including the ability to relay information to previously untouched customer populations. For example, a 2011 survey by Accenture[1] reported that Chinese doctors (particularly in rural areas) are anxious to discover more about Western medicine, in whatever format is available, thus making digital a great pathway of getting education and information to those who need it to provide better health care for patients. From one end to the other, channel management is all about making connections.

Other successful and often replicable practices include:

Emphasize influence. Pharmaceutical companies excel at building and leveraging influence-based models. In this industry, the entity that influences product selection (the physician) is neither the consumer of the product (the patient) nor the organization that usually pays for the product (an insurer, hospital, government entity, or the patient himself). In such an environment, virtually nothing is more important than the collection and communication of useful information. Other industries do follow this model (CGM companies, for example, exert influence through trade promotions). However, companies in many other industries could also benefit by using information to inform and collaborate with the people who really influence the product choice (i.e., the "influencers").

Collaborate. In the pharmaceutical business, collaboration is key. Drug companies generally work with a huge variety of knowledge leaders—making discoveries and generating information that finds its way back into product development and training, as well as sales and marketing. Companies in other industries may perform point surveys and gather voice-of-the-customer data, but this isn't the same as an ongoing process of deep, joint, intellectual collaboration. It is not unusual for pharmaceutical companies to partner with competitors—coming together not just for breakthroughs in therapeutics but to create access-related synergies in sales and jointly positioning several products as part of a larger health solution. Colicensing, alliances, and franchise management tend to be more common in the pharmaceutical business than in other sectors.

Innovate with tablets. With the goal of reshaping how reps sell, one pharmaceutical company recently set a strategy to purchase roughly 20,000 iPads. Each tablet is loaded with relevant content, giving the reps the ability to make the most of often brief conversations with a broad range of information available instantly. In the past, a salesperson could represent only a small number of products. Now, he or she can carry far more information on a wider variety of subjects—technical information, promotional materials, client-account data, market research, and even feedback from the scientific and user communities. The sales representatives are more productive; in other words, they can carry more products than before and they are getting greater customer satisfaction through more intelligent and informed interactions.

Analyze. Importantly, the use of more channels and the technological enablement of these channels enables a closed-loop customer relationship management (CRM) capability, which allows real-time customer interaction to be analyzed. The result is more targeted interactions and more informed leverage of sales channels to optimize return on marketing and sales investment.

Insights from the Insurance Industry

Several trends are changing the way insurance products are sold. One such trend—substantiated by countless surveys—is that customers in general are becoming less trusting, less loyal, and more demanding. Another is that demand for insurance products is tending to drift toward opposite poles. One group insists on more personalized, value-added service and advice, and complex products that can be configured to make them more relevant to individual customers. At the other end of the spectrum are those who are more inclined to treat insurance products as a commodity—choosing standardized, no-frills products at the lowest price option via a direct-sale website or through a price-comparison service. Surveys also reveal that customers want more channels through which to engage with insurers. Not only do they want more innovative, convenient channels at their disposal, but they are tending to use different channels for different types of interaction—for example, insurers' websites to research their options, agents to buy a policy, and call centers to initiate a claim.

The net effect of these trends is an industry that is "reparsing" itself. At the generic, low-price end, aggregators are helping increase insurers' market share by stressing low prices, quick response, and ease of purchase.[2] This is creating a dilemma for many insurance companies: If they refuse to collaborate with aggregators, they yield a big part of the market to competitors. If they get on board, they generally must accept lower margins. At the high end, agents (both captive and independent) remain essential to the sales process. However, competing at the complex end of the market is costly and requires new capabilities like developing multichannel distribution strategies. More analytics also are needed to understand and segment customers, and to develop, measure, and refine personalized customer treatments.

How Are Insurance Companies Responding?

Many insurers are reacting to the above trends by reinforcing traditional channels: empowering agents and using technology to improve call center management; creating "single views" of the customer; and more fully enlightening agents as to a customer's needs, buying priorities, and contact history. At the same time, many insurers are investing heavily in new channels such as mobile apps, social media, price-comparison websites (aggregators), and online sales and servicing.

Some insurers also are concluding that they cannot compete effectively in the distribution realm. Instead, they're concentrating on developing new products and becoming easier to work with. Some are establishing relationships with distributors such as brokerages, other insurance companies, and even nonindustry partners through which the company might be able to leverage assets. Examples of the latter include organizations with large customer/user bases (e.g., a retail chain or bank) or large sales networks (e.g., a direct sales organization). New relationships also are being sought through social media. Insurers have realized that many consumer decisions regarding choice of insurance product and provider are influenced by recommendations that travel through social media.

Last, the use of aggregators is becoming common. In the United Kingdom, aggregators have grabbed more than 50 percent of the motor insurance market and are starting to make their presence felt in life insurance. Some insurers listed with aggregators have gained market share but at the cost of profitability. These companies may be hoping to enhance their combined operating ratio when the economy improves and pressure on premiums eases. Other companies are using aggregators to sell loss-leading basic policies, which they then try to make profitable by selling add-on features such as third-party liability or car radio or windscreen covers. Some companies have even created their own price-comparison services.

What Sales-Related Innovations Are Working in Insurance and How Can Other Industries Benefit?

Most insurers recognize that their products are becoming more commoditized. This fact—combined with customers' increasingly jaundiced view of financial institutions (which tends to negate brand strength)—has raised the importance of personal relationships between consumers and independent agents. Add in the fact that certain classes of insurance product are ever more complex and diverse, and it's clear why more customers value unbiased assistance.

So the question becomes: How do insurers excel at persuading independent agents to sell their products instead of those of their competitors? The obvious answer is to have better products and better customer service. However, this is not always possible. And even when it is, there is nearly always a cost premium. Another obvious answer is to give independent agents higher sales commissions. But this is not permitted in all markets. And where it is permissible, such arrangements often must be disclosed, which potentially erodes customer confidence in an agent's objectivity.

The highest-potential strategy, therefore, is to help the agent succeed. To do this, companies can help agents become more conversant by implementing better training programs, increasing access to (and quality of) product information, and providing sales tools that raise the agent's effectiveness and efficiency. In the insurance business, good examples of helpful tools include mobile time and prospect-management applications, collaboration systems that bring product experts into the selling relationship, and analytics solutions that help segment prospects and schedule tailored treatments. Insurers also can work to improve service levels by accelerating application- and claims-response times, and helping agents' businesses run more smoothly.

The overarching goal is getting the agent to view the carrier as his or her ideal partner. In support of that goal, here are some other selling-related strategies—ideas that could also be advantageous to companies outside the insurance industry.

Develop a "new life distribution vision." As the insurance environment becomes more complex, some insurers are realizing they cannot be competitive on all fronts. One option is to "stick to their knitting" and focus on their underwriting and product development capabilities. Like manufacturers in other industries, such firms will be open to working with a wide array of parties—from independent advisors to aggregators—that can deliver their products. Although their brand may not follow the products all the way to the ultimate customer, these insurers will develop specific pricing and delivery strategies that will allow them to be the most selected provider. This may imply establishing a model where they are easy to do business with; can create and maintain the range of products consumers are demanding (from simple policies that can be sold online with minimal if any advice, through to complex, personalized products that require competent advisors to sell them); and provide clear, compelling product information, as well as effective education and training. They also must have the nimbleness to rapidly shape new products at the behest of important distributors.

Embrace "holism." Holism refers to an insurer's managing of five key, disruptive technologies—mobile, analytics, social media, collaboration, and digital marketing/gaming—in an integrated way to transform sales and distribution. Holism represents an extraordinary opportunity for insurers to build innovation into their distribution strategies, helping to improve results and sales gains. The practice provides a key enterprise capability that can improve the overall return on distribution resources for a carrier while creating a more effective emotional connection with consumers, especially the underinsured Millennial and Gen X populations. By leveraging the integrated nature of the aforementioned technologies, insurers can communicate information to customers in the time, place, and format of their choosing—which could help insurers transform their relationship with customers, from one in which customers are "sold" products to one in which customers are actively engaged in educating themselves and collaborating with agents and other desired channels to "buy" products.[3]

Master digital enablement. For most personal-lines insurers, agents are an unmatched source of strong person-to-person customer relationships and distinctive experiences. Insurers can sustain, and even extend, this advantage by fully enabling their agents. On the one hand, that could be as simple as ramping up your web presence. Take Progressive Insurance®, which has partnered with Web.com to offer website templates and search-and-display marketing packages at reduced rates to independent agents. This allows customers to receive online quotes without jeopardizing the relationship with their agent. It also can enhance lead generation. Fueled by advances in real-time experience optimization and configurability, online technologies can further help carriers personalize their customers' digital experiences and integrate unique value propositions for specific customer segments that are likely to value an agent relationship. Carriers also can extend their digital support to help agents connect with customers via social media by providing starter kits, training, best practices, content, seamless access to quoting, and other transactional capabilities. They also can help their agents steer clear of regulatory problems and provide tools for monitoring and improving the effectiveness of their social media investments.

Develop and test new channel approaches. Many insurers' multichannel distribution tactics seem to be working: Analytics and predictive modeling are helping insurers plan and implement a more diverse array of customer-contact points and experiences. Enhanced websites and mobile apps are making it possible for diverse groups of customers to engage more effectively with the insurer. And new and often radical approaches are being invented and tested for use in emerging markets, where customs and infrastructures may be very different from those that insurers are used to. For example, UAP Insurance in Kenya enables farmers to buy crop insurance by using their mobile phone to send in a photograph of the barcode on a bag of fertilizer or seed which they have bought, and to pay premiums using the M-Pesa mobile banking system.[4] Another example: Max India and its partner New York Life Insurance extended their virtual network throughout India by distributing scratch cards through small retailers. Customers paid irregular premiums as and when they could by buying a scratch card and texting the concealed code to the insurer, which credited the amount to the customer's account.[5]

Insights from the Electronics and High-Tech Industry

Reliance on indirect channels is increasing dramatically in the electronics and high-tech (EHT) sector. Five years ago, the percentage of industry revenues coming through the indirect channel is believed to have been 30 percent or less. Estimates now put that total at around 60 percent.[6]

There are many reasons for this jump. One is that indirect channel partners can provide EHT vendors with effective entry paths to emerging, small and mid-size markets. Channel partners bring established local-level relationships and are well positioned to integrate cross-vendor products and serve as trusted advisors. Research bears this out: Often an EHT customer asks the partner for his or her recommendation about what technology solution and brand to purchase, and the customer often accepts the recommendation.

Changes in the EHT business also are the result of "consumerized IT"—devices originally geared to the consumer market (smartphones, tablets, mobile apps) incorporated more and more into businesses' day-to-day operations. The impacts of this trend are broad as well as deep. Most significant may be that employee behaviors, rather than CIO directives, tend to define B2B and B2C companies' interactions with high-tech companies. As a result, vendors' solution-development missions are more experience-based, with dominant considerations being versatility, ease of use, and quality of the user interface. IT professionals are less likely to be drivers and more likely to be intermediaries. The net effect is that tech companies frequently need to realign their sales approaches to communicate more directly with end users.

Another trend—convergence—is highly familiar to EHT companies. For more than a decade, formerly separate disciplines and EHT sectors have been coming together:

- Media companies and retailers are joining the high-tech device market.
- High-tech manufacturers are getting into media (music, video, books distribution) and services (telco networks managed by equipment vendors, printing sold as services rather than devices, etc.).
- Service operators are becoming systems integrators and technology resellers.
- Computer and office equipment manufacturers are acquiring systems integration or outsourcing services companies.
- Internet portal companies are fast becoming the largest vendors of online computing and storage.

As with virtually every industry, EHT companies also must find new ways to sell effectively in emerging markets—to understand unfamiliar cultures, deal with regulatory barriers, identify the right intermediaries, and overcome distribution and channel-development obstacles. But the globalization agenda affects high tech more than most sectors for two reasons. The main reason is that emerging markets move toward mature-market status largely by developing their own high-tech industries (think China with its leading network equipment vendors and computer manufacturers). To counter the threat created by these emerging-market multinationals, high-tech companies need to expand into the territories of these new competitors. Another reason is that the EHT market is largely (though not completely) coupled with the economy and countries' growth in consumption. So growth for EHT companies is to be found in emerging markets—which isn't as true for other industries such as pharmaceuticals, where aging populations continue to spur demand for new compounds, even in mature markets.

How Are EHT Companies Responding?

EHT companies know that their most lucrative customers are tech literate. As a result, many are working harder at listening—for example, through social media and digital channels, which are important to tech customers—to what people say about them and their products, and which rapidly undulating trends are affecting retailers. Armed with these insights, EHT vendors may be better equipped to identify market shifts, communicate ideas, fix problems, influence public opinion, and promote and sell new products and services. Like few other industries, EHT is able to manufacture its own ecosystem for marketing, selling, and customer relationship management.

Still, evolving markets and increasing reliance on indirect channels are causing some EHT companies to reexamine their selling approaches. Many are questioning their channel models' scalability. Others are seeking better ways to collaboratively market, sell to, and service end customers. Still more are reassessing their partner segments—the offers, value propositions, and engagement capabilities needed to collaborate effectively. One example is that, with messages shifting more toward employees and consumers, EHTs are less inclined to sell with technical specs and more likely to emphasize experiences. As a result, they need salespeople who are less tech-intensive and more demo and relationship savvy—those who identify more closely with customers.

Furthermore, EHT companies also invest significantly in sales processes, training, and tools that allow their sales forces to address their clients' business requirements. So the shift, particularly in the B2B space, is toward the experience *and* the business need, and away from technical specifications and fact sheets. An example is the use of business requirements-based parameters rather than technical requirement input sheets to help the salespeople zoom in on the right combination of products, software, and services to address a specific business situation at an enterprise client. The other impact of this trend toward "solutions addressing business requirements" instead of "products meeting technical requirements" is the need for collaborative selling: An EHT company doesn't sell alone; instead, it assembles pieces of the solution from its offerings and other companies' catalogs, working collaboratively with the vendors of these other elements.

Another burgeoning need is for easily reconfigurable, multichannel approaches. Fast-changing markets and rapid-fire introductions of new products make this a necessity. The balance of direct and indirect must be flexible. Reliance on a particular digital channel (e.g., social media) should be able to ebb and flow according to user groups' often-capricious tastes. Adoption of channel-management analytics and segmentation approaches are increasingly vital to ensure that the right KPIs are used to reward top channel partners. Capabilities must be in place to cross-sell and up-sell partners' solutions.

What Sales-Related Innovations Are Working in EHT and How Can Other Industries Benefit?

There are many selling areas where electronics and high-tech companies naturally excel. One is utilization of multiple media. Take Dell® and Microsoft®, which have created online forums and special events for top influencers in social and industry-related media. Given their reach and credibility, such influencers can be powerful extensions of the selling force.

It can't be a surprise that EHT entities are particularly web savvy and media literate. As a result, most industries have much to gain by emulating EHT's technology-driven monitoring, listening, and engaging practices, as well as other EHT-honed capabilities that are somewhat less obvious:

Excel at "channel surfing." This is not about empowering the remote-control-dependent couch potato. It is about knowing customers, understanding how market segments change and, as a result, moving smoothly between channels as customer needs shift. Consider how quickly Apple adopted direct sales—building an impressive network of retail stores without disenfranchising existing channel partners. Or how rapidly Alcatel® shifted from direct to indirect selling in the enterprise space. Or how Dell repeatedly altered its direct/indirect strategy—responding each time to smart assessments of market shifts.

Build superstacks. Superstacks are aggregations of companies whose selling efforts are aided by the collaborative use of others' channels. Benefits include sales forces that are literate in a broader range of areas and the chance to concurrently leverage several companies' marketing and communications infrastructures. Numerous companies leverage this selling-ecosystem approach: Cisco®, EMC®, VMware®; Google®, Samsung®; Microsoft®, Nokia®; and SAP® and—as described in detail in Chapter 11—Accenture.

Develop new approaches for addressing emerging markets. One of the unique advantages of emerging-market multinationals is that they're good at selling in markets with characteristics similar to theirs. Myriad companies have much to gain by understanding and emulating these practices. Ideas for emerging markets also may spring from innovation-focused collaborations. For example, the SAP Co-Innovation Lab® offers a hands-on opportunity to develop new ideas and solutions by bringing together independent software vendors, system integrators, technology partners, and customers.[7]

Excel at consultative solution selling. SAP® and Oracle® have become very good at this. The core mission is developing an iron-clad business case: helping customers understand why it is beneficial to invest significant dollars in a software license. These approaches now are increasingly being used by other tech companies such as printer and network equipment manufacturers.

Understand the potential of moving from a product-only focus to more of a service focus. The best and simplest example of this is the software-as-a-service (cloud) concept. However, there are many others in the EHT arena, such as managed network services, online storage, and managed printing services. Entire industries such as online travel booking are essentially services.

"Copying" Is Encouraged

The most important message this chapter contains is that almost no selling innovation should be thought of as exclusive to one industry if you take the time to look beyond the surface. The real innovation opportunity comes from isolating what caused the sales model to change in the other industry and look for the level of change it could bring to your sales model. Take consumer goods manufacturers, many of which have been point-of-sale innovators. But using smartphones as sales tools and data-collection devices should hardly be the sole province of consumer good companies. The same holds true in pharmaceuticals, a sector whose companies often excel at "influencing the influencers." Who are the influencers in other industries and what potential might they have to regrade the playing field? Then there's the insurance business, which has been forced to deal with inroads made by price-comparison websites (aggregators). Despite the probability of lower margins, some insurers have turned lemons into lemonade by building their own price-comparison capabilities and/or positioning aggregator sales as loss leaders. Might a similar tactic be possible in other fields? Last, electronics and high-tech companies have emerged as superstack leaders: builders of powerful multicompany sales forces. Not surprisingly, EHT companies are also pioneers at repositioning products as services or even more comprehensive solutions. What other industries might do the same?

The obvious conclusion is that there are myriad, industry-agnostic ways to strengthen the selling function: better collaboration, greater channel diversity, more-advanced technology utilization, keener market insights. However, there are many broadly applicable sales capabilities that are just as vital but more subtle. One is adeptly navigating customers' increasingly complex and drawn-out decision-making processes. Another is correctly identifying and connecting with all of a potential customer's power brokers—including the naysayers who never show up during the sales process but can still kill a deal. Perhaps no specific sector is dominant in these areas. But finding the leaders, learning how they do what they do, and making those practices your own, is nonetheless a worthy goal.

SECTION

II

The New Agile Selling Model and Strategy

Making the Agile Selling model work requires companies to adopt a vast range of new capabilities. As they do so, companies likely will encounter an array of challenges and issues they must address. Some areas of the organization may already have well-developed processes in place and leaders who firmly believe in what they've been doing to date (both of which will be hard to change). Other areas may not have been touched in years, or decades, and are ripe for a refresh (but aren't a priority for the team). Still others may be attempting to take advantage of major changes in markets and technology, but may lack in-house skills to succeed in those initiatives. This section outlines the key areas that companies must address to move toward Agile Selling and how to get started.

For instance, in the Agile Selling ecosystem where a B2B company's sales and service life cycle is no longer a linear process, but rather a multidirectional network, how does the company identify, prioritize, contact, manage, and convert sales leads? In our experience, the answer involves a demand-generation approach that relies on advanced analytics to target the right accounts and prioritize leads, is supported by a sophisticated lead routing and nurturing capability and processes that are tightly aligned across all channels, and is paired with a mechanism that enables the company to closely track and measure the results of all leads.

To generate leads more effectively, companies need a tighter focus on the customer buying experience. Indeed, although specific offerings are still the lifeblood of companies, in today's more sophisticated selling ecosystem the most powerful competitive differentiator is how well a company can create and deliver an experience that matches customers' specific needs and preferences. To create such an experience, companies should begin by rethinking the selling process using self-service as a reference point, and creating a new, pull-oriented selling process that is designed around the customer by using insights driven by analytics.

Incentives and pricing also are vital today, just as they always have been. However, the complexities of an Agile Selling model require companies to approach these core capabilities in different ways. For example, companies have always had difficulty truly understanding how well incentives work. In a scenario with more complex selling relationships, determining the ROI from incentives is even harder. Organizations that get the best return on incentives make sure they align incentive programs around their go-to-market model and customer experience blueprint; manage and measure incentive spending as an integrated portfolio at multiple levels; and use advanced analytics to design, test, and dynamically manage incentive programs.

It's the same situation for pricing. Setting the right price to maximize volume and profit has always been a difficult proposition, and it's one that gets even harder the more—and more independent—sales channels a company employs. For these companies, achieving "channel harmony," not cross-channel pricing party, is the name of the game. To achieve such harmony, a company must execute pricing effectively—which requires a company to be able to segment, both its customer and channel base, set the pricing strategy and actual prices for each channel focused on a particular customer segment, and negotiate with profit as well as revenue in mind. Technology tools (especially analytics) and data, appropriate rewards, relevant metrics, and strong governance are enablers that are critical to building a strong pricing capability.

As should be clear by now, a key theme running through the aforementioned capabilities is analytics. Indeed, in our experience, creating and operating an effective and sophisticated Agile Selling model is impossible without the use of modern analytics tools. But analytics also can play a much broader role in significantly improving a company's performance at every step of the sales cycle. Leading companies are using powerful new analytics tools to complement their salespeople's intuition, judgment, and experience, and enable them to make more effective, fact-based decisions. By thus injecting science into selling, companies can exert greater influence on those in the sales process who matter most, evolve from segmented to personalized selling, and get an earlier and more accurate read on sales performance.

In this section, we dig more deeply into these capabilities and how they have helped a number of leading companies enhance the effectiveness of their broader selling ecosystem.

Advanced Strategies for Customer Targeting and Lead Generation

Lan Guan and Golnar Pooya

Chapter Summary

- More ways to interact with customers, more business partners, more uncertainty and simply more variables mean more complexity—but staying the same is not an option for companies with a growth plan.
- In an Agile Selling model, a company doesn't have a linear process for its sales and service life cycle. It has a multidirectional network to manage.
- Multiple dimensions are critical for building a leading demand-generation engine including advanced targeting analytics, integration of lead generation and distribution, multichannel process alignment, and strong focus on return on investment (ROI) measurements.

In recent years, many companies have tightened their belts, and few business functions have been squeezed more than marketing. In these "right-size" marketing organizations, customer targeting and lead generation are the most common and serious casualties. This is not surprising, because marketing can have a somewhat esoteric image. In many business-to-business companies, lead times from lead generation to sales conversion can be long, and multiple entities can be involved along the way. As a result, it can be tough to track marketing's role and value in a final sale. Thus, in a selling environment that is increasingly complex, marketing teams are challenged to do more with less, producing more productive leads while reducing the average cost per lead to improve profitability.

This chapter looks at what organizations can do to optimize customer targeting and lead generation in an Agile Selling environment characterized by profit pressure and a process path (from lead generation to sales conversion) that now has more twists, turns, forks, intersections, and decision points than ever. An obvious cornerstone is using analytics-driven insights to create a scientific and sustainable way to identify, prioritize, contact, manage, and convert leads.

Lead Generation's New Profile: More Channels, More Challenges

It's tough to thrive in today's B2B selling environment. More ways to interact with customers, more business partners, more uncertainty, and simply more variables mean more complexity. In this environment, traditional mass lead generation techniques are less effective and increasingly expensive. Everyone has to work harder. As the Red Queen said to Alice in *Through the Looking-Glass*, "Now, here, you see, it takes all the running you can do to stay in the same place."[1] But staying the same is not an option for companies with a growth plan (which is, in essence, all of them). Lower budgets mean sales and marketing teams must find more effective mechanisms to target fewer, higher-quality leads—all with a lower average cost per lead.

But are things really that different? After all, the number of enterprise accounts for a typical B2B company has long been in the thousands (and the market is far larger if you include small- and medium-size businesses). What specifically has changed? And what new actions and resources are needed to stock the kind of pipelines that maximize salespeople's time, talents, and conversion potential?

The answer to the first question is *yes*: It really is a brave new selling world. Consider, for example, how many ways there are to interact with customers and deliver products and services through intermediaries (Figure 6.1). Couple this with extended sales cycles involving multiple buyers and influencers throughout the process, and the account targeting and lead generation process is complex. More players. More

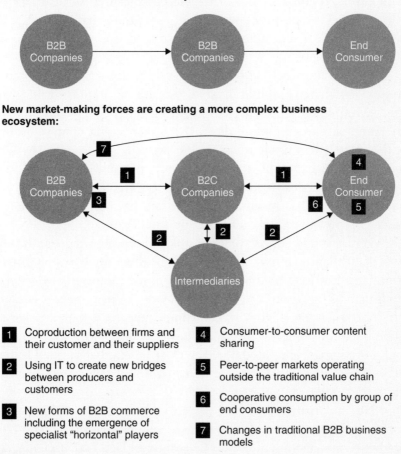

FIGURE 6.1 Today's Lead Generation Environment Is More Complex Than Ever Before

handoffs. More handshakes. More variables (e.g., the B2B prospect's buying path and the structure of the provider's offer). New metrics for measuring success.

In this new ecosystem, a B2B company doesn't have a linear process for its sales and service life cycle. It has a multidirectional network to manage. Each salesperson thus has a more-networked role, with information and leads coming from multiple intermediaries. As a result, sales teams must figure out the right strategic role to play with each intermediary. First and foremost, this means making good choices about channels—an increasingly vital skill as organizations home in on joint customers through their alliance relationships. All in all, today's multichannel selling processes require more information, more technology, more collaboration, more investment dollars, and more skills and training.

Beyond more selling channels, modern-day leads literally come from everywhere: traffic at a retail location, an inquiry from a web visitor, responses from a direct marketing campaign, follow-up from an event, hits from mobile devices, interaction via contact centers. It therefore is less viable to assess and prioritize all leads in the same manner; there are simply too many sizes, types, and variables. Adding more fuel to the lead-complexity fire is the increased likelihood that an organization has recently added selling partners or expanded its product portfolio through a merger or acquisition.

With so many sources of leads, quality becomes significantly more important than quantity. This potentially alters the entire marketing paradigm. For example, launching additional campaigns to generate leads may be more likely to cause "lead fatigue" than make a salesperson more successful. Nor can companies repeatedly mass market the same set of customers. Customers have become more sophisticated, and more impact is needed to shape their buying behaviors. Overtargeting customers and deluging them with information will probably harm the relationship more than help it.

Not surprisingly, the best place to find examples of higher customer sophistication is online—a place where buyers (B2B and B2C) are better informed than ever. The reality, in fact, is that many companies are nowhere close to turning online marketing into the lead-generation gold mine it could be. To maximize sales opportunities and returns on their marketing investments, companies must do a better job of understanding how online behavior integrates and interacts with offline behavior. This is where analytics comes in—the single best tool companies have to track leading indicators and understand buyer conversations, preferences, and trends.

So what's the bottom line in this new customer-empowered, lead-choked, partner-intensive environment? Without the right technology—framed by a new account targeting and lead management strategy—companies likely will incur higher costs per lead and therefore higher costs of sales and stifled growth. With more channels, too many (but too few quality) leads, and no good way to separate the wheat from the chaff, marketing's ROI will probably suffer. Salespeople may be less productive and funds misspent (e.g., pouring marketing dollars into poorly performing channels and campaigns). Sales resources could be inappropriately or unproductively allocated. Longer term, there's the potential for diminished share and reduced ability to crack new markets.

Responding with Technology

Recognizing (at least part of) the problem, many companies are investing in tools to improve marketing effectiveness and optimize lead generation. In fact, a recent study among business-to-business (B2B) marketing organizations indicated that nearly one-fourth of the B2B organizations surveyed lack a marketing automation platform plan to invest in one.[2] However, improper deployment and misperceptions about these tools' capabilities often undermine those entities' lead-management enhancements and may even produce a rise in manual (workaround) processes. For example, several organizations have sought to improve demand generation by investing in sales pipeline management and marketing resource management (MRM) technologies. But these have improved a single silo of the process at best. Others have invested in advanced reporting tools—focusing on a single set of metrics and results tracking, but not concentrating hard enough on where demand is coming from or which customers and prospects to prioritize.

Even analytics can misfire without supporting data-management capabilities and tight alignment with the sales process. The problem arises when companies position analytics as *the* solution, instead of a key component of the solution. The other key ingredient is clean, accurate data available in large quantities. Analytics without high-quality *and* high-quantity data is like feeding junk food into a healthy body: It fills you up but there's no real value.

For these reasons, at least in part, one-third of respondents to the B2B marketing study use their marketing automation platforms only occasionally. Furthermore, less than half (43 percent) of those surveyed have translated their investments into improved lead conversion rates.

In sum, today's demand-generation reality is often a well-intended but disjointed collection of investments: all or most of the right ingredients but no proven recipe for creating a synergistic end product. What's needed is an overarching strategy for integrating and aligning new tools with account targeting approaches, lead-generation processes, lead-nurturing methods, and clearly defined sales approaches. In the next section, we suggest ways to make that happen.

A Leading-Practice Approach to Demand Generation

Acquiring more and better leads—and fully leveraging their value—requires sophisticated strategies, advanced tools (e.g., predictive analytics, lead generation, campaign management), and a clear sense of mission: targeting the right accounts with the right offerings, the right engagement methods, and the right messages. There are five dimensions to such an approach:

1. Utilizing advanced analytics to target the right accounts.
2. Integrating analytics capabilities to prioritize leads.
3. Backing up the lead generation process with intelligent lead distribution capabilities.

4. Aligning processes across multiple channels.
5. Implementing a measurement and result-tracking capability.

Utilizing Advanced Analytics to Target the Right Accounts

A precursor to setting marketing objectives and lead generation methods is developing a clear understanding of the customer engagement experience across the company. Sales, marketing, service, and other customer-facing organizations must work together to define a holistic customer engagement experience that is inclusive of each customer interaction across both online and offline channels. The customer engagement design serves as the overarching blueprint for demand generation programs. (For more on the customer buying experience, see Chapter 7.)

The first step toward improved account targeting is gaining better customer intelligence. By combining existing customer data, secondary research, and interviews with subject matter experts, the B2B marketing team can create a single, consolidated view of specific customers and customer types. It can then use advanced analytics to model customer behaviors and help go-to-market teams gain insights about high-potential targets and markets. Leading companies use analytics and statistical modeling to build an account-targeting engine that provides insights about target accounts and assesses prospects as sales leads (Figure 6.2). The modeling process is built on a rigorous methodology for customer segmentation: creating customer categories that align with the company's business objectives. The idea is to group customers based on the statistical significance of certain variables (e.g., industry, purchase volumes, propensity to buy) and thus obtain a clear data picture with which to define marketing objectives.

One company in the communications industry with which Accenture works has aggressively built such an account-targeting engine. To counter strong competition and achieve growth, the company

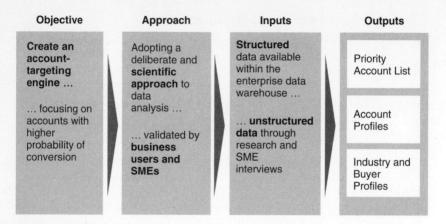

Objective	Approach	Inputs	Outputs
Create an account-targeting engine ... ... focusing on accounts with higher probability of conversion	Adopting a deliberate and **scientific approach** to data analysis ... ... validated by **business users and SMEs**	**Structured** data available within the enterprise data warehouse ... ... **unstructured data** through research and SME interviews	Priority Account List — Account Profiles — Industry and Buyer Profiles

FIGURE 6.2 Using Analytics to Target the Right Accounts with the Best Sales Intelligence

needed deep customer insight and targeting along with better channel alignment and development. Business analytics from SAS® helped the company to redefine the medium business customer in less than three months by aggregating a variety of external and internal data sources into a 360-degree view of the customer.

The new approach allowed the company to understand who its medium business customers were well beyond their industry codes—providing a complete customer-centric view. Questions they could answer included: Where is the customer located—including its headquarters and branch offices? What's the corporate structure? How many employees? How many and what type of communications services did the company use across voice, data, IP, and managed services?

Armed with this 360-degree view, the company could statistically segment its mainstream and premium customers into micro-segments, grouping various businesses in unexpected new ways. In turn, this allowed the company to determine the right channel treatment and solutions for each customer segment. Essentially, with a 360-degree view, this communications company can determine which customers require what coverage because they know so much more about them.

Integrating Analytics Capabilities to Prioritize Leads

When a company has a large number of leads to work from, it requires a method for prioritizing them. Prioritization is a predictive analytics' key contribution to lead generation and management. Predictive analytics look historically at what kinds of leads have a higher conversion rate—what types of customers were attracted by which offers—and finds the potential leads that "look" like the historical successes. By identifying key characteristics of past successful campaigns and applying this understanding to the potential population, the analytics define the leads with a higher propensity to be converted into sales.

It's important to note that there are two basic kinds of analytics. Descriptive analytics (the more basic and established) provides a way to look back at historical data and answer questions such as what happened, why it happened, and how much it hurt or benefited the organization. Predictive analytics use quantitative methods to derive forward-looking insights from data. Predictive analytics leverage descriptive analytics, but add sophisticated statistical modeling, forecasting, and optimization to gauge potential business outcomes. Predictive analytics also can help companies forecast demand at very granular levels, and even determine in advance how to respond to disruptive events such as market shifts and product-supply disruptions.

Sophisticated analytics users are better equipped to understand what kinds of leads have high(er) conversion rates and what types of customers are (more) attracted by which offers. In effect, these companies know more about what the best potential leads "look like."

Lead qualification with analytics requires two lenses: a value lens and a win-potential lens.

1. *Value-based qualification*: Understanding the importance of each customer based on his or her buying history, sales-growth potential, and strategic positioning.
2. *Win-rate-based qualification*: Calculating the likelihood of closing a sale with a specific customer or prospect.

Companies that have an engine in place to process large amounts of data and a large number of variables can tag different scores to sets of leads. They thereby have a mathematical method to rank different prospects and leads in a multitude of ways that result in more productive leads while using fewer resources.

By using advanced analytics for predictive targeting, companies are more likely to be offering the "right touch at the right time" and are thus able to generate more qualified leads, have more customers respond to marketing campaigns, and make sales strategies more effective.

Backing Up the Lead Generation Process with Intelligent Lead Distribution Capabilities

Although lead generation mechanisms that are enabled by advanced analytics will produce higher-quality leads, those leads also must be managed and nurtured across the extended selling network. Leading companies ensure that a well-structured and optimized lead routing and nurturing capability exists before investing in pure lead-generation advances. Such a capability deploys lead-scoring and routing approaches to align the highest-potential customers with the right resources at the right time. A national insurance company implemented analytics-driven lead distribution that resulted in a net gain of $118 million in 12 months. And by implementing a lead-nurturing program, one global telecom company was able to achieve a 400 percent improvement in qualification rates.

Aligning Processes across Multiple Channels

Delivering on the promise of the customer experience requires that organizations are highly integrated across the end-to-end process from lead generation to customer retention. There are multiple dimensions to such integration.

Sales and marketing have long struggled with the handoff of leads between the two organizations. Sales evaluation of leads is often based on what they know about the customer: a combination of perception and experience. Marketing tends to use scientific methods for lead generation and analysis, especially when the above advanced analytics are in place. Thus, it is paramount to reach agreement between sales and marketing on the criteria for determining a qualified lead so there is a consistent process for how and when leads generated by marketing are pursued by the sales team. The key here is close integration between marketing and sales, with common approaches to defining customer value, executing handoffs, and managing data flows. This is particularly critical in an Agile Selling environment where there are both direct sales teams and channel partners involved in the lead management process.

Integration across the multichannel environment is also increasingly important. Not only are there multiple entities (marketing, sales, and channel partners) pursuing, and communicating with, the target account, there are multiple channels by which the customer is receiving and offering information that may be important (think social media such as LinkedIn®, the call center, or your website as starters). Thus, leading companies develop a means to coordinate and integrate these multiple channels and multiple contact mechanisms in their lead nurturing efforts.

Implementing a Measurement and Result-Tracking Capability

A critical part of improving the return on investment from lead generation is measuring that such progress is being made. Thus, companies need to develop key performance indicators for lead tracking and management and implement end-to-end measurement of the process' effectiveness. It is particularly important to develop a feedback loop for continuously testing and learning from responses.

Winning companies have taken a strategy decomposition approach to develop and prioritize key performance metrics. By taking this approach, companies can create tight linkages between strategies, value drivers, causal drivers, and key decisions (Table 6.1).

TABLE 6.1 Strategy Decomposition Approach

Strategic Theme	Value Driver	Causal Driver	Key Decisions
Grow net adds	Share of mass market revenue	• Marketing activity levels • Marketing tactic productivity • Pipeline strength • New acquisitions • Disconnects • Renewal rate • Churn • Backlog	• How do we allocate the marketing mix to target the appropriate target customer segments? • How do we best price our services to retain existing customers (early adopters, fast followers)? • What is our price sensitivity relative to our competitors? • Why do we have backlogs in certain regions? • What approaches should we adopt to close a high percentage of high-propensity leads? • How do we improve our customer qualification process?

Lead Management's Leading Edge

The earlier approach can help deliver what many sales organizations need:

- The opportunity to create more targeted campaigns with better-quality leads.
- A broad, multichannel mix of lead sources, with messages, offers, and lists optimized through testing.
- Stringent, analytically driven lead qualification.
- Valuable, ongoing guidance for the sales organization. Scoring and prioritization is provided for all leads. Leads can be rescored and reprioritized as they travel through the sales pipeline and updated information is acquired.
- End-to-end alignment: Marketing and sales share responsibility for lead generation and management. Standard best practices apply globally to both sales and marketing. Key performance indicators, accurate data, and analytics work together to assess performance.

B2C businesses have worked to optimize many of the components of this approach for years. Based on our experience, selected B2C companies have grown year-on-year market share by as much as 30 percent, increased sales by up to 50 percent, and reduced customer attrition by 40 percent. These results suggest B2B companies could also benefit from employing advanced analytics for account targeting and lead management as described here to potentially deliver a high return on investment. The main reason is the strategy's concentration on five imperatives:

1. Working smarter than competitors by making better use of advanced analytics.
2. Using analytically derived insights to fully understand individual customers and specific segments of customers.
3. Formulating prioritization strategies based on targets' value and conversion likelihood.

4. Creating clear, channel-based approaches for optimizing customer touches in cooperation with sales partners.
5. Aligning lead-generation and management advances with established or upgraded sales and marketing processes.

To some degree, this may sound generic, but the reality is that
few B2B sales and marketing organizations do it successfully. Virtually
every B2B company—particularly those selling through an ever-larger
network of partners—must excel at lead generation and management.
And currently, not many do.

A Renewed Focus on the Differentiated Customer Buying Experience

Ron Ref and Ami Palan

Chapter Summary

- The message is clear: More and more customers want things that traditional sales approaches may not provide: context; relevance; and deep product, service, application, and market insights that resonate with customer needs.

- Research shows that nearly half of all surveyed firms with annual revenue exceeding $1 billion believe that "the customer buying experience is a significant competitive differentiator."[1] However, those executives' actions speak far less loudly than their words.

- The time and money spent to create a differentiated customer buying experience are among the best and most fundamental sales-related investments a company can make.

The basis of selling used to be about products and services: "What our product can do for you." "How our service can enhance your business." "How what we sell benefits what you do." Products and services are still the heart of any selling ecosystem. But more and more often, the defining variable is context: creating, managing, and leveraging a positive, motivating *customer experience that is matched to the customer's specific needs*.

Numerous trends are behind the increased focus on the customer buying experience. The most obvious and long-standing is a steady rise in customer power. Although still happening, for the most part it is old news: Power has been shifting toward the consumer for years, with most every innovation and innovator (think Walmart®, Amazon.com®, and Expedia®) bringing more power to the people. Add to this other forces such as increased commoditization, declines in customer loyalty, empowerment through information sharing, and so forth, and the power shift is nothing short of seismic.

These trends point to an inconvenient truth: Organizations that neither hear nor respond to the "voice of the customer" will lose ground to entities with more keenly developed senses. And corporate sales organizations that fail to create different selling approaches for different customer segments will be less likely to recognize and cater to the issues and concerns that are most important to the customer.

As customer power increases and customers' buying processes become more sophisticated and complex to navigate, many B2B organizations are challenged to serve the varying needs of their customer base in a way that adds value but is also efficient. This chapter analyzes the customer-experience phenomenon and offers insights for building customer-centric sales approaches and support systems that optimally serve.

The Forces of Change: What's Driving the Emphasis on Customer Buying Experiences?

Across many industries, the process of reaching the customer and influencing his or her decision making is becoming logarithmically more complex. Power rests more than ever in the hands of the customer whose needs, expectations, and requirements are rapidly evolving. Concurrently, innovations in technology and changing market dynamics are also driving the need for sales organizations to better understand their customers' buying behaviors. Here is a broader look at why today's sales teams must center their selling approaches on the customer's buying preferences.

Power to the Customer

If we acknowledge that customers are now in the driver's seat, it stands to reason that those same customers are using new benchmarks to make their buying decisions. After all, they're better informed; technology has made it easier for them to do their homework. Consequently, they know that whatever product or service they're considering is not the only game in town. Chances also are good that they know more about an item's strengths and weaknesses, and even what the seller's costs are (consider how accepted it now is for auto buyers to demand a look at the dealer's invoice). Last, customers are acutely aware of how many ways there are to acquire the same item. In effect, people depend less on the salesperson as a source of basic information. Customers expect to buy the way they want to buy. They expect an experience that is targeted to their needs.

All that knowledge cannot help but undermine a buyer's loyalty. Loyalty by definition is relationship-based, but most companies have come to assume that customers are loyal because (1) "we give them the best deal," (2) "what we sell is what they've always needed," or (3) "we're 'the devil they know'—loyalty persists because our customers understand what they're getting." None of these justifications hold up in a highly customer-centric world. Loyalty must be built on other foundations.

It thus follows that empowered customers (particularly in B2B, where insights and expertise are highest) are less impressed by traditional sales skills. For many, the sales event may actually add little or no value to their core mission: identifying and procuring the right solution. According to an Accenture study of the chemical industry, 70 percent of customers surveyed do not believe that salespeople are a valuable part of the buying relationship with their supplier.[2]

The message is clear: More and more customers want things that traditional sales approaches may not provide: context; relevance; and deep product, service, application, and market insights that resonate with customer needs. They want a relationship that begins with the customer—not the product or service. And they want the ability to buy through the channel of their choice, which implies that sales reps must understand certain parts of a customer's business better than the customers do themselves. In effect, the rep's job is increasingly consultative and the customer experience is largely fashioned by listening.

Technology as a Driver of Change

Twenty-first-century selling clearly features a different kind of buyer: more informed, harder to please, and less inclined to be loyal. In turn, connecting with that buyer requires a different kind of selling venue—not just different pitches, terms, and tactics, but a largely new selling environment that feels different, focuses on different things, and emphasizes different outcomes. A great many innovations and events have helped fashion that environment.

Social media has been one of the most powerful accelerants of increasing the power in the hands of the customer. Via social media, customers receive objective and (even more importantly) *subjective* information from people they know and respect—friends, acquaintances, business connections. In such situations, good news travels fast, but bad news travels even faster.

It's almost impossible to talk about social media without mentioning mobility. Like social media, smartphones and tablets have altered the nature of information and the speed with which it travels. Because of mobile technology flooding into use in the workplace, business customers are more often using the same technology at home and at work with almost instantaneous opportunities to acquire information, forward feedback, and voice grievances. Sales reps are theoretically available 24/7. Mobile device use in the workplace is changing how businesses procure products and services as well as how companies connect with customers—which looks more and more like how they would connect with consumers. For selling organizations, mobility is a huge change driver.

The "everything as a service" phenomenon is also a great example of how the customer experience paradigm is changing the purchase of technology and technology-related products. The advent of cloud computing and software-as-a-service is, in effect, a transition for the buyer from buying a product to buying a service. How the product is purchased, how quickly it can be implemented, how postcontract service is provided are all aspects of the buying life cycle that are redefined by the cloud. To the buyer, cloud means "I can get it fast," "I can pay as I go," and "I get the latest innovations for free" (among other mind-set shifts). This is a completely different value proposition for the seller to deliver against than the old world of selling software implemented on the customer's hardware.

Unique Buying Preferences of High-Growth Markets

Last, to capitalize on some of the world's fastest-growing and potentially most lucrative markets, companies must find effective and efficient selling approaches that meet the specific needs of those markets, which may be very different from the buying preferences of enterprises in mature markets. Simply consider the small- and medium-size business market (SMB), which companies often reach through a distributor or reseller. As we explore in Chapter 12, the SMB buyer's need for education and service as well as his or her preferred method of buying and interacting with vendors is very different from a buyer in a multinational corporation reached through a direct sales force. Similarly, a corporate buyer in China may have very different preferences and needs than one in Western Europe or Brazil.

Companies Have Been Slow to Change

The argument for building the selling process around the customer's preferred buying experience is strong: more powerful customers, shifting buying criteria, evolving technology, and fast-changing expectations and needs. Yet research shows that most companies are slow to make the transition. According to one study, nearly half of all

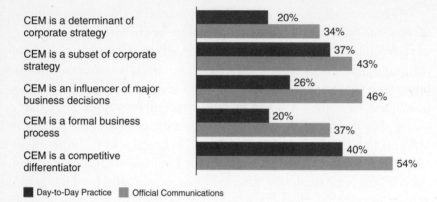

CEM is a determinant of corporate strategy — 20% / 34%

CEM is a subset of corporate strategy — 37% / 43%

CEM is an influencer of major business decisions — 26% / 46%

CEM is a formal business process — 20% / 37%

CEM is a competitive differentiator — 40% / 54%

■ Day-to-Day Practice ■ Official Communications

Ranked by: Impact on Corporate Strategy

FIGURE 7.1   Top Management's Official Communications about Customer Experience Management (CEM) Relative to Their Day-to-Day Actions

Source: 1st Annual ClearAction Business-to-Business Customer Experience Management Benchmarking Study, ClearAction, 2010.

researched firms with annual revenue exceeding US$1 billion believe that "the customer buying experience is a significant competitive differentiator."[3] However, those executives' actions speak far less loudly than their words (Figure 7.1). The reality, in fact, is that companies devote as little as one percent of their annual revenue to understanding and enhancing the customer buying experience.

Similar findings were revealed in another study: Almost half of researched companies with US$1 billion or more in revenue do not have a clear understanding of their customers' buying processes or how those processes affect the company's internal sales processes (Figure 7.2).[4] The bottom line: How to optimize the customer buying experience is still undecided in a great many organizations.

So why haven't companies done more to create differentiated customer buying experiences? Part of the problem may be that change is happening so fast that sales organizations simply can't keep up. Large companies, for example, generally have multiple business units, myriad stakeholders, and untold selling and customer relationship

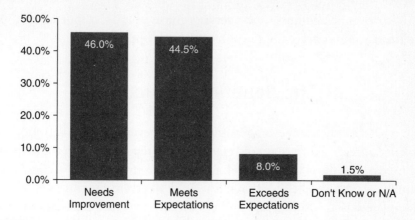

FIGURE 7.2   Companies' Understanding of the Customer Buying Process

Source: CSO Insights, Sales Performance Optimization Research, 2012.

management (CRM) processes. Even if they use standardized selling approaches, these are not necessarily easier to alter: New, pan-organizational agreements and alignments relating to segmentation, process consistency, territory coverage, and so on, must be forged and implemented, and this is tough to achieve when most decision making happens at the business-unit level.

In addition, ownership of the customer experience is still undefined in most organizations. So rather than address the complete end-to-end experience, companies are more comfortable with bite-size pieces: Identifying and addressing discrete opportunities or areas of notable customer dissatisfaction.

Finally, many B2B organizations struggle to meet diverse customer buying needs in a way that adds value but is also efficient. Despite efforts to manage the variability and complexity of their market through sophisticated customer segmentation, B2B companies are ultimately falling short in making such segmentation actionable or embedded throughout the enterprise. They fall back on an efficient, "one size fits all" treatment that fails to address customers' individual preferences, or they employ a segmented approach that results in poor and inefficient allocation of sales and marketing resources: Overserving less-strategic customers, underserving those of most importance, and failing to align effectively to capture growth opportunities.

The Benefits of Change

So what exactly are we suggesting? We believe that time and money spent to create a differentiated customer buying experience are among the best and most fundamental sales-related investments a company can make. We also believe that it is feasible to create a highly adaptable, template-based, world-class, and comprehensive customer experience despite the huge variability in customer mix that most B2B companies must manage. We further believe that any sales organization that truly connects with customers (i.e., that builds sales processes around the customer) will enjoy a steadily increasing edge in the marketplace.

To fully align cost-to-sell and serve with customers' evolving needs and expectations, B2B companies should create formal "customer buying experience strategies." The reason is simple: Developing a differentiated B2B customer buying experience will drive incremental value for the organization. As illustrated in Figure 7.3, there are three dimensions to this truism:

1. Lower costs: Decreased front-office selling costs and reduced sales operations costs. With a formal, standardized, customer buying experience strategy, companies can lower their costs to sell and serve by improving overall sales-related efficiencies. For example, a clear-cut strategy makes it easier to optimize specific parts of the sales and marketing mix—identifying and implementing high-return investments. The same strategy can help a company identify the most cost-effective mix of personnel, as well as the right technology investments to support specific sales objectives. And a formal strategy allows a company to migrate less-important or easy-sell customers to less-costly channels, thus freeing up funds to create more unique experiences for high-value customers.

2. Higher revenue: Improved customer-acquisition capabilities, opportunity to sell more to existing customers, improved

customer retention, and more chances to sell highly profitable solutions and services. Companies with advanced customer buying experience strategies do a better job of capturing opportunities and identifying and correcting performance gaps. They are better able to see what changes to make internally to deliver what customers desire, as opposed to what sales protocols are required by company management. For example, does a company require customers to adhere to payment plans they do not like? Or is it bundling SKUs for its own convenience instead of based on what appeals to its customers? Is the company selling what and how the customer wants to buy?

3. Other (intangible) benefits: Increased customer loyalty, improved net promoter scores, and greater customer satisfaction. Customer-centric sales processes are key to enhancing loyalty. Salespeople's interactions become more personalized. Sales metrics become more valuable, more accurate, and easier to formulate. Sole-source contracts become easier to secure.

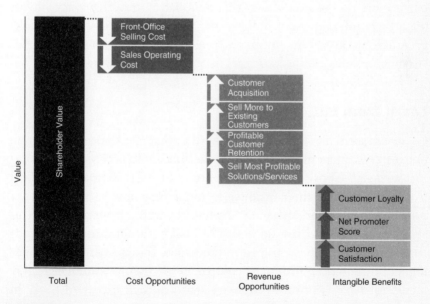

FIGURE 7.3   The Value of a Differentiated B2B Customer Buying Experience

A Structured Approach to Optimizing the Customer Buying Experience

Strategies for creating selling processes that are fully aligned to the customer buying experience have two primary pillars: (1) rethinking the selling process using self-service as a reference point, and (2) creating a new, pull-oriented selling process that is designed around the customer. There are six "key design principles" to consider.

Acknowledge the Need for Self-Service

Offering a self-service channel has become more the rule than the exception. This is not simply a way to shunt customers to a less-convenient but more economical venue. Instead it is an increasingly vital part of a larger menu of connection options. Some customers will prefer this alternative. Other, lower-priority customers may have to be "steered" toward it. Either way, a self-service channel is key, but it must represent a highly accommodating experience for buyers (e.g., by emulating the simplicity and user friendliness of Facebook® or Amazon.com). This implies stronger mandates, not so much for "user acceptance testing" but for "user experience testing."

Learn from B2C

Generally speaking, B2C companies are further ahead when it comes to putting customers first (perhaps the best example is consumers' comfort with self-service). Thus it's important for B2B companies to learn from the leaders—the consumer-facing companies that already have executed a consumer experience strategy. Learning from the B2C firms also is important because so many B2B buyers are now using stipend-based business models: Instead of the procurement organization buying and distributing products, companies are giving employees allotments to make approved purchases that are then expensed back. In these situations, buyers are essentially interacting with companies as consumers.

Think and Design to How the Customer Experiences the Enterprise

Design internal sales processes based on customers' buying experience and their intentions when buying—such as how they intend to compare offerings or their intent to pay using a certain method of payment. This is, in part, a culture thing: inverting the company's perspective from a psychology of selling to a psychology of buying. In effect, the best sellers think like buyers; they empathize. This helps them formulate tailored approaches that speak to what the *customer* wants.

Empower Channel Partner

Our experience is, in the high-tech industry for example, that approximately two-thirds of the time, a channel partner is predisposed to recommend a specific brand to a customer. The customer usually accepts that recommendation. The channel can be very influential in a customer's buying decision. To generate the greatest return on channels, companies must be sure that the segments they are targeting for growth are aligned with the channel partner's targets. They also can motivate channel partners to sell their products by leveraging their scale to take on activities (such as marketing) that will decrease channel partners' costs and make it easier for them to sell to joint targets.

Think Solutions, Not Just Products

The distinction is important. Even if customers are seeking something as simple as a printer, that printer it still a solution to a problem: People need to print something. To do so, they need paper, printer ink, possibly a cable, and some may even need consulting on how to set it up within their network. Too often, companies bundle SKUs and services based on what they are offering instead of developing bundles from the perspective of what the customer wants or needs to buy. Consider a high-tech company moving in the small and medium-size business (SMB) market. The SMBs have very different needs than the company's enterprise customers, and yet the company offers its enterprise solution to this market. Why? Because it was very difficult to engineer, configure, and support the bundled solution the SMB market needs because the organization isn't structured to do it. Companies that think in terms of solutions find ways to overcome these issues and bundle and present their offerings in the way the customer wants to buy.

Diagnosing Customer Needs

Companies seeking to redesign their selling process around their customers' buying experience generally do so as part of a broader redesign of the customer experience across the organization. However, for the sales organization the process can generally be broken down into two parts: diagnosing customer needs, and then designing and building selling processes against those needs. The diagnosis is based on gathering and synthesizing a variety of customer and market information to produce an integrated segment-by-segment analysis of customer needs and value propositions. (See Figure 7.4.)

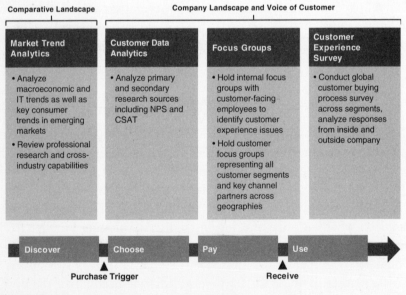

FIGURE 7.4 Diagnosing Customer Needs

Several data sources can be combined to provide the insights for diagnosing customer needs.

Analyze Market Trends

Study technological, socioeconomic, and industry trends and events; assess their relevance to the company; and use these findings to create future-state process-design parameters. Examples of trends and events might include the growing impact of social media, cloud computing, mobile technologies, and software-as-a-service, as well as the consumerization of IT, the growth of emerging markets, and the ability to use predictive analytics and granular segmentation to understand and anticipate customer expectations.

Analyze Existing Data

Begin by identifying existing customer touch points to determine the moments of truth in the customer's existing buying life cycle. Gather voice-of-customer information to help identify current and future requirements and expectations. Compiling needs and preference data from customers can take significant effort, time, and resources, but online tools and analytics can make the job easier. Such technologies can help a company create meaningful customer segments, understand buyer values, determine customers' willingness to pay, identify key purchase drivers, measure "why" and "how" customers make decisions, and detect common themes and buying patterns. For the most part, such technologies use analytics to understand data and look ahead to formulate differentiated customer buying experiences that will be relevant over the long term. They also can help align each customer's preferences with the most relevant messages and offerings.

Launch Focus Groups

The objective here is to use a representative cross section of customers to provide direct insights that help feed the design of a future-state sales process—a cohesive, best-of-breed purchase experience. Internal and external groups are organized more or less the same way, with similar discussion points (moments of truth, current-state priorities, future-state priorities).

Conduct Customer Experience Surveys

Consider developing a customer survey focused on determining future-state preferences to provide a quantitative data source for supporting the development of a customer experience blueprint and sales process. Methodologies such as value stream mapping can be very helpful in customer needs diagnosis and experience design. They help to document information and material flows across customer segments and regions, and can help participants understand the potential impact of new customer-experience-centric processes. For example, such a tool might help assess the incremental revenue bump generated by a new customer-friendly payment option. Conversely, it could help quantify the negative consequences (lost opportunities, higher costs) associated with an organization's current sales-centric processes.

Designing and Building the Experience

Understanding the specific needs and variability in the customer mix is fundamental to a B2B company's ability to efficiently align its resources to maximize revenue and profitability. By splitting customers into like groups according to their needs and key characteristics identified through the process above, companies should be able to create unique and deliberate buying experiences that allow the company to become the number one choice at customer accounts where it seeks a high share of wallet and future growth, while still keeping it competitive at other customers that, taken together, are important for the company's bottom line.

Many factors contribute to a customer's overall buying decision. However, most customer-supplier relationships can be characterized by a single factor that directly or indirectly dominates the customer's decision to choose a supplier. This buying orientation is a primary means by which customers can be segmented and different selling strategies can be deployed.

For this reason, the first step in designing a customer-experience strategy is to identify the distinct principal buying orientations that represent the company's customer base. Although the principal orientations of buyers must be defined by each company, the following buying orientations are most common to B2B markets[5]:

- *Price orientation*: Customers are most interested in price and will generally default to the best deal. A long-term relationship with the supplier is of low importance.
- *Transaction orientation*: Customers buy according to how well a vendor meets the customer's expectations regarding the buying process. Some customers may want an easy, intuitive transaction that is predictable and hassle-free. Others may desire a more engaged and consultative buying process.
- *Basic solution orientation*: Customers want low prices and standard product and service offerings. They place the most importance on the high reliability of supply and the low total cost of ownership.
- *Reliability orientation*: Reliability of products and services is paramount—often because the customer's operations depend on it. These customers will invariably choose the most reliable offerings over those with the lowest price.
- *Quality and performance orientation*: Customers desire the best product and service quality and are willing to pay a premium for it. High reliability is assumed. Customers that place a premium on the supplier's sustainability record may also be placed in this grouping.
- *Brand and image orientation*: Customers place a lot of trust in the supplier's and the product's brand, reputation, and market history.
- *Relationship orientation*: Customers emphasize their history with the supplier and the knowledge the supplier has of their business. Long-entrenched relationships between various parts of the customer and buyer organizations are key, and these relationships act as a barrier to the entry of new suppliers.
- *Customized solution orientation*: Customers want niche solutions that are available only to them or a very narrow group of other

customers. The supplier's ability to innovate to meet customer-specific needs is very important to this group, and the customer often relies on the supplier to support the former's own differentiation efforts. Characteristics such as quality, performance, and reliability are a given.

Two important factors should be considered when determining buying orientation. First, the needs expressed by customers may not always convey their principal buying orientation. To illustrate, consider a company whose procurement, manufacturing, and marketing groups have different supplier-selection priorities. Procurement may emphasize best price, manufacturing may focus on supply reliability, and marketing may value a specific product attribute that enhances the differentiability of the company's own product offering. If the buying decisions are primarily price-driven and do not recognize the input of manufacturing and marketing, acting on the price-centric buying orientation is key to winning the business. Second, what matters when winning the business is not always the same as what matters after the business is won. Once a sale has been made, sustaining and growing the relationship often means meeting the needs of stakeholders other than those involved in the buying decision.

Acknowledging the above codicils, sales executives can start by selecting the minimum number of buying orientations that best fit their industry and current customer base. These orientations should accommodate a large number of customers, have measurable size and purchasing power, reflect different customer responses to the marketing mix, and represent an actionable opportunity for the company.

Once a company selects these principal buying orientations, it should classify every customer into at least one group. Subsequently, it should divide customers on the basis of their overall strategic importance to the company. While a number of attributes can define the strategic value of the customer, two criteria apply well in most situations. The first is the current financial importance of the customer (often measured as contribution margin), and the second is the achievable growth potential at that account.

Segmenting the customer base by using a composite view of customer value and buying orientation then provides a map by which

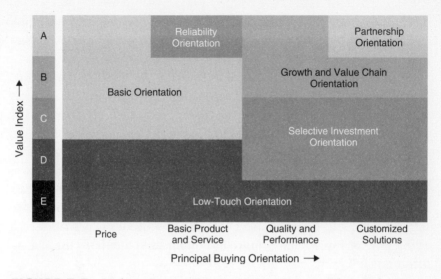

FIGURE 7.5   Linking Buyers' Primary Orientations to Their Value as Customers (Illustrative)

companies can use their customer insight to develop new, pull-oriented selling processes that are designed around the customer's needs (Figure 7.5).

To implement this approach in an organization, it is key to identify "points of differentiation": how certain jobs will be done differently, how the interaction between certain roles will shift, the manner in which certain critical processes might be executed, and the talent, skills, and tool requirements for each sales model. The "points of differentiation" that distinguish each segment can vary depending on the business situation and the segments created.

For example, the way the company interacts with the customer will be different for each segment. In the illustrative model in Figure 7.5, for the "Low-Touch" segment, the company needs a mechanism for efficiently serving a large number of smaller and less strategically important customers. As such, it may rely on web-based self-serve channels in place of a direct sales force. Customer service may be provided online as well, and there may be extra charges to handle any unique customer requirements with respect to order delivery.

In contrast, interactions within the "Partnership" segment of important customers may involve relationship building among the senior executives of the company, extensive engagement of technical personnel, and collaboration with select groups within the customer to enhance their success.

The segmentation could also direct how sales resources are assigned. In the "Growth" or "Partnership" segment in the example in Figure 7.5, the company may want dedicated coverage, with anywhere from one to five accounts per rep, depending on the size and complexity of those key accounts. In the "Basic" and "Selective Investment" segments, the accounts are smaller and the level of effort is pared down. Therefore, the number of accounts that a sales rep can serve could be higher. For the "Low-Touch" sales model, an inside sales group could easily support 150 or more accounts per sales rep, as the level of investment required to understand any one customer is substantially lower.

Customer Experience Case Study: Chemical Company

Following a detailed study, executives at a leading chemical company concluded that the company's customer base comprised four primary buying behaviors:

1. Those seeking the lowest possible price.
2. Those desiring a basic set of services along with good price.
3. Those that place the most value on quality and performance.
4. Those that select suppliers based on the latter's ability to provide customized solutions.

By querying the organization's most seasoned commercial personnel, analyzing past customer experiences, and applying logic-based decision trees, the company was able to place almost all of its 5,000-plus customers into one of the four above-mentioned segments. The company then overlayered these classifications by segmenting customers into five distinct groups according to their overall strategic value. Combining these two dimensions allowed the organization to create six distinct sales models—each of which supports a redesigned customer experience that balances customer needs with the company's sales, marketing, and revenue-generation goals.

In our work with B2B companies, we have seen this market-facing approach be a powerful mechanism to optimize sales resources, support, and infrastructure, all the while boosting control over the sales and customer-facing functions. It helps boost top-line revenue through an increased focus on underpenetrated accounts, a higher pipeline conversion rate, better premium product penetration, and quicker achievement of sales proficiency among reps serving strategic accounts. Furthermore, the customer buying experience design serves as the foundation for integrating the sales methodologies and customer-facing processes, for directing the sales organization's needs from enabling technologies, and for building a performance framework for sales talent.

In all, a sales approach that is centered on the delivery of differentiated customer buying experiences enables a company to develop stronger and more efficient sales and marketing organizations, thus increasing shareholder value through both top-line revenue growth and decreased cost.

8

Price Strategies in a Multichannel World

Tom Jacobson, Cecilia Nguyen, Tiffany Gilbert, and Julian Short

Chapter Summary

- Pricing is a key piece of an Agile Selling strategy: Getting it right can be exceedingly difficult; getting it wrong can be disastrous.
- Mastering not only "setting" the pricing right but also "getting" the price is critical to maximizing value.
- To leverage pricing across multiple channels, companies must address three key areas: (1) segmentation of customers and channel base; (2) setting the pricing strategy and actual prices for each channel; and (3) negotiating for profit as well as value.

Pricing is a key piece of the new B2B sales model and Agile Selling strategy. Getting it right can be exceedingly difficult; getting it wrong can be disastrous. History is littered with examples of pricing decisions that seemed to make sense at the moment but ended up reconditioning the customer base in detrimental ways (the automotive industry's almost mandatory need for incentives and retailers that can't seem to sell to customers without a steep discount are two examples that immediately come to mind). The indirect sales channel presents a number of further complications in presenting the appropriate value proposition to customers and holding the line in negotiations with them to achieve the right balance between sales and profit.

In this chapter we explain how to determine the right pricing structure as part of a new Agile Selling model—the strategies and tactics that sales executives can use to set pricing across channels. In particular, we explore how companies with multiple channels to market should set prices that achieve harmony across these routes to market—harmony that ultimately influences sales channels and shapes customer behavior most effectively.

The True Meaning of "Price"

Sales executives know that what their company charges for its products and services has an enormous impact on revenue and profit growth. Price too high and revenue can plummet as customers turn to lower-cost alternatives. Price too low and risk forsaking substantial profit.

Just as critical as the immediate financial impact is what price says about a company's product or brand: Selling too high might provide an entry point for competitors, but going too low might signal to a customer that the product doesn't have the quality that competitors' products do. On the other hand, trying to maintain parity strips away any differentiation a company might have.

Yet despite the importance of price to a company's financial position and brand image, we have found that many B2B companies aren't rigorous enough about their pricing. This is particularly true for those that sell indirectly and thus are one step removed from the price paid by the end customer. For these companies, understanding the give and take between price and functionality or level of service—and determining their pricing philosophy with respect to their channels before setting the prices themselves—are ongoing challenges that B2B companies must address to grow and thrive. But how?

The best place to begin our discussion is to define what price really means. Price is not just the number with a dollar sign in front of it that is visible to the customer (whether end customer, wholesaler, or retailer)—or, in other words, the money a company is asking for the product or service itself. It's not just the amount a customer sees in a price catalog or an auto dealer's sticker inside the window glass with the suggested retail price.

"Price," when broadly considered, can be much more than the visible price of a good. It includes all the terms and conditions of the deal, both cash and noncash—the totality of the commercial relationship with the customer. What do we mean by this? Consider a manufacturer that sets a price for its product, sells it to a customer at that price, and then takes multiple phone calls from the customer to explain how to use it. Many companies don't factor in those postsales phone calls when determining their up-front price; the calls were not in the original terms and conditions. Yet the manufacturer has to pay customer support people to take those calls. If the customer makes too many calls, the cost of handling them erodes the profitability of the product sold. In fact, products with razor-thin margins can easily become unprofitable if they require much higher-than-expected customer support. In this case, the company needs to consider its pocket margin: the profit that remains after subtracting from the list price all costs related to the transaction as well as cost of goods sold.

Companies also must understand that this requires a mastery of both "setting and getting" the price, or selling a good or service for what was originally intended. Unfortunately, many companies experience the all-too-common scenario in which they invest an inordinate amount of time to set the right price for a product only to watch it all come undone because their sales process's only response to a customer's complaint that "It's too expensive" is to cut the price. In our experience, companies leave substantial money on the table—between 15 percent and 30 percent—when their sales force too readily resorts to discounting to close the deal. Pricing is not just about setting the right price at the outset, it's also about actually getting that price from the customer—a price that is determined by explicit terms and conditions.

With this in mind, the way to think about price is not as a static element of a product, but rather as an item that must be dynamic. Classical marketing theory considers price almost as a static feature of a product, much like its color or weight. However, modern pricing theory states that price should be set within the larger context in which the customer buys and uses a product. In fact, companies can use price to shape how customers use the product and what channels they buy through. Airlines do this regularly. They offer lower prices for customers who purchase tickets from their websites rather than through a call center. Customers who want a representative's personal attention have to cover the additional cost of that channel in the form of a higher-priced ticket.

Pricing was once far simpler. Before the Internet allowed anyone to easily compare prices on everything from airline tickets to automobiles, price was a game of checkers for companies. They could set a price and stick with it for weeks or months before customers found out what other companies were charging. Those with especially hot products could raise their prices to capitalize on heightened demand. But today, pricing has become a game of chess. In addition to the Internet, B2B buyers have skillful procurement professionals whose job it is to intimately understand each vendor's price. B2B company pricing policies are thus far more transparent to customers and to channel partners.

But there's one aspect of pricing that hasn't changed: Price must reflect demand and competition. Pricing effectively requires sales executives to not only understand the relationship between price and demand, but also how their prices and products compare to what competitors are offering and charging. For example, when a customer says he or she can get a competitor's products for a lower price, a salesperson must know whether the customer is using a less-expensive channel (such as the web) and exactly what the competitor is including in its price. Without knowing that, it's impossible for the salesperson to make an apples-to-apples comparison and, thus, know whether his or her company's pricing is fair.

Pricing to Account for Multiple Channels to Market

Price is a powerful tool for B2B companies that use both direct and indirect channels to sell their products. Pricing enables these companies to optimize the value each channel can deliver. Today, most companies need multiple channels to market to maximize growth. Customers expect to have multiple ways to interact with providers, with some preferring the direct approach (which companies such as Dell have turned into multibillion-dollar businesses) and others preferring to deal with intermediaries such as wholesalers and resellers. Furthermore, many companies (especially in B2B or business-to-business-to-consumer [B2B2C] markets) whose products need considerable customer handholding to get the sale (think business software or life insurance) require parties that can do the local selling for them. This is especially true when customers are numerous, fragmented, and individually don't account for significant revenue.

To get the greatest return from investments in both direct and indirect channels, B2B companies should use pricing at the outset of the customer's buying process to guide them to the right channels. In some cases, this means pairing customers with channels that are appropriate to their volume, cost to serve, and profitability. Although all (profitable) customers are important to B2B companies, some invariably are far more important to the top and bottom line. But that doesn't mean companies should chase away the less-profitable customers. In fact, they should embrace these customers, but convince them to use lower-cost channels. Higher-margin customers should be given higher-touch, higher-cost channels of interaction.

Companies frequently make the mistake of cutting loose their low-volume, high-cost customers. They stop sending a salesperson to the customer's site or no longer invite them to the annual customer event. But instead of "firing" such customers, a company could provide an incentive—for instance, lower unit prices—to buy through its website. Whatever companies do with their less-profitable customers, they must clearly define the type of interaction these customers can expect at each price point. The interaction includes what channel the customer will use (Internet, direct sales force, indirect sales force, retailer, or other) and the after-sale service the company will deliver to that customer.

Sometimes customers prefer *less* interaction, and are willing to pay extra for it. Take Navistar®, the $14 billion manufacturer of trucks and truck parts. Truckers who need parts for their rigs can buy them from one of more than a thousand[1] Navistar dealers around the United States, or they can buy them online or by phone and have them shipped directly to them. If truckers choose direct delivery, they pay more than if they picked it up at the distribution center. In this case, they're paying for convenience—not having to spend valuable time and mileage to pick up the part. In this case, less human interaction can actually provide more value than more interaction. The point is that companies must determine what customers value, which may be more or less service interaction.

But directing different customers to different channels and services isn't the only way B2B companies can maximize revenue and profit through pricing. They can shift customers from one product to another. This has long been a strategy in retailing, where retail chains have used a "good-better-best" approach to differentiating a set of products that solve the same problem, whether snow shovels or clothes dryers.

Companies also can use pricing to entice buyers to products that aren't selling as well as expected. Hotels have done this since the 1990s, turning over rooms to online aggregators such as Priceline®, Expedia®, or Hotels.com®. They help lodging operators sell excess rooms by lowering the price or conducting online auctions. In these cases, companies must set the conditions under which such aggregators offer rooms at discounted rates or else risk unprofitable business. Apparel manufacturers have followed a similar approach long before the Internet. They have sold excess inventory through factory outlet stores or off-price retailers for decades. In fact, the first outlet malls in the United States cropped up in the 1930s. And through the web, many clothing companies offer lower prices on excess or outdated clothing. They maintain higher pricing on newer and more popular products sold through retail chains.

But the reverse works as well: Companies in all sorts of industries use dynamic pricing to raise prices in real time on products in short supply but high demand. For example, more than half of the Major League Baseball clubs at the beginning of the 2012 season reportedly were using dynamic pricing[2] to adjust ticket prices for games based on demand, opposing teams, or other factors.

The Complexities of Pricing across Sales Channels

We don't mean to paint a picture that pricing across sales channels is straightforward. In fact, it isn't. As a consequence, many companies struggle with it. Those that do struggle can suffer from a host of bad and unforeseen consequences—including rampant discounting that turns profitable prices into unprofitable prices, channel warfare among direct and indirect sales forces, and angry customers confused by a welter of competing offers from the same company and overrun with salespeople trying to get in front of them.

Companies often grapple with pricing across channels for two reasons. The first is lack of a channel strategy. In this case, companies typically have operated with direct and indirect channels but without an overarching strategy that delineates the role of each channel as part of the whole. For example, a company may have no strategy for directing customers to different channels based on their needs and the company's cost to serve them. In other cases, companies do not allocate products effectively across channels to minimize overlap. That is, different channels sell the same offerings often to the same customers.

When this happens, a company's sales channels end up competing with one another, which can create significant conflict. In nearly every case, the result is "price leakage," a euphemism for what often becomes unprofitable selling. Like floods seeking lower ground, customers flee to lower-price channels that aren't necessarily less expensive for a supplier to serve. We saw this played out in a merger. The two companies combined their operations and had a direct sales force and distributors selling its products in the same markets. Operating almost as competitors, the two channels sold against each other. Savvy customers recognized how they could get a lower price—"Just ask Joe to beat Sam's price." All kinds of discounting followed.

The second barrier that companies face when pricing by channel happens when they try to institute a one-size-fits-all approach to channel management. Some companies treat all their channels the same, offering the same price and customer support. But that doesn't provide the critical incentives for channel partners such as sales agents and distributors (especially those that don't sell competing lines) that could be far more motivated to sell the company's products—if they purchased it at a favorable price.

All relationships with channel partners can be characterized as falling somewhere on a spectrum between symbiotic or parasitic. Symbiotic relationships are those in which agents or distributors don't sell competing lines, have strong relationships with end customers, and are usually willing to share customer data to help the supplier better determine its pricing and the value proposition. Such data can have a wealth of benefit to the supplier. Parasitic relationships are just the opposite.

It makes intuitive sense for a company to provide better prices, incentives, and support to partners that are more likely to tie their success to the company's products (symbiotic relationships) than partners for which the company's products are just part of a broad set of offerings from many competing vendors (parasitic relationships). Yet, many companies don't. Most B2B companies focus their market segmentation (if it exists) on their end customers. But it is as important to segment the base of channel partners as it is to segment the end customer base. Unless a company knows how it should treat different types of channel partners, it likely will take the one-size-fits-all approach—or just as bad, to treat each channel partner differently based on its unique demands. That's a recipe for pricing chaos and thin margins.

But less profitable pricing isn't the only consequence. The shortcomings in pricing that we've described earlier can have many more negative impacts. They can drive business to a channel with higher costs to serve or one that demands lower prices. They can encourage customers to "game" a company to get the best price or drive channels to cannibalize one another. And they can obscure a company's value proposition or make it difficult for a company to understand and quickly react to competitors' actions. In all of these cases, the end result is that a company can leave a substantial amount of money on the table.

Getting a Handle on Channel Pricing

No B2B sales leader wants higher costs, cannibalized channels, customers fleeing to lower-priced channels (without a commensurate reduction in the cost of serving them), or the other negative impacts of poor pricing practices just mentioned. To leverage pricing when there are multiple channels to market, companies must *execute pricing effectively*. This requires success in three key areas:

1. Segmenting both the customer and channel base.
2. Setting the pricing strategy for each channel—channels that focus on a customer segment.
3. Negotiating for profit as well as revenue.

Companies that succeed in all three dimensions should reach a state in which pricing generates substantial value for all three parties: the company itself, its channel partners, and its customers. It's a state called *channel harmony* (Figure 8.1). Channel harmony maximizes revenue and profit, and minimizes channel conflict that confuses customers and channel partners. Channel harmony greatly enhances a company's market position—one that poor pricing practices can erode rather quickly.

As companies develop a broader set of channels and sales models, they must pay close attention at all times to whether and how their

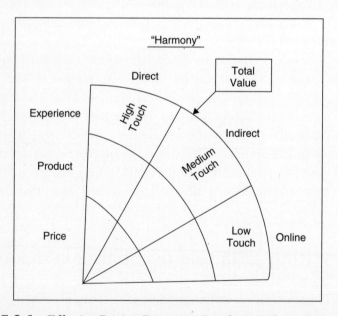

FIGURE 8.1 Effective Pricing Execution Results in "Channel Harmony"

prices and models for each channel should differ. This has become crucial today because of the ever-increasing ease with which partners and end customers can find prices. Just a few keyboard entries in an online search engine are all many, if not most, channel partners and customers need to find out how much a company is charging at retail and wholesale. Just a few inquiries in an online social network such as Facebook or LinkedIn can reveal unpublished prices, or the pricing that a company gives favored customers. Rising price transparency makes it essential for companies to have their pricing strategies clear—and adhered to.

But this is not a conversation that we hear in many companies. In most, the discussion about channel pricing is typically one about how to keep prices in parity. That's the wrong conversation to have. As we established earlier in this chapter, all of a company's sales channels should *rarely* have the same price. Rather, the prices for each channel must be in harmony with each other. The way to achieve such harmony is to price a company's products or services in a way where differences in prices by channel can always be explained based on the value proposition of a channel. To use the Navistar example, sending truck parts directly to customers is more expensive because it saves them the time and cost of picking them up. Price differences by channel also can be explained by the types of customers each channel serves, a company's product mix, cost to serve each channel, and the overall experience each delivers.

To summarize, if a company creates harmony across its sales channels, it reduces cannibalization and leaves less money on the table to customers. That is, it will be far less likely to have to reduce prices because the customer can get the same product and overall value proposition from a lower-cost channel. Creating channel harmony also reduces the risk of annoying and losing customers who don't understand the company's pricing rationale across channels.

So exactly how does a company create channel harmony? Let's explore the three tactics in detail.

Segmenting the Customer and Channel Base

Creating harmonious pricing across channels begins with segmenting the customers and the channels to them. Just as not all customers are

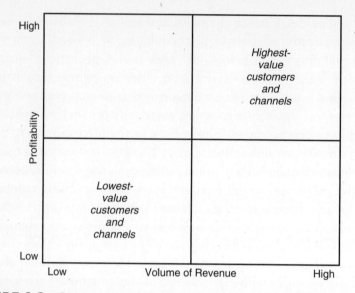

FIGURE 8.2 Segmenting Channels and Customers by Value

alike, not all channel partners are created equal. In both cases, the economic value—revenue and profit—that each can generate can vary
dramatically.

Thus, the first step in maximizing channel pricing is dividing both
customers and channel partners into groups. The segmentation should
be done along two dimensions: volume of revenue and profitability
(Figure 8.2). Customers and channel partners in the top-right quadrant (those that generate high sales volume and profit) are a company's
most valuable customers and partners. Those in the lower-left quadrant (low sales volumes and profit) are the least valuable. By segmenting customers this way, a company can determine which customers it
should serve with higher-touch, service-oriented channels (those in the
top-right quadrant), as well as those it should shift to lower-cost, self-
service channels (lower left quadrant).

This segmentation also guides companies in differentiating the
roles they assign their channel partners and their expected contribution to the company's overall profit. Partners in the top-right quadrant
clearly are a company's most important ones. They deserve special
attention and support, and they also may deserve preferential pricing.

Once a company segments its customer and channel base this way, it will gain a much deeper understanding of its costs to serve each segment, the willingness of customers to pay, and the competitive responses it should expect. With this information, sales leaders can begin determining how to differentiate their price points and service models. That will serve as a rational basis on which to develop the offer for each channel.

The formulation of each channel offer then becomes the basis of channel differentiation and—as importantly—communication. Airlines, for example, have become very effective at differentiating the way they price flights in each channel (through aggregators, their websites, travel agents, and their own call centers). Customers generally understand that service levels and prices are different by channel. They choose what channel to use depending on what they need.

Setting Pricing Strategy and Price

After segmenting channels and partners, a company is ready to set its pricing strategy and pricing for each segment. The first part of this—setting pricing strategy—requires more than just calculating costs, competitor prices, and the value that customers perceive. An effective pricing strategy is an overarching framework that defines what a company is to its customers and who it aims to serve with its pricing. It's also a framework that helps a company proactively define these essential elements rather than let customers or competitors define them. As such, a company's top leadership team should be deeply involved in pricing strategy—as well as overall marketing and brand strategy. And they need to be involved in follow-on discussions as the market evolves and customer needs change.

A company must clarify its pricing strategy to not just its sales leaders and salespeople. Everyone who needs to articulate the firm's pricing policies must be able to easily understand the strategy—customer service agents, public relations (PR) people, channel partners, and the like. A key component of marketing strategy, pricing strategy must promote a company's core objectives and reinforce its desired brand image. It must also be comprehensive enough to cover all channels, customers, products, geographies, competitive actions, and changes in cost.

After crafting the pricing strategy, the next step is to set the pricing. Drawing on the results of the segmentation exercise we described previously, sales leaders will be able to determine whether and how pricing should vary by segment. Because customers and channel partners in a quadrant will have similar characteristics, all should be treated the same way through consistent pricing. However, the channel through which partners operate and customers buy will further influence pricing in a segment.

Consider two channel partners, both of which are in the upper-right quadrant (high volume, high profit, and thus very important). One partner sells the company's products through online channels, while the other partner has retail stores. The company could set different pricing for each partner based on how they deliver products to customers. For instance, the one that uses the Internet ships the company's products; the other delivers them through its stores, which implies higher delivery costs.

The Navistar example we mentioned earlier in this chapter illustrates this concept well. For certain select and highly important channel partners, the truck manufacturer sets up dedicated storage facilities near the partner. That gives the partner a ready supply of spare parts at all times. There's a cost to Navistar for building and operating those facilities, and the company factors in that cost in determining the prices those partners pay (higher than those of some other partners). In turn, those partners factor in those costs in what they charge the end customer—truckers who need replacement parts to keep their rigs on the road. Truckers who need replacement parts immediately—that is, those facing loss of income because their trucks won't operate—realize the premium price they must pay is worth it.

One of the most difficult aspects of setting prices for indirect sales channels is that the price a company sets for partners is the only price it can truly control. Still, that "control" is not absolute; the price the end customer strikes with a channel partner greatly influences the price a company can set for that partner. One of the most prominent examples of this is the automotive industry. Automakers can suggest whatever retail prices they want. But just because they set that price doesn't mean that dealers—the industry's core channel—must adhere to them. Anyone who's ever haggled with a car dealer knows that the sticker price on a car is not the "real" price.

Our point is this: To make sound pricing decisions—ones that will increase the probability a product sells at the highest possible margin—a company must know the price paid by the end customer. Thus, when setting the channel price, companies must consider the market value the product has for the end customer. That value is reflected in what the end customer pays for it. Imagine the hypothetical case of a manufacturer of bottled water that charges a channel partner $100 for each bottle. That price is based on a number of factors: the relationship between the two entities; how often the partner purchases from the manufacturer; the degree of integration of their supply chains; how much support the partner needs; and the cost of making the product.

The channel partner is not likely to sell each bottle for $5 (unless it wants to quickly go out of business). Instead, it will try to get more than $100 to make a profit. But would a $100 price be in line with what customers perceive the value of the bottle to be? The answer to that question depends on many factors, including the degree of competition in bottled water. Are there competing bottles of water for $200 or even $500? Or are most competitors' products selling for less than $100?

We use this admittedly exaggerated example to argue that before companies set a price for channel partners, they must have a good idea of what their products command in the market. There is no better information of this type than what customers actually are paying for those products. As a result, a company should try, to the extent permissible, to get much greater visibility from partners on its own products, point of sale data—but how? That generally requires giving partners the right incentive—such as providing more support and services to a partner (for example, training or technology) that helps it sell the products, or exclusive offers that other partners don't receive.

There are limits to transparency, and companies must understand their tolerance for sharing. As much as a company has to decide how much transparency it wants to give to channel partners, it also has to decide how much it is going to demand back from them.

It's clear from the preceding that setting pricing for channel partners is not easy. But four principles can go a long way to clarifying the ambiguities:

1. **Designing to a price point**. For many years, companies designed products and services to achieve a certain cost of manufacturing. Starting with a long list of potential features, they eventually would winnow that list when they determined the cost of producing them. Today many companies instead design to a price point that implies a share of market (not manufacturing costs). This has revolutionized how companies think about what they offer. Some B2B companies have taken this concept to the next level: by determining customer choices and the channel cost to serve those customers. For example, customers who purchase a product through an online channel most likely need lower prices, ready access to the product, and the ability to easily return it. When designing the product and its pricing for that product, a company has to understand the cost to serve the customers who use that channel. If customers want ready access to the product, the company must incorporate the cost of fast shipping. If customers want to be able to return or exchange their purchases easily, the company must be ready to accommodate massive amounts of returns and exchanges. In other words, when setting its pricing the company must account for those functions, buyer needs, and factors that drive cost to serve up or down.

2. **Rethinking the pricing structure**. Like most aspects of a product or service (features, functions, etc.), pricing cannot remain static. B2B companies must periodically or more frequently revisit the commercial terms they've set with customers because their needs change over time. Are more customers interested today in the outcomes of the product—the benefits that it generates for them? If so, the offer, commercial terms, and conditions—including price—must change accordingly. In other words, companies must continually bring innovation to their pricing efforts. Companies have done so in the past by including leasing or financing for customers who need help with affording a purchase. (For companies such as General Electric®,

this practice goes back a long way. In 1932, GE introduced consumer financing for appliances.[3]) Other examples of pricing innovations include pay-for-performance, value-based deals, and free shipping (case in point: Amazon.com's Prime® service). Another way to change pricing is to bundle other products or services and determine a new price for that bundle. The issue is how to add ancillary products or services that customers need at a price point that doesn't erode profitability. And still another form of pricing innovation is paying for usage, something that the aerospace industry has long employed with regard to aircraft engines. In the 1960s, the concept was given a name—"power by the hour"—by Bristol Siddeley Engines Ltd®, a British aerospace engine manufacturer, and reinvented in the 1980s by Rolls Royce®, which trademarked the term.[4] Under this concept, a manufacturer provides an engine and complementary replacement parts to its airline and defense customers for a fixed fee per hour an engine is used. The arrangement enables the customer to more accurately forecast its operating costs and avoid having to buy and stock costly replacement engines and components. The power-by-the-hour concept also is popular among manufacturers of tires used in industrial applications.

3. **Determining elasticity of demand**. The most fundamental aspects of pricing strategy can be summed up in one phrase: "price elasticity of demand." This concerns whether a company understands the end customer's demand for its offers and how price changes impact that demand. Companies long ago gave up using a "crystal ball" to predict customers' response to price changes—that is, essentially raising or lowering prices to see what would stick. Today, most large companies depend on sophisticated analytics technologies and the math behind them. This includes quantitative and qualitative variables that draw on statistical algorithms embedded in enterprise software-class transactional systems. Through such systems, companies can in theory more effectively forecast demand and competitor response to price changes. They also can target marketing messages to consumer segments, manifest supply, and optimize both cost and price to achieve their strategic goals (e.g., increase market

share versus raising profitability). Intimately understanding the relationship between price and demand requires companies to use new technology and new techniques: analytics, optimization transactional software, competitive intelligence, customized marketing communications, training, and a host of support processes. Companies often struggle with all of these.

4. **Making sure pricing is in line with what customers expect for the products, services, and prices they get in a given channel**. Not too long ago, B2B companies made most of their pricing decisions in private. Even their published price lists were known to be directional at best and not taken literally. But with advancements in online technologies (e.g., web crawlers that search websites for prices) and mobile devices, increased procurement training, and the eroding confidence of many sellers, it's not hard for many customers to find a better price—even from another department in the same company. Searching the web to obtain a better price has become an established practice for many. Additionally, most customers now have a distinct idea of what they expect in an offering and "experience" for a price they are willing to pay and a channel they are willing to use. To provide a simple example, most customers know that when they order a product online, they will get a lower price but not much (if any) personalized service. But when they buy the same product in a high-end boutique store, they expect much higher prices yet also a much better buying experience—one that makes them feel special.

Our last point is perhaps the most important. If a company's pricing and other aspects of its offer are not at all what customers in a segment expect, the consequences can be disastrous. Companies must carefully decide what bundle and price will work best for each segment. They must also communicate clearly with customers so they understand what they're getting for that price point.

In this regard, the 2011 experience of Netflix® holds lessons for all companies. To offset rising costs, the hugely successful movie rental firm in July 2011 decided to increase prices. Customers had been paying $9.99 per month for DVDs and unlimited online streaming. That July, Netflix priced the DVDs and streaming each at $7.99/month, which translated into a price increase from about $10 to $16 per month. Customers were frustrated and, in just a few months, it was reported that an estimated 1 million customers canceled their Netflix subscriptions. This forced the company to lower its growth projections, and the stock fell.[5]

Subsequently, CEO Reed Hastings apologized in a letter to customers: "I messed up," Hastings said. "I owe everyone an explanation. . . . I see that given the huge changes we have been recently making, I should have personally given a full justification to our members. . . . It wouldn't have changed the price increase, but it would have been the right thing to do."[6]

Negotiating for Profit

After segmentation and setting price strategy and prices, the third element of executing pricing effectively across channels is about negotiation. As we mentioned at the outset of this chapter, good pricing is not just about "setting" the right price. It is also about "getting" that price. In contract and sales negotiations with customers, that "right price" often is negotiated down substantially, sometimes to a point when there's very little margin left for a B2B company.

This happens more and more these days given the substantial pressure on customers to reduce costs. Cost-cutting measures will likely require a B2B company to face a customer's procurement department. Unlike B2C companies, B2B firms deal with businesses that often force much more complex negotiations than most consumers induce on companies. As a result, the potential for profit leakage in B2B is severe.

All this requires B2B companies to stay in tune with their sales forces. Sales leaders must embed a new pricing strategy in the negotiation and contract management processes that their salespeople use. And they must also connect their computer systems that run the front office (sales and marketing) and back office (finance, accounting, etc.). Only by doing this can salespeople know how much of a gap there is between the price the company "sets" and "gets."

These problems play out in many ways. Consider the concept of setting "discount bands"—the amount that salespeople can reduce a product's price. (These are also known as "price windows.") Let's assume that a company sets its price at $20 for Partner A (which sells to end customers through an online channel). The partner complains about the price, saying "I do tons of business with you, so I want a volume discount," or "That's great, but I can actually get this from your competitor for $15." Whoever negotiated with Partner A and signed the contract must go through a series of negotiations. If the company hasn't provided the right level of authority to that person—and if that person doesn't know that the company can't waver from its $20 price—then Partner A may erroneously hear that a lower price is coming. That's going to create a problem—a dissatisfied partner (after hearing the lower price is not possible) or a dissatisfied vendor (unhappy to discount).

The more that customers view a product and the channel through which they buy it as a commodity, the less flexibility that a B2B company has with its price windows due to commodity price pressure. However, as more companies move to selling "solutions," not just products, they will have to work collaboratively with their channel partners to create the optimal offer at the optimal price. That will require a more flexible price window at the point of sale.

Key Enablers to Effective Pricing

All the practices that we've described in this chapter are critical to setting and getting the optimal price, channel by channel. However, we would be remiss if we didn't discuss other "enablers" to effective pricing—elements that can be quite technical and can sound quite tactical, and thus can easily be glossed over by a company's pricing strategists.

The first of these enablers is technology and pricing data. In most companies, the data necessary to price optimally resides in many different enterprise applications—supply chain management, customer relationship management, enterprise resource planning, and others. This data also can be found on technologies that employees take home or on the road with them—spreadsheets, customer lists, and other information stored on PCs, laptops, and (increasingly) mobile devices like smartphones and tablet computers.

To price effectively, sales leaders must be able to pull all the relevant data housed in these systems. They then need the software that can crunch the data and help them make sense of it. Only when that happens can they create relevant pricing for each channel and customer segment.

So what kinds of technologies make this possible? The amount and type will vary from company to company depending on its channel, market, and product complexity. But as a baseline, every large or complex B2B company needs pricing technology that enables critical pricing decisions. This, in turn, means technology that provides insight on customer and channel profitability, enables "what-if" model analyses, captures data from different markets, and continually churns through information. All of this will give B2B companies the ability to conduct "test and learn" processes that allow them to make pricing decisions that produce more predictable results.

To go a level deeper, such pricing technologies should have the following key characteristics:

- *It's uncomplicated*. A company with a small number of customers, stock-keeping units, and channel partners may be able to get away with Excel spreadsheets. B2B companies with more customers, products, and partners typically will need more sophisticated software.

- *It allows pricing professionals to understand costs, monitor supply and demand, and track and maintain prices*. These tools are at the heart of moving from reactive to predictive pricing. By using these tools, pricing conversations shift from wondering why revenue and profitability are at the levels that they are, to determining whether the underlying strategic, competitive, and customer assumptions that a company makes are indeed valid.

- *It can integrate with other information systems and shift data to industry-standard databases*. These other systems include transaction (e.g., ERP), business intelligence, and operational systems (e.g., finance, accounts receivable and payable). Much of the financial and management reporting systems that B2B companies have today are designed to create financial statements. The task of shaping and pricing deals—and thus the ability to reach the company's profitability goals (its "profit destiny," as we like to say)—has depended on far less sophisticated systems such as spreadsheets, or note sheets (which aren't based on software at all). Modern pricing technology brings to the table ERP-class, "closed-loop" analysis (i.e., analysis that enables a company to use its experiences to continually refine pricing). The technology enables sales leaders to understand the behaviors of salespeople (and others) that result in profit leakage through price negotiation and discounting. It also helps them determine more targeted pricing strategies and prices—that is, those relevant to a certain customer segment and segment of channel partners. The ability of pricing technology to integrate with other corporate systems can help a business run more profitably at not only each price negotiation but also at the portfolio level.

- *It incorporates a strong backbone for analytics*. For example, having visibility into customer and product profitability allows companies to better understand where they are making money and, thus, where to focus their resources. Analytics tools give sales executives a strong foundation for determining pricing strategy and pricing decisions before they negotiate deals. Increasingly B2B sales executives need such data because channel partners and end customers come armed with their data.

The second often-overlooked enabler of effective pricing is rewards (which we cover in detail in Chapter 10 on sales and marketing incentives). A company can only excel in pricing if it provides the appropriate incentives and rewards to its sales force. This is not the case in many B2B companies today. In these companies, the sales organization rewards salespeople primarily or only on the revenue they generate, not the profitability of that business. If salespeople are only rewarded to sign up more channel partners—regardless of the price agreements they strike with them or the cost to serve them—their company will fail at pricing effectively. They won't be able to set prices that create channel harmony and maximize profits.

Quantified metrics and reports are the third key enabler. What kinds of metrics and reports are we referring to? Just about every B2B company must enter into complex contractual pricing and negotiations with channel partners and customers. Understanding the full cost to serve each customer or channel partner—and how those costs change over time (and the behavior causing those changes)—is crucial, as we have explained. Metrics and the reports written about those metrics enable sales leaders to adjust pricing practices continually. These metrics typically take the form of price waterfall charts (which can visually display how pricing has changed over time and factors that may play into it), price bands (the range within which a product can be priced as dictated by competitive intensity and the perceived value of the product to consumers), whale curves (which indicate how money-losing customers affect total profitability), scatter plots, and value maps (a tool that tracks customer perceptions of products). Although pricing software will help managers produce these graphics, they must know ahead of time what form, measure, and value they want to get from them.

Strong governance is another key enabler of effective pricing. Somebody in an organization must be charged with pricing, either an individual or a team. The centralized pricing "organization" must define each person's role in the pricing process and receive regular reports on pricing performance. As well, the pricing function must look for opportunities to improve pricing, part of which is making sure the sales force is compensated for its role in maximizing profitability from pricing. The pricing group must also spend time with top management to revisit and (if necessary) adjust the company's overall pricing strategy.

If the pricing team is empowered to develop highly customized pricing reports—reports that influence functional managers (sales, marketing, service, etc.) and recommend changes that improve how they set and get prices—the group can play a powerful role. Having a pricing team that intimately understands the types of reports pricing technology can deliver and the types of reports managers around the company relate to best will help the company choose the right pricing software.

The key is creating a culture focused not just on increasing revenue but also on boosting profitability. In that kind of culture, managers and salespeople recognize the importance of pricing, as do other employees from top to bottom. In such a culture, salespeople are recognized as top performers not based on the sales they generate but rather on the profitability their sales generate.

A Job Never Completed

A final note on pricing: It's not a "one-and-done" project that is ever completed. Sales leaders must execute the process we have laid out in this chapter continually. Pricing strategy and execution are dynamic phenomena because the market to which pricing is applied— customer needs, competitors' actions, and other market developments —continually changes. Any given pricing strategy should be expected to have a short shelf life—and even shorter in the future.

To price their offerings to generate maximum profitability, companies must make sure that their prices and price execution are relevant and sustainable. By relevant, we mean that the price strategy reflects the current reality. By sustainable, we mean price execution practices that are in compliance with the price strategy and don't backslide into profit-robbing behavior.

As we've stated, the larger and more complex the business (more products, channels, customers, etc.), the more apt it will be to make sure that its pricing strategy and execution are up-to-date and in sync with one another. Yet even small- and medium-size businesses need to put effective pricing structures in place. They, too, can't regard pricing as a one-shot exercise to be done every 10 years or so.

The industry in which a company operates also will influence the frequency with which it must revisit its pricing. For example, those in industries with short product life cycles (e.g., high tech) and extremely dynamic markets (rapid technology change, new entrants, etc.) will have to rethink their pricing far more frequently and act on their findings faster. On the other hand, slow-moving industries with little new competition and customer demands (e.g., parts suppliers for old cars) can revisit pricing far less often.

The most important issue is that when a company must change its pricing strategy, it must have the right capabilities to change it.

Conclusion

Even the best-laid sales models can become ineffective when the pricing strategy component is flawed or not updated soon enough. Companies with the right approach to pricing strategy—those that set the right prices—take the first big step. They segment both the customer and channel base, determine the overarching pricing strategy as part of brand and offering strategy, and determine the best prices for each channel and customer segment. They then negotiate for profit, not revenue.

But that is just about "setting" the right price. "Getting" the right price is just as important. It means working with channel partners to understand the ultimate prices that end customers are paying, looking at competitors' pricing and offerings, and then deciding whether and how the pricing strategy must change.

Bringing Science to Selling

Jan Van der Linden

Chapter Summary
- Powerful new analytical options have emerged to augment intuition, judgment, and experience to dramatically transform sales performance.
- Analytics can be applied across the end-to-end selling process and can address critical blind spots.
- Analytical platforms around customer analytics, pipeline management, lead management, and talent mangement are some of the biggest levers being used by leading selling organizations.
- Successful companies are focusing on seven key guiding principles to drive the analytics-focused cultural change while prioritizing and focusing their efforts.

As discussed in the opening chapter, as the business environment grows more challenging, companies of all kinds are under ever-mounting pressure to grow and grow profitably. Yet sales organizations—the chief instrument for growth at most organizations —often struggle to uphold their end. The numerous research studies we've already cited clearly indicate that many sales organizations struggle to master the key tenets of high-performance selling: having a deep understanding of what customers value; managing and deploying new capabilities; hiring and developing talent; and getting the most return on these investments.

However, the tide is turning. Powerful new options for improving sales performance are emerging that enable companies to take a more scientific approach to selling. These options—new analytical tools that complement salespeople's intuition, judgment, and experience, and enable more effective, fact-based decisions—are core elements for making the Agile Selling model work. Just as analytics has helped companies improve the effectiveness and efficiency of their supply chain and marketing functions, it now can help boost sales performance.

Analytics at Work

When applied to core business functions—both strategic and operational—analytics can generate significant competitive advantage. In supply chain management, for instance, scientific approaches have delivered impressive results. Decision support systems for production, inventory, and transportation problems emerged during the 1960s and 1970s, and now permeate all aspects of supply chain management: activity-based costing, statistical quality control, demand forecasting, network optimization, simulation, linear programming, and capacity planning, to name a few. These tools have delivered tremendous payback: from reducing costs, to better leveraging assets and partnerships, to minimizing waste caused by misallocated resources.

Marketing also has embraced analytics, starting with sample-based consumer research and expanding into other areas such as segmentation analysis, brand attitude, and brand awareness research. More recently, sophisticated techniques for advertising and promotion-effectiveness analysis, price elasticity analysis (which we touched on in the previous chapter), and media mix optimization have helped marketers get more out of their marketing investments. These techniques also have given marketers a much keener understanding of customer needs, behaviors, and preferences—enabling companies to target more precisely and allocate resources more effectively.

So what about sales? Pockets of analytical support for sales certainly exist in some companies. The most common uses of sales analytics include mining of prospect databases (although this is arguably a marketing function) and providing sales reps with analytically driven customer-segmentation schemes. However, compared with other business functions, the use of analytics in sales is still in its infancy. Perhaps this is not surprising, given the number of obstacles to bringing more science to selling.

- Attitude: The prevailing wisdom at many organizations has been that analytics and selling do not mix. Instead, these companies have relied on the good instincts and strong relationships of experienced, well-connected sales reps.
- Data: Traditionally, the sales function has been less data-rich than other functions—particularly the marketing or supply chain organizations.
- Tools and techniques: Until recently, few tools and techniques were available to support sales analytics; and those that were available were not widely accepted.
- Inactionable insights: Companies that experimented with sales analytics often found it difficult to make analytical insights available to the sales force in a useful manner.
- Additional B2B challenges: In a B2B setting, applying analytics is more challenging. B2B relationships generally are complex and long term, and the "customer" is not a single individual but rather multiple decision makers and stakeholders.

The Turning Tide

Despite these historic obstacles, the desire to inject more analytics into the sales process is building in the corporate arena for two reasons: the increased availability and sophistication of enabling capabilities and solutions, and simple necessity.

In the past decade, widespread adoption of enterprise resource planning (ERP) and customer relationship management (CRM) systems improved the availability and quality of sales and sales-related data. Many companies deployed opportunity or pipeline management systems, creating a central repository of sales opportunities. These repositories make it possible to analyze success rates and other factors to derive insights on how to accelerate opportunities through the sales pipeline. Also, many companies working with external channel partners deployed partner portals to gather important sales data. In many cases, this dramatically improved their visibility into partner sales activities.

Sheer necessity also has contributed to the growing demand for sales analytics. In one survey, 23 percent of respondents said the number of products or services their companies offer more than doubled during the previous five years. Seventy-six percent said the complexity of their product and solution bundles also increased.[1] Such complexity makes it increasingly difficult for individual sales reps to make effective decisions about prospecting, customer targeting, cross-selling, and other key sales behaviors without having a strong analytics capability to support these decisions.

Another factor compounds these challenges—attrition. Sales reps turn over faster today, which limits the level of experience and customer intimacy within the sales force. This lack of product and customer knowledge also forces heavier reliance on tools and analytics.

Last, customers simply have become more demanding: They expect salespeople to understand their needs and to match product or service offerings precisely to their preferences and circumstances.

Eliminating Blind Spots with Analytics

Once a company recognizes the potential of analytics to improve its sales performance, its first consideration is where and how to apply analytics capabilities. We recommend starting with the traditional end-to-end sales process, from customer segmentation and planning through to postsales support. As shown in Figure 9.1, common "blind spots" in the sales process undermine performance. Most readers would agree

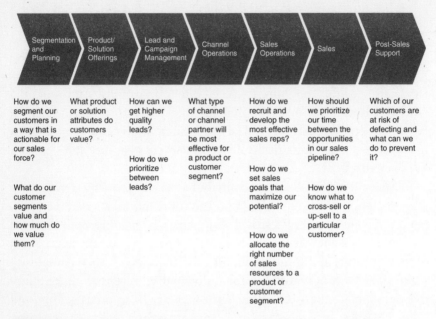

Segmentation and Planning	Product/Solution Offerings	Lead and Campaign Management	Channel Operations	Sales Operations	Sales	Post-Sales Support
How do we segment our customers in a way that is actionable for our sales force? What do our customer segments value and how much do we value them?	What product or solution attributes do customers value?	How can we get higher quality leads? How do we prioritize between leads?	What type of channel or channel partner will be most effective for a product or customer segment?	How do we recruit and develop the most effective sales reps? How do we set sales goals that maximize our potential? How do we allocate the right number of sales resources to a product or customer segment?	How should we prioritize our time between the opportunities in our sales pipeline? How do we know what to cross-sell or up-sell to a particular customer?	Which of our customers are at risk of defecting and what can we do to prevent it?

FIGURE 9.1   Common Blind Spots across the End-to-End Selling Process

that these blind spots are both typical for most sales organizations as well as critical to address. In these areas, sales reps often base their most important decisions on personal judgment and intuition rather than on facts and insights. Judgment and intuition are useful qualities to have; stemming from experience, they can be highly valuable, accurate, and even indispensable. At the same time, judgment and intuition are significantly enhanced by analytics, enabling better informed decision making at critical points in the sales process.

Figure 9.2 shows how analytics can support virtually every step in the sales process and help provide visibility to the blind spots across the process. This list is not exhaustive, and not all items on the list are relevant or feasible for every company. However, nearly any company can create significant value by adopting a number of these capabilities and extending their scope and reaching throughout the sales organizations—in other words, by bringing more science to selling.

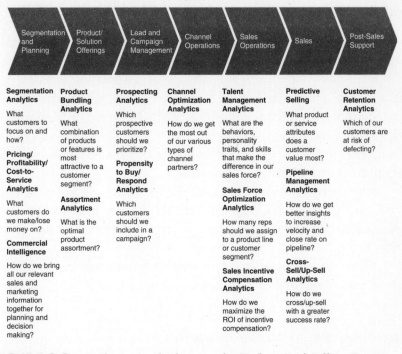

FIGURE 9.2   Analytics Applied across the End-to-End Selling Process

Key Outcomes Sales Analytics Can Drive

As discussed, sales analytics can be applied across the end-to-end sales process and drive significant value in each of these areas. Specific value delivered will vary across industries, selling models, and partnering models. However, there are four key outcomes that apply across most organizations and industry sectors where sales analytics play a major role:

1. Evolving to greater differentiation between customers.
2. Exerting greater influence on customers.
3. Evolving from segmented to personalized selling.
4. Getting an earlier and more accurate read on sales performance.

Differentiate between Customers

Many companies are striving for greater differentiation in how they interact with their customers because they recognize the one-size-fits-all model is no longer effective. Customers expect interactions that more closely align with their preferences, but under "one size fits all" some customers receive treatment elements they care little about and others they care a great deal about. Other customers may experience the reverse situation. By better matching treatments to preferences, overall customer satisfaction increases.

Another reason companies seek greater differentiation is the one-size-fits-all model is no longer affordable because it offers the same treatments to all customers irrespective of the customers' value to the company.

Three categories of analytics are needed to support greater differentiation in customer interaction.

Customer Buyer-Value Analytics

What do customers value when it comes to how a company interacts and transacts with them? What do they want to hear? What kinds of behaviors might influence a particular customer segment or customer type? What sales behaviors turn certain prospects off? Is there a potential segment that responds particularly well to product demos? Is there a definable group that places an exceptionally high value on relationship selling? How much of a premium might a particular segment place on a salesperson's technology skills or the company's provision of technology assistance? What postsales service elements are particularly valued by a customer segment?

Finding answers to questions such as these is an established discipline, with several customer research techniques available to uncover insights. Some companies apply shortcuts by gathering this information from the sales force. We caution against this approach as it can lead to documenting the "conventional wisdom" that can be based on misconceptions and assumptions. This type of research, done right, often can produce surprising findings in how customers want to be sold to. Commercially available tools have emerged based on the concept of choice modeling that greatly simplify this analytical process and transform it from a "study" into a continuous data-gathering process. This is vital, because data that reflects a single point in time is far less valuable than data that is constantly updated.

Customer Value Analytics

How valuable is the customer to the company? What is the current contribution of each customer to the company's profitability? Done right, and with the correct level of granularity, this kind of analytical research often yields unexpected results and typically will uncover a number of customers on which the company is actually losing money, even without taking fixed-cost allocations into account. This analysis of current profitability should be augmented with a view of future or potential value of the customer (often referred to as share of wallet). Combined, these analytical metrics help determine for which customers or customer segments it makes sense to maintain or invest further in treatment elements versus those for which doing so does not make economic sense. Customer value analytics tells a company what it should change now and what it should prepare to do differently in the future.

Cost-to-Serve Analytics

What is the cost of specific offerings and sales behaviors? Conversely, what is a company saving by implementing (or not implementing) certain approaches for various customers or customer segments? Like customer value analytics, the mission here is assessing the relative worth of individual customers and customer groups. However, cost-to-serve analytics goes further by modeling the economic impact of various sales approaches to various customer segments. It combines "what's" with "what-ifs."

Understanding in advance the financial impact of changing certain sales behaviors is extremely valuable. It obviously is good to invest more in high-value customer segments if those new investments are aligned with what targeted customers or groups truly value, and if there is good reason to believe that increased loyalty and/or revenue will result. What is *not* acceptable is making investments where overall cost-to-serve goes up. The primary purpose of implementing differentiated sales models should always be growth at an equal or reduced cost to serve, and this is what cost-to-serve analyses help a company determine.

Armed with data pertaining to these three objectives—buyer values, customer value, and cost-to-serve—companies can begin parsing their sales and service models by segment and create more relevant and differentiated messages for each.

Exert Influence

The traditional approach to organizing and deploying sales resources is based on coverage: territory coverage, industry sector coverage, coverage of customers of different sizes, and so on. For some time, this has been considered the right way to optimize a company's selling resources. However, as buying processes become more complex, the notion of exerting influence on customers is gaining in importance. It is a statement of the obvious that a salesperson is trying to influence a customer or prospective customer to buy something. However, many companies do not explicitly take the notion of influence into account when planning their sales strategies and tactics. And yet there is a wide variety in how much influence can be exerted on certain customers versus others, as well as in the right approach to exerting influence. This is where analytics, coupled with old-fashioned relationship building, comes in.

Today's companies must make "influencing sales outcomes" their core sales mission—identifying and implementing strategies for driving customer-buying decisions. Underlying this mission are other goals. For example, if the influence a company can exert on its customers is limited, it must discover who influences the buying decision. From there it would make "influencing the influencer" a top priority. As we profiled in Chapter 5, a good example is pharmaceutical companies that target "opinion leaders," typically physicians who are leaders in their field and are very influential with their peers. It takes a great deal of data and analytics to first identify who the opinion leaders are and second to understand what matters to them. Another example we discussed in Chapter 5: consumer products companies that sell to retailers by providing caches of relevant insights about retailers' shoppers and markets. They have learned that the way to sell a new product or a promotion is to understand the retailer's priorities and develop the right analytical insights to prove that the new product or promotion contributes to those priorities—for example, by driving more shopper traffic or by increasing the shopper's basket size. In other words, they have learned how to influence retailers by applying analytics, speaking the retailers' language, and adopting their metrics.

In short, exerting influence is significantly more strategic and rewarding than emphasizing blanket coverage. However, the former requires a much deeper understanding of a customer's business and priorities. Exerting influence involves gathering, interpreting, and presenting useful information—building trust with facts and insights. To build a compelling case, a company needs analytics.

Evolve to Personalized Selling

Earlier, we discussed how companies can use analytics to segment their customer bases and create differentiating messaging and offerings for each segment. Segmentation has proven to be an effective way to group customers into meaningful and manageable categories, thus making it easier to target products and services to them.

However, leading companies are taking this a step farther by evolving from segmentation to personalization in their interactions with and offers to customers. As opposed to treating all customers in a segment as a single entity, personalization involves tailoring communications and products or services to individual customers based on a unique set of data about those customers.

Great examples of personalization can be found in the pharmaceutical industry, where companies are using an analytics-based approach called *closed-loop selling* to drive personalization. Here's how it works: As the sales representative prepares to conduct a sales call with a physician, he or she uses customized presentations that are tailored to the characteristics and requirements of the type of physician the rep will be calling on. The presentations can include visual aids, clinical reprints, opinion leader videos, case studies, physician surveys, and other such tools.

With a tablet PC, the rep shares these presentations with the physician in an interactive session. Software built into the tablet records a variety of data in real time about each sales interaction—including the order in which materials were presented and how much time meeting participants spent discussing specific materials. This information, combined with the outcome of the sales call, is sent electronically back to headquarters, where it is aggregated and integrated with other data sets from other sales representatives. A team then analyzes the data set to determine what type and sequence of messages and visuals are most effective with a particular physician segment. Using these insights, reps can refine and improve the selling content and the selling story, which are redelivered to the sales force in an automated manner via their tablet PCs. The next time the sales rep is in front of that physician, the selling messages will be more personalized to what that physician cares most about. The diagram in Figure 9.3 illustrates the closed-loop nature of this approach.

Brand Strategy and Customer Segmentation
Brand teams define customer segments aligned with their product strategy

Reporting and Tracking
Data transmitted back to HQ for aggregation, integration with other data sets and analysis

Graphic Content Development
Brands create effective content tailored to the segments and have it approved by regulatory/legal team

Sales Execution
Sales reps use the segmentation to target physicians. The tablet PC facilitates the delivery of messages using engaging multimedia visual aids

FIGURE 9.3 "Closed-Loop" Selling Analytics

This closed-loop selling approach can have a significant impact on a company's sales. For instance, at one pharmaceutical company that used it, the majority of the company's sales representatives exceeded their growth targets during the initial rollout of the process. Moreover, the average rep saved 30 to 40 minutes of administration time per day as a result of the integrated tool set and selling content. Brand teams benefited from the instantaneous analytical feedback from sales interactions. And the company realized significant cost savings due to the transition from paper-based to electronic selling materials.

Another way to personalize selling with analytics is through an approach called *predictive selling*, which uses a robust analytical tool to help sales reps more effectively match offers with what customers really want—which is not always what they *say* they want. Predictive selling is particularly powerful because it doesn't require any preexisting data—the data is generated as part of the analytical process. This is something that is especially interesting and value-adding for industries where customer data is sparse, which is the case in most B2B sectors.

In predictive selling, a rep on a sales call guides the customer through an interactive dialogue with the tool (using the rep's laptop or tablet) to reveal the customer's true preferences in terms of product attributes or service elements. As part of the conversation with the customer, the rep asks the customer to make trade-offs between different combinations of product or service attributes. By instantaneously analyzing and summarizing the results of this conversation, the tool gives both the customer and the rep the basis for a rich conversation about what type of product or service is truly right for this customer—often revealing what matters to a customer to a degree of explicitness that the customer may not have been able to articulate.

A chemical company adopted predictive selling as a way to significantly increase the effectiveness of its sales force's selling interactions. In addition to using the underlying tool in actual sales calls, the company made the tool available on its website and encouraged current and prospective customers to go through the trade-off dialogue by themselves. This functionality became a great source of sales leads for the company, especially because the tool generated such rich and deep insights on customer preferences and needs.

The level of personalization that approaches such as closed-loop selling and predictive selling allow is a clear source of competitive differentiation. In addition to leading to a more effective sales inter-action (which, in turn, can boost revenue or margin), personalization creates greater loyalty among customers. Customers will recognize the steps a company is taking to really understand what is important to them and will more likely reward them for that effort.

Getting an Earlier Read on Sales Performance

In many companies, sales forecasting has deteriorated into guessing with a process wrapped around it. It's often plagued with inaccuracy and it places a major drain on sales resources who should be spending their time with customers.

Current challenges notwithstanding, getting an early read on sales performance remains critically important for several reasons. It provides vital input to a company's annual or quarterly business plan, and depending on the industry, it can feed into some form of supply or capacity planning across multiple time horizons. It also enables a company to identify opportunities to make appropriate interventions or reallocate resources to respond to specific trends or market developments—for instance, running a special promotion or campaign, allocating sales resources to areas of weakness, or redirecting efforts to areas of accelerating growth.

Yet despite its importance, few companies can claim to have cracked the code on sales forecasting. In the vast majority of com-panies, the sales forecasting process is very labor intensive, not to mention often dysfunctional and nonvalue-adding. It gives sales management (at all levels) the illusion of control, which is why the process is perpetuated. Part of the root cause of the problem is that sales forecasting gets confused with sales target setting. This only heightens the stakes and the emotion associated with this process. In some organizations, the repeated calls for updated forecasts put a significant drain on the sales rep or sales manager's productivity and take away precious customer-facing time.

The process is typically also judgment driven with very little math applied to it. Sales management tends to rely on regional or divisional sales managers to provide forecasts for their slice of the business. These managers, in turn, rely on their teams to provide a bottom-up forecast for their districts or accounts. This process then gets repeated multiple times (when management doesn't like the forecasts) or across multiple time horizons (e.g., yearly, quarterly, or monthly). The problem is, many factors (overall economy, client industry growth, price changes, promotions, competitor moves, new product introductions, etc.) can affect sales results in varying ways and degrees. It is next to impossible to use judgment to make sense of the likely impact of this collection of factors on ultimate demand for a company's products. As a result, sales reps tend to simply take last year's results and make a percentage adjustment to it. This may work under conditions of extremely stability, but we all know those are rare.

So what is the answer? It is a combination of analytics augmented by sound judgment where it makes sense. Companies must go back to using statistical techniques to arrive at fact-based forecasts. The statistical discipline of econometrics and demand forecasting has been around for a very long time and has been honed and refined in the field of economics. In manufacturing industries, it has wide application in supply chain analytics for the purpose of SKU-level, short-term demand forecasts to establish how much a company should produce of each SKU it sells. In the area of sales forecasting, however, which takes a longer-term view and operates at a higher level in the product hierarchy, the application is relatively rare. Where it is being applied it can be very successful and it resolves the pain points described earlier.

How would it work? Let's examine the analytical process to inject more science into the sales forecasting process.

The starting point would be to include causal factors into the forecasting process: even when companies use statistical demand forecasting techniques they often limit themselves to extrapolating previous years' demand. This will reveal trends and cyclicality in demand, but will not predict turning points in demand that are a break from past trends. Needless to say, it is precisely these turning points that are most critical to predict. The better approach is to include other variables into the forecasting process that are causally related to the demand the company is trying to forecast. As mentioned earlier, these factors can include expected overall economic growth, planned price changes, planned promotion or campaign activities, anticipated competitor actions, and other such actions. Obviously, data availability on these causal factors will be the limiting factor; but including some of these factors will dramatically improve the quality of the sales forecast.

A company also should determine the appropriate level of detail of the forecast. Fundamentally, three dimensions define the level of detail at which a company can create a forecast:

1. Customer (ranging from some grouping of similar customers or customers within a geographic region to individual customer).
2. Product (ranging from product category all the way down to SKU).
3. Time horizon (ranging from year to quarter to month to week).

In theory, a company can apply sales forecasting at any level of detail or aggregation. However, too high a level will make the forecast less actionable and too low a level will undermine the accuracy of the forecast. Thus, the right level for sales forecasting purposes is typically:

- Customer: A grouping of customers in a particular sector or within a geographic region (large regions, not sales territories).
- Product: A broad product grouping or brand.
- Time horizon: A yearly and quarterly outlook.

Finally, a company should validate the forecast with judgment, to confirm the forecast "makes sense." The company should conduct a quarterly meeting with key sales and marketing leaders to critically review and debate the forecasts that were generated by the analytics. For the numbers to be acted on, they not only must be robust, they must be bought into. Often this involves tweaking some of the findings to build a group consensus.

The Time Is Now, But How?

At the beginning of this chapter, we discuss the opportunities to use sales analytics across the end-to-end sales process. We also provide examples of how the application of analytics to specific areas of the sales process has reaped significant benefit. Now, we turn our attention to the more practical challenge of making sales analytics happen in a company. Toward this end, we provide seven guiding principles for introducing sales analytics into an organization.

Find the Starting Point

Once a company recognizes the potential of analytics to improve its sales performance, the first consideration is where and how to apply analytics capabilities across the end-to-end sales process—from customer segmentation and planning through postsale support. Focusing the introduction of analytics on one or two places in the sales process is most realistic and practical.

It is important for a company to be judicious about choosing its starting point. Analytics can only be successful if they are acted on, and that means the use of analytics must be connected to decision making. This will require some organizational change, not in the sense of structural change, but in the way information flows and decisions are made. If there is skepticism or resistance in the organization, a company needs a good success story to win over the critics. If analytics is alien to a particular company's culture, the organization will need to demonstrate with solid (case-based) evidence how making fact-based decisions will strengthen the culture.

A company could take several different routes to finding the best starting point. One route could be to choose a high-profile problem, an area that has caused major headaches in the recent past or that has been a nagging and well-known issue for a while. For instance, the sales organization may frequently be surprised by shifts in demand in the marketplace. Or there may have been a gradual decrease in demand that was hidden by pushing more and more inventory to the channel and suddenly the problem is exposed. Using major or well-known problems such as these as a starting point has two advantages. First, it addresses a real problem and thus has greater potential to create value; and second, it is perceived as valuable by the broader organization and, as a result, will benefit from broader support by top management, by other functional groups (e.g., supply chain management, finance, marketing), and, perhaps most importantly, the company's own sales organization.

A second way to identify a good starting point is to follow the value. This one is obvious, but often not used. A company may want to choose its starting point in areas that are true levers for growth or that support its chosen growth strategy. If the company's focus is mostly on cost, it might want to investigate its biggest cost pools, such as the total cost of the sales force, the money spent on trade promotions and channel programs, or the money lost as a result of the gray market for the company's products.

A third guide to the right starting point is the company's strategic objectives. Most sales organizations have a small set of key objectives to guide how they work and go to market. If, for example, one of these objectives states, "focus on our fastest-growing customers," the company can look for analytical approaches that emphasize this handful of top customers to better understand them, their customers, and how the company can make them even more successful. Analytics are often a way to take very specific action on what can be generic objectives.

Don't Turn Sales Reps into Number Crunchers

Many large sales organizations have at some point conducted time-utilization analyses to find out how salespeople divide their time between the different activities in which they are engaged: face time with customers, sales call preparation time, internal meetings, time to create internal presentations, administrative tasks, preparing sales reports, and so on. The results are invariably depressing for sales leadership because actual time spent with customers is so low.

The last thing a sales leader wants to do is exacerbate this problem by forcing salespeople to engage in more number crunching and analyses of their territory, accounts, and products. In addition to adding an even greater, noncustomer-facing burden, it also doesn't play to their strengths. Most salespeople do not have the appetite or the temperament to spend significant amounts of time generating analyses. However—and this is important—they should have the capability and the willingness to act on the results and outputs of analytics, whether that means understanding and accepting that different customers should be approached differently from others, or introducing the results of analytics efforts into the sales process and into the sales conversation.

An illustration of these principles involves a large mobile communications provider and its efforts to reduce churn among large business accounts. These accounts were managed by account reps at the overall account level, with limited insight into individual subscriber behavior. A specialized offshore analytics team was set up to do the data mining and use predictive analytics to identify subscribers within the accounts who were at risk of defecting. Insights generated by this team were handed off to a churn-reduction program manager, who coordinated the interaction with the sales organization. Jointly, they developed appropriate retention methods for proactively preventing at-risk customers from leaving. These actions helped the company reduce B2B churn by 12 percent. The point of the case study is to illustrate how the sales reps were not burdened with the actual analysis or even with the thought process on how to act on the findings. Instead, a process was set up to seamlessly integrate the findings *and the implications* of the analytics into the sales organization's way of working

Selling on the basis of facts and insights is a crucial skill for a successful sales professional and will become dramatically more important in the next few decades as market complexities increase and analytics as a competitive advantage comes closer to maturity. Just don't ask sales people to chase those facts and insights themselves.

Create a Sales Analytics Support Function

To avoid burdening salespeople with "number crunching," a company should create some type of support function that does the analysis. If a company is already making a push into analytics (within or outside of the sales area), it may very well have set up some type of analytics support group or analytics center of excellence staffed with statisticians and data management experts. In that case, the company should leverage this capability. If not, it probably has some form of sales operations or sales capability function. These groups tend to be good places to initially house the sales analytics support function, as long as they contain a base of talent on which the company can build.

Whatever the situation, a company must understand the specific requirements of sales analytics (as opposed to other forms of analytics) placed on this support function. In many marketing or supply chain or finance teams, for instance, it is perfectly feasible for a statistician to run a sophisticated analysis and hand over the raw results to the marketing, supply chain, or finance professional, who then takes the time to figure out how to translate the findings into business implications and (subsequently) into a set of decisions and actions. *This model rarely works in sales*. In sales, analytical insights must be processed and packaged *before* they are handed over to the salesperson. This means:

- The analytical insights must be applied to the scope of responsibility of the sales person; for example, his or her territory or account(s), or a specific subset of the products he or she sells.
- The actions the salesperson is expected to take on the basis of the analytical insights must be clear and unambiguous; for example, "use this messaging or product positioning with this customer."
- If the salesperson is expected to weave analytical insights into his or her conversations with customers and use data to support the conversation, it is helpful to create customized charts and presentation materials the rep can take to the customer with minimal rework. For example, analytics may have uncovered insights into buying patterns or preferences of a customer's customer. The analytics support function should weave these insights into a presentation deck tailored to that customer and then provide this material to the salesperson.

Understandably, the level of processing and packaging will depend on the nature of the sales interaction and the level of homogeneity between customers. In industries such as consumer products, electronics, and pharmaceuticals, this level of "mass customization" can be pushed significantly. For example, one consumer products company with a sales organization numbering in the thousands periodically runs analyses on its sales data and on syndicated market data. This process uncovers trends about its own products as well as those of its competitors. Automated analytical decision rules then define implications and suggested actions for each customer. Finally, the system generates a presentation for each customer containing the relevant facts and figures, implications for the customer's business, and customized recommendations. This presentation is routed to the relevant salesperson who typically makes minor changes and then takes it to the customer on his or her next sales call.

In terms of level of automation and sophistication, this is an extreme example and usually not viable for many sales organizations. Where solution selling is more prevalent, analytics are just as relevant but the level of what processing and packaging the support function can realistically do is more limited.

Tie Analytics to Specific Sales Strategies and Embed Them into the Sales Process

The example in the previous section also illustrates the importance of embedding sales analytics into the actual sales process. For instance, at the consumer products company, analytically derived insights were not simply sloughed off on salespeople, who then could choose to use them as they saw fit. That approach would clearly lead to poor adoption and inconsistent use. To the contrary, the analytics enabled a very specific step or set of actions the salespeople were expected to take as part of their selling activities. Proper use of analytics-based information elevates the impact of the selling process and, as a result, the effectiveness of the salesperson.

This principle is further illustrated by a case study on how sales analytics were implemented within a division of a chemical company selling products where use is highly regulated. End users of the product have to involve certified intermediaries who must approve or recommend the use of the product. The company was not effectively interacting with these intermediaries, who were very important influencers of the choice of product by the end user.

Because the product is regulated, all approvals and recommendations are filed with regulatory authorities. The company identified a data source that captured these approvals. Analytics performed on this data allowed the company to understand the approval and recommendation behavior by the intermediaries. It allowed the company to determine the company's market share versus its competitors with each individual intermediary, as well as uncovered deep insights into the behaviors and preferences of the intermediaries with regard to different products and different uses of the products. The company was then able to cluster the intermediaries into detailed segments and prescribe the right actions and messages for the salespeople to take to these intermediaries. That information was pushed to the sales CRM tool and the salespeople now use it to plan and execute their sales calls. In this company, analytics are an integral component of the sales process. They provide the sales organization with a way to successfully execute its new sales strategy of calling on intermediaries with relevant and targeted sales messages.

Foster an Analytics Culture in the Sales Organization

Many companies have strong organizational cultures, and sales organizations often have their own subculture as well. This culture may not be tuned in to the use of analytics and may experience it as somewhat alien. If that is the case, sales leadership should encourage the acceptance of analytics and foster more of a fact-based culture through a number of actions.

Asking for Facts

Sales leadership can achieve significant culture change by simply asking for facts to back up assertions. If, in every key internal sales meeting or account planning meeting, decision makers ask for hard facts when an assertion is made, the broader sales organization will quickly understand that leadership is serious and they will seek out the right facts and insights in preparation for the next meeting.

Rewarding Use of Analytics

By visibly rewarding, even promoting, salespeople who have a passion and a knack for seeking out and using analytics in customer meetings, sales leadership will demonstrate to the broader sales organization that using analytics is important to their own success.

Setting the Example

Sales leaders can set the tone by applying analytics. For example, the annual strategy presented by sales executives should be informed by insights and analytics on the broader market; on customer and competitor trends; and on market opportunities uncovered by analysis. They can demonstrate that they, too, are driven by facts and not simply opinions and intuition.

Communicating Analytics Success Stories

These stories should not focus on the supposed brilliance of an individual salesperson in applying analytics. Rather, the example should demonstrate how analytical building blocks the broader sales organization has put in place came together and worked in the way they were intended. This could include the data, the analytics, the insight generation, the process to deliver the insights to the salespeople, and then (crucially) the choice that a particular salesperson or sales team made to effectively bring the insights to bear as part of a customer interaction. The full process should be celebrated and highlighted so other salespeople can see that it is not hard to incorporate analytics with the high level of support that will be available to them.

Recognizing the Changing Profile of Successful Salespeople in the Future

Increasingly, the ability to communicate analytical insights within the company and, more importantly, to customers will be critical to a salesperson's success. By explicitly and repeatedly communicating this changing profile to the broader sales organization, leadership sends a strong message to the current sales force about the type of salespeople the company will recruit, and how today's salespeople need to evolve to stay relevant and successful.

Don't Be Discouraged by Lack of Data

Some sales leaders believe their companies have insufficient data to make a push into analytics. It is true that the amount of information industries and companies have about their customers and product sales varies widely. At one extreme are sectors such as communications and financial services where, as a result of direct and data-intensive interaction with customers, purchasing patterns and usage trends in products and services can be closely analyzed. At the other end of the spectrum are industries such as chemicals, industrial products, and high tech, where interaction with customers is typically through one or more layers of intermediaries. In addition, if the customer interaction is business-to-business—where "the customer" is actually multiple decision makers—the data picture can get even murkier. Many other industry sectors fall somewhere in between these two ends of the data-availability spectrum.

A company should acknowledge various data limitations where they exist, but it should not become discouraged by them. Doing impactful sales-analytics work does not always require terabytes of customer data waiting to be mined. In certain cases, the analytical process creates its own data—as was illustrated earlier in the discussion of predictive selling. Another example is talent management analytics, where a survey instrument is used to collect detailed data on top sales performers along the dimensions of personality, behavior, and competencies. Analytics-based studies are then conducted to identify factors that truly drive top performance within a particular sales organization. One high-tech company used this approach to profile high performers in its sales organization. The profile became the basis of the company's recruitment and career-development strategies as well as its training approach.

Analytics can also rely on internal data sources that are almost always present but may not be thought of as typical data sources. For example, most sales organizations have opportunity management systems that help capture and track sales opportunities as they progress through the pipeline. This data can be mined for insights on what types of opportunities have a higher probability of culminating in a successful sale. One communications company, for instance, used sales-pipeline analytics to uncover insights on the types of opportunities (e.g., product type, product combination, deal size, and gross margin) and the types of customers (e.g., size of customer, industry segment, previous purchase history, and timing of previous purchases) most often associated with a successful sale. The company augmented its internal data set with external data from data vendors such as Dun & Bradstreet®, InfoUSA®, and Experian®. The insights allowed the sales organization to properly prioritize the many opportunities in the current pipeline and allocate resources more effectively.

Other examples of sales analytics that rely on widely available internal data sources are pricing analytics and cost-to-serve analytics. Invariably, the data needs to be processed in some way first, but data sources are generally available.

Incorporate Market-Sensing Analytics into the Future Vision

While it is crucial to find the right starting point for an analytics effort, even before that, a company should start developing a future vision of sales analytics to communicate and work toward. This vision will ensure that the analytics journey has direction and is understood by the organization. It could include a number of analytical areas such as the ones described in Figure 9.2. It could also include a vision for a decision-making framework emphasizing how to incorporate analytical insights into the day-to-day running of the business. Or it could include a different type of analytics that we refer to as "market-sensing analytics." Most of the sales analytics areas described in this chapter involve some form of optimization based on current or historical data. However, market-sensing analytics are designed to monitor and provide insights on business volatility by processing large amounts of unstructured or nontraditional data and spotting patterns in the data. Recognition of these patterns can allow a company to get a competitive edge by spotting market developments early.

An increasingly popular example of this (particularly among consumer goods companies) is brand sentiment monitoring, where specialized tools trawl through social media such as Facebook and Twitter® to uncover positive or negative trends in the way a brand is perceived. Other interesting examples are starting to emerge. When UBS Investment Research® issued its second-quarter 2010 earnings preview for Walmart®, it noted the use of private-sector satellite companies to tally the number of cars in the parking lots at Walmart stores.[2] By counting cars in a sample of 100 Walmarts, analysts were able to get a sense of customer flow and use regression analysis to predict the company's quarterly revenue.[3]

In a similar example, Illinois-based analytical firm Lanworth Inc.® is using infrared and microwave images taken from satellites to monitor agricultural commodities globally.[4] Such techniques enable Lanworth to accurately estimate the total number of acres planted per crop. Using infrared images to assess chlorophyll levels in the plants, and microwave images to assess moisture levels in crops, Lanworth analysts can monitor the health of crops over time and spot any changes that might affect supplies in the commodities market.[5] Imagine the value of this type of information to a sales organization that directly or indirectly serves the agribusiness sector.

As the examples show, market-sensing analytics can be truly game changing—a source of significant competitive advantage by picking up signals from the marketplace earlier or in a more accurate way than the competition. And because no one is closer to the marketplace than the sales organization, sales leadership has a responsibility to start thinking through what market-sensing opportunities exist for their company.

A Final Word on Developing a Sales Analytics Capability

Given the wide array of analytical areas that now enable organizations to apply science to selling, it is important to understand what these areas have in common. Most analytical areas rely on the same or similar data sets, as well as similar analytic approaches and technologies. Consequently, the same core group of analytical resources can support multiple areas. Furthermore, several analytical areas build on each other. For example, many use segmentation as a foundation for other analytical capabilities. Similar mechanisms can and should be used to integrate analytics into day-to-day sales processes. A similar approach to change management can be used to facilitate adoption by the sales force.

These similarities allow companies to consider two approaches to adopting a more scientific approach to selling. The first approach is to focus on one analytical area that is expected to provide high value and then (once this area is established) expand into other areas. This approach is pragmatic, focused, and low-risk. However, the implementation sequence may limit opportunities for synergies with other areas and could require more time to achieve true competitive advantage.

The second approach is to lay out a vision and roadmap for evolving the entire sales function toward a broader use of analytics. This option allows the organization to apply analytics in a logical sequence, while building out the foundational elements needed to support a more scientific approach to selling. This option also requires clearer strategic intent and greater commitment to the concept at the outset.

Regardless of the approach taken, by applying analytics to key areas across the sales process, an organization can use objective fact-based information to help sales people use their time more effectively and boost their overall sales effectiveness. Adhering to the principles outlined in the chapter will help ensure that new analytical insights turn into meaningful gains in revenue and profit performance.

10

Incentives That Drive Performance

Motivating the Right Behaviors with the Right Sales and Marketing Incentives to Optimize ROI

Jason Angelos and Gary Singer

Chapter Summary

- Bonuses, commissions, incentives...companies spend billions of dollars "inspiring" their internal and external sales forces, and then on tracking, planning, and processing these.
- Many times, the spend is spread across silos, which limits the companies' ability to measure "cause and effect" and thereby the return on their investments.
- Leaders get four things right to maximize the return on investment and then build the scalable mechanisms to continuously optimize.

Incentives. Promotions. Rebates. Commissions. Companies collectively spend billions of dollars annually on sales and marketing incentives to "inspire" their internal and external sales forces to sell more products and services. These organizations believe strongly that monetary motivators are key to effective selling. They also tend to be comfortable with the amounts they're spending—from 5 percent to as much as 20 percent or more of revenue in many cases.

To be sure, companies spend innumerable hours tracking, planning, and processing marketing incentives such as trade promotion investments. And they invest significant sums tracking incentive compensation for their sales force—both direct and indirect. The more difficult issue they wrestle with is whether their sales and marketing incentives are as effective as they could be. Are the rewards they're paying out commensurate with the value they receive? Are all those dollars driving the right sales behaviors—spurring salespeople, agents, and channel partners to reach their maximum potential? Are the company's strategic priorities fully reflected in its incentive structure? Might a different distribution of dollars help fuel more profitable growth?

We have found that the companies that enjoy the highest return on sales and marketing incentive programs do several things right. For example, high performers clearly align incentive programs around their go-to-market model and customer experience blueprint. They recognize that it's all about motivating behavior to drive intended outcomes—unaided consideration from consumers and qualified leads; channel partner promotion, affinity, and mindshare; and the right sales actions in moments of truth with the customer. They also measure and manage incentive spending as an integrated portfolio at multiple levels, and they use advanced analytics to design, model, track, and dynamically manage incentive programs.

This chapter examines innovative approaches Agile Selling leaders are taking to infuse more science into the art of incentive design and employ analytics to better inform incentive program decisions that drive desired business outcomes—all with an eye toward driving profitable growth with optimized investment levels in sales and marketing incentives.

The Incentive Conundrum

Sales and marketing leaders have multiple variable investment levers at their disposal that collectively drive the likelihood and profitability of sales: advertising and media spending; marketing incentives (which, depending on the industry, may take the form of trade promotion or channel incentives); sales incentives for those directly interacting with customers (such as a sales employee, channel partner, or independent broker/dealer); and discounts on pricing. Each plays an important role at various stages in the sales cycle. Some of these levers are addressed in other chapters (for example, Chapter 8 on pricing and Chapter 6 on lead generation strategies). In this chapter, we focus on the sales and marketing incentives companies use to influence specific outcomes at "moments of truth" to sell, service, retain, cross- and up-sell customers.

Incentives are hardwired into most companies' sales and marketing strategies. Virtually every sales initiative features incentive programs. In marketing, incentives may not be as ubiquitous across industries, but they are nonetheless a huge component. Simply put, incentives are front and center of most companies' sales and marketing strategies. They frequently reside at the core of those strategies—a primary way to reinforce desired behaviors in internal sales reps and channel partners to drive intended business outcomes. Small wonder that incentives are so ingrained and so dramatic in terms of dollars spent.

How dramatic? Well, companies generally spend between 3 and 10 percent of revenues on sales incentive compensation.[1] High-tech entities may spend 5 percent or more on sales incentives. Global banks may commit up to 7 percent of revenue to sales commissions. Insurance companies have a long history with sales incentives—often paying commissions and bonuses equivalent to 6 to 10 percent of revenue. On the marketing side, incentive spending can be just as striking: Each year, U.S. consumer packaged goods manufacturers spend an estimated $200 billion—15 to 20 percent of revenues—on retailer incentives.[2] Other industries with high levels of marketing incentive spend include pharmaceuticals, telecommunications, and high-tech (the latter two in the form of channel incentives).

It's perfectly clear what companies' incentive payments are trying to do: From a sales standpoint, the mission is to get internal and external salespeople to sell more stuff. From a marketing standpoint, the goal is a bit more esoteric. But it basically comes down to encouraging channel partners to market and sell more aggressively on your behalf.

However, many things are not so clear. For example, the relationship between what companies are paying and what they're getting. Or the assurance that incentives are helping reps or channel partners sell or promote the *right* things. Or the knowledge that incentive payments are being allocated to the right people and business entities in the right proportions. In short, most companies can't tell for certain that their incentive dollars are driving the specific outcomes most important to the business. So in the end, the most important question is "How can we achieve the greatest return on our incentive-related investments?"

Most organizations (including Accenture) believe that companies' typical investment levels in sales or marketing incentive programs are appropriate. However, most companies don't think their incentive programs are particularly effective. According to research conducted by Accenture and CSO Insights,[3] only 10 percent of researched companies (all with annual revenue exceeding $1 billion) believe their incentive compensation programs drive precise selling behaviors. And among the survey's 1,500 executive respondents:

- Forty-one percent said their salespeople don't have a clear idea of their company's goals and objectives.
- Any given year, 36 percent to 47 percent of salespeople will fail to achieve their individual quota.
- Nearly half of companies believe their incentive plans either do not, or only occasionally, drive intended behavior.
- Thirty-seven percent acknowledged a limited understanding of the cause-and-effect relationship between sales incentives and sales performance.

In the marketing-incentives arena, manufacturers and retailers also have made minimal progress improving trade promotion effectiveness. This is particularly disconcerting given today's economic uncertainty, increasing competition, and more demanding customers with an increased propensity to switch across providers and products. These circumstances are creating great pressure on manufacturers to either lower prices or find creative ways to convince shoppers their product is a better choice. The net effect is that companies continue to pour money into marketing incentives, despite a lack of clarity as to what they're actually getting in return.

Parsing the Problem: More Art Than Science?

Why has it proven so difficult for companies to establish tighter cause-and-effect relationships between sales and marketing incentive programs and the results those programs engender?

Historically, incentives have often been viewed as the "third rail" of sales and marketing programs: hundreds of millions or, in many cases, billions of dollars of annual spend where the prevailing view was one of "best to leave good enough alone" with the sales force and channel partners. Approaches to incentive designs were more incremental art and tinkering with a "more is more" predisposition—a belief that more spending (and more programs) would continue to yield higher sales performance. Incentive effectiveness measures and analytics were typically viewed at a macro level, in aggregate, and often months in arrears. All of this limited the ability to clearly gauge cause and effect at an actionable level and inhibited abilities to clearly derive return on investment (ROI).

One important challenge is that sales and marketing programs generally function as silos rather than as a collective investment portfolio. Too many companies design and fund sales and marketing incentive programs on an independent, piecemeal basis—instead of creating synergistic efforts. Organizational silos between sales and marketing—as well as *within* sales and marketing—are common. Separation exists among brands and product lines, among channels and customer bases, and around "levers" such as trade promotions and advertising. These siloed approaches—beyond producing limited insights and ambiguous returns—also make it difficult to tie activities to results. For example, in the technology industry, performance is often self-reported by channel partners, which makes it easier for them to "double dip"—that is, participate in legitimate overlapping incentives payments from different sources for the same marketing activity or sales performance.

The silo default also has different ramifications depending on whether it's a sales or marketing incentive. In sales, companies may spend a lot of time developing a customer experience model (see Chapter 7), but the way they align their incentive programs doesn't follow suit. For example, these organizations may look closely at the specific behaviors they are trying to drive, but they do so at discrete points. As a result, they don't measure or track the impact of behavior changes across the sales life cycle—from getting someone's attention to closing a deal with them. This leads to unintended consequences for the organization, including unearned incentive payments and potential channel conflict.

Sales organizations also tend to unintentionally encourage conflicting behaviors by setting up different types of sales incentives within the same business. In the publishing industry, for example, sales managers may be paid on gross advertising sales while publishers' bonuses are based on gross profits. This can result in sales managers—in their efforts to boost sales revenue—approving excessive numbers of low-margin sales, which hurts the company's overall profitability (as well as the publisher's income).

It's also common for sales and marketing incentive programs to fall behind the pace of evolving business models. In the technology sector, for example, many vendors now sell solutions and services (e.g., selling "in the cloud")—implementing and operating the technologies they manufacture. However, those same organizations' variable compensation systems might still be product-centric. Take software: Firms that offer traditional on-premise software are now building software-as-a-service businesses. These new operating models must be supported largely by new sales compensation strategies. If different selling models are not implemented—one for on-premise software and one for software as a service—the likely result is confusion and conflicting motivations across sales channels.

Another field, insurance, is increasingly characterized by rising consumerism and the proliferation of digital marketing and direct-selling platforms. These moves call into question a variety of long-standing sales practices, such as using a one-size-fits-all commission model and rewarding agents and brokers for their existing book of business (which puts the emphasis on maintenance as opposed to growth).

The bottom line is that companies cannot power new business models with old approaches to incentive compensation. There must be an explicit link between a company's incentive investments and the revenue those investments generate.

Companies have made significant investments to identify and control what they are spending in aggregate. Trade promotion management systems, for example, help consumer goods companies do a better job of capturing spend data, tracking shipment and promotion information, understanding claims, making payments, and resolving disputes. These advancements clearly deliver improved efficiency and insight to data. What they often *don't* do is help companies improve "how" and "where" they are spending.

Research conducted by Accenture and the Promotion Optimization Institute (POI)[4] bears this out. Sixty-five percent of surveyed consumer packaged goods manufacturers were found to have strong capabilities in sales transaction management, while 58 percent perform well when it comes to allocating promotion funds. A surprising number, however, lack the data, tools, and systems to understand things like category profitability and the impact of promotions on shopping behavior. Only 27 percent surveyed are equipped to fully evaluate promotions post-event. Only 17 percent plan collaboratively. Only 13 percent do a good job of predicting and planning for a promotion event's impact. The bottom line: Promotion trade funds are being managed more efficiently and accurately, but *trade productivity*—the return companies get on their promotion investment—is not rising commensurately. As a result, promotion budgets as a percent of revenue continue to increase, even as programs designed to improve trade promotions are pared back or canceled because of companies' inability to understand returns. Small wonder that only about one-third of trade promotion events generate incremental profit.

All this is not to say that companies are failing in some easily rectifiable way. Transaction management is obviously easier than decision management; and it is far simpler and often more permissible to push volume, given competitive pressures and Wall Street's intolerance of temporary losses of share. As a result, quick-return mentalities usurp longer-term solutions. Like people, companies also tend to be comfortable with the status quo, and they're frequently put off by the notion that new, "unproven" approaches will be too expensive, too work-intensive, and too reliant on perfect data or ultra-advanced technology or technological sophistication. Besides, "how do we *know* that we'll see better returns?"

Sales and Marketing Incentives: Developing ROI-Focused Approaches

Whether you're talking sales or marketing, we believe companies that achieve consistently high returns on their incentive investments do the same few things right. For one thing, they make sure their incentive programs align with their go-to-market models and partner/customer experience blueprints. They understand, in other words, that the heart of any initiative is interactions with customers. So that's what they define, track, and measure: the relationship between sales/marketing behaviors and customer/buyer outcomes.

Leading-practice companies also excel at portfolio allocation and management: controlling and measuring spend as an integrated portfolio at multiple levels. This means they look at all sales and marketing spend as a suite of options, such as moving funds from trade spending to ad spending, or from sales incentives to channel incentives. They're equally inclined to think about spend as a portfolio decision *within* a spending category, such as moving funds between various incentive programs, or tactics for a particular product or channel or across products or channels. A good example might be using marketing mix analytics to determine the best allocation of spend by brand within a category. Similarly, sales performance and compensation analytics can help to evaluate the effectiveness of special incentive contests or

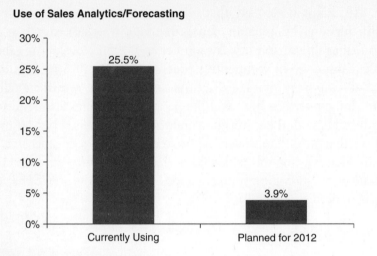

Use of Sales Analytics/Forecasting

FIGURE 10.1 Few Companies Use Analytics to Identify Problem Spots and Prospective Opportunities

Source: CSO Insights, Sales Performance Optimization Research, 2012.

promotions—assessing the correlation among business results, sales credit participation, and payout ratios—before extending them for another quarter. Organizations can do a better job of designing, modeling, and adapting incentive programs by using analytics to help perform value assessments, quantify spending tradeoffs and (subsequently) reformulate strategies, tactics, and fund-allocation approaches. At the moment, moreover, analytics may provide a significant competitive advantage because few companies currently use it to optimize their incentive programs (Figure 10.1).

Optimizing Spending

More than they may realize, organizations can optimize their spend on incentive programs without compromising sales performance or discouraging or alienating salespeople. In many cases, nearly one in 10 incentive program dollars spent yield little or no return for the organization.[5] Companies can improve effectiveness and drive significant financial performance improvements by aligning and allocating incentive spending against strategic imperatives, conducting more thorough analysis to identify the most valuable targets and reevaluating policies within the performance period. Specifically:

- *Redesign and align incentive plans.* Think anew about whom you want to incentivize for sales, the desired salesperson behavior, your ability to measure and track sales impact, and what the eligibility requirements for compensation should be (think sales contribution relative to sales credit and sales credit participation ratios). Reassess the use of thresholds, caps, and accelerators. Make sure bonus/overlay programs reward incremental sales improvements. Changes like these can bolster the effectiveness of incentive spend by up to 7 percent.

- *Set new targets and/or quotas.* Move past the "historical-plus-XXX-percent" approach to setting next year's revenue targets and quotas. Rely instead on opportunity-based analyses of the factors that contribute to more profitable revenue and/or growth.

- *Identify and end overpayments.* Increasing payment accuracy can cut commission spending by up to 8 percent. Companies do this by improving their compliance-to-pay policies, building better spend/quota-management programs, and closing incentive plan loopholes. Overpayments also may be stanched by better processes and tools. It isn't uncommon, for example, for poorly synchronized processes, systems, and data to result in miscalculated commissions and credits. And it's not just about improving accuracy. Often, incentive programs are working as designed but not as intended—resulting in unearned incentive payments. For example, take the case of a high-tech firm where, in spite of intended policy to the contrary, sales reps received 100 percent sales credit for the sales of "noncommissioned" third-party products.

- *Increase insights from data.* The key here is not so much capturing data as leveraging data and doing so in a more timely fashion with greater frequency: using correlative analytics, econometric modeling, and advanced forecasting to recognize profit-generating and productivity-optimizing opportunities more readily, deploy salespeople more effectively, and more-tightly align incentive rewards with sales-performance results.

Case Study: Banking

A global bank recently analyzed its incentive payment program and confirmed what its executives had long suspected: In certain areas, overpayment rates were running as high as 10 percent of total incentive spend. Two culprits were identified: a high number of exceptions and overdependence on manual processing. By correcting these and other problems (i.e., by rationalizing policies, strengthening controls, and improving the integrity of commission data), the bank has since avoided more than $15 million in annual incentive overpayments.

Case Study: Telecommunications

After extensive research, a large telecommunications company discovered that it was awarding outsized commissions on third-party dealers' wireless products and contracts. The crux of the problem was residual commissions: Shortcomings in key processes and systems were allowing dealers to receive commissions beyond the eligible term—long after consumers changed contracts or began purchasing equipment directly from the company. This represented potential savings opportunities worth more than $10 million per year.

- *Reinforce specific sales behaviors that increase revenue.* Again, using analytics, identify the behaviors and associated key performance measures that drive profitable sales. From there, it's possible to design better pay-for-performance programs that tie partner/sales incentive payments to the execution of those specific behaviors.

Building the Underlying Capabilities

Optimizing incentive spending requires improving timely insight to actionable data, altering decision frameworks, business processes and policies, and even organizational structures. We've outlined innovative actions companies can take to maximize ROI on the hundreds of millions of dollars spent annually on incentives—reducing sales and marketing incentives spend as a percentage of sales (or revenue) while contributing to profitable growth. But what must an organization do to fully embrace and integrate these improvements and sustain their benefits, making sales performance and incentive spend analytics part of business as usual for the company?

The following is a five-stage approach to identify the right tools and build the underlying capabilities to sustain incentive spending benefits, provide greater agility and speed to market for new programs, and help bolster sales productivity.

Select/Plan/Pilot

We recommend beginning with an assessment of key incentives and promotion planning and execution requirements as they relate to industry practices, strategic and operational requirements, and value-creation potential. To gather this information for trade promotion, you can use shipment data or consumption data—whichever is available; it isn't necessary to connect shipment, wholesaler, and retailer point-of-sale data to get the insights you need. Diagnosing sales incentives capabilities should consider: core compensation administration while looking upstream at the "quote to commissions" process; the sales coverage model; the number of individuals receiving sales credit per individual order (aka sales credit ratio); and the correlation between company performance, average quota attainment, and average payout ratios.

Once a company identifies and prioritizes its requirements, it can select a software solution, develop a preliminary plan that emphasizes the most-desirable capabilities, and establish an implementation schedule. Examples of some of the most desirable capabilities are those that reliably contribute to improved flexibility and speed to market for new programs, the ability to execute more targeted incentives, better insight to data, and improved accuracy and traceability with incentive payments. Some companies may design a preliminary process to select a solution, and then identify one or two technology providers for a pilot or proof-of-value phase. In the case of a trade promotion optimization solution, a pilot generally includes one or two account teams and a subsegment of brands or product categories.

Among other benefits, the selection, planning, and piloting phase helps achieve alignment across the organization and demonstrate proof of value. For this reason, it is vital to have cross-functional participation.

Rethink/Redesign Decision-Making and Execution Processes

This is where many companies fall down. As noted earlier, they expect technology alone to improve returns, without concomitant changes in the way spend decisions are made. Another common mistake is failing to coordinate planning and execution processes across brand marketing, corporate sales planning, field sales, and supply chain management. After all, each group handles spend planning and execution differently. On the other hand, companies that excel at updating and aligning processes, making decisions, and even altering operational structures to improve sales and marketing spend ROI nearly always:

- Collaborate with marketing, sales and sales planning, and sales operations (e.g., incentive program tracking and management) teams when formulating incentive programs and budgets.

- Use pay-for-performance incentive methods to "motivate" captive sellers and channel partners to demonstrate intended behaviors and deliver business results.
- Optimize spending allocations by using econometric modeling and target ROIs that vary by promoted product groups, in the case of marketing incentives, or by product, territory, named customer account, and other dimensions for sales incentives. In effect, top-performing organizations demand approval and accountability for deviations at both an aggregate portfolio level as well as with individual incentive plans.
- Develop incentive and promotion plans using a formal process, standard fact base (e.g., opportunity-based target setting by geographic territory or named customer account), and standard analytic methods that leverage a common planning platform.
- Use analytics to elicit buy-in and increase adoption for sales and marketing incentive programs to individual sales people and channel partners.
- Develop operational and financial metrics. Operational metrics can include planning cycle time, number of account plans confirmed by retailers, and number of course corrections made and implemented. Financial metrics may include incremental volume and margin gains, and incentive spending as a percent of sales.
- Cascade metrics and dashboards—making sure that (1) the information is accessible at all organizational levels, and (2) the right information and level of detail is available (e.g., at a high level for executives, versus specific data on promotion events and their performance for account teams).
- Conduct post-event analyses and formal evaluation sessions that result in specific actions: for example, as inputs for annual operating plans and as suggestions for helping marketing, sales account teams, sales planning, and sales operations make course corrections throughout the year.
- Use analytics "centers of excellence" to ensure consistent evaluation and application of sales and marketing incentive data–performance results and payouts. These centers can be centrally

managed and/or locally dispersed. Either way, they are the repositories for the company's predictive and optimization models for incentives.

Deliver and Scale the Solution

Every company has its own way of designing and deploying enabling technology. However, companies that stand out usually excel at model and data preparation. They recognize they're not building transactional systems so much as "decision enablers," whose core technology is grounded in a flexible, rules-based engine and econometric statistical models. The difference is key, because most of the time used to design these solutions must be spent on thoroughly documenting the business use cases—performance results the incentive programs drive—and structuring the analyses needed to develop analytic models across product lines, sales channels, and customers.

Advanced statistical modeling is vital to optimize incentive spending investments and plan targeted incentive programs that boost sales. But making these capabilities part of a technology solution requires that data be prepared: cleaned, meta-tagged, and readied for modeling usage data at a transactional or point-of-sales level.

Support and Measure

Like any initiative, key performance metrics should be built into new processes and applications. Only a handful may be required, such as pay accuracy, sales lift, and incentive spend ROI. A compliance measurement function also should be part of this stage. This enables companies to proactively identify and address capability-adoption hurdles during implementation. We recommend creating a change-adoption-measurement function that has sole responsibility for identifying implementation/adoption problems, suggesting solutions for resolving them and monitoring corrective actions. When the spend optimization implementation program is completed, the change-adoption-measurement function can transition into a formal performance-measurement function whose primary goal is continuous performance monitoring and course correction.

Manage Programs

The cornerstone here is a dedicated program-management team headed by people with a strong background and stake in the company's sales and marketing incentive initiatives. Effective program-management attributes are depicted in Figure 10.2.

▄Case Study: Consumer Goods

To improve profitability, a global CPG food manufacturer analyzed its trade promotions across three brands covering more than 100 product groups. The manufacturer wanted to find ways to improve trade spending ROI, while delivering new analytical capabilities to its sales organization. After analyzing its trade spending ROI and building a promotion-planning and forecasting tool, the manufacturer was able to identify ways to improve market share and profitability. Toward this end, it:

- Built econometric models to predict the volume and profit lifts associated with promotion events, tactics, and timing across promoted product groups, channels, and accounts.
- Developed proxy/surrogate lift coefficients for new products and tactics.
- Developed new end-to-end trade promotion planning and execution processes.
- Supported group training, and one-on-one, on-the-job coaching for U.S. sales personnel.

Among the most impactful results were return-on-sales improvements of 0.5 to 4 percent across product groups, a 50 percent reduction in promotion forecasting error, and the discovery of opportunities to reduce inventories by about 30 percent.

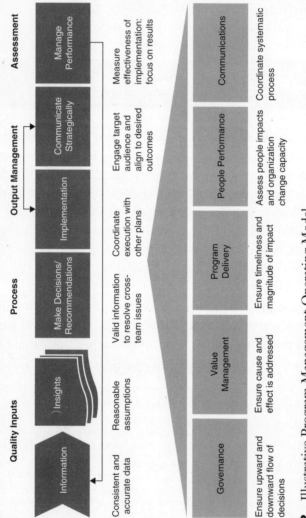

FIGURE 10.2 Illustrative Program Management Operating Model

What's It Worth to You?

Creating a tighter connection between sales/marking incentive investments and sales performance returns takes a lot of work. In either case
(sales or marketing), improved access to data and analytics, new technologies, processes, and skill sets and even operational structures may
be needed. So are all these efforts worthy of an organization's time
and dollars?

We believe that the potential gain can significantly overshadow
the short-term pain. On the sales side, materially higher revenue and
profits—typically coupled with lower incentive spend (as a percentage
of sales or revenue)—are the frequent result of changing the way you
manage incentive programs:

Higher revenues. These come primarily from driving or reinforcing the behaviors that most directly improve sales performance and
productivity, and raise customer and salesperson satisfaction. Accenture researchers[6] have found that a $1 billion business could boost its
pretax profit by $23 million simply by using motivational tools and
incentive programs that work together to raise salespeople's performance. In effect, you're creating programs, policies, support systems,
and work environments that drive better sales performance, reward

---

Case Study: Insurance

A U.S.-based, multiline insurance carrier found opportunity by
moving from a one-size-fits-all approach for broker sales incentives to a commission program focused on broker segmentation.
A tiered commission rate structure—based on producer segment
and the value of the producer's book to the company—was also
adopted. Combining these innovations with new performance
thresholds for items such as reimbursements for appointment fees
helped the carrier reduce its annual incentive spend by $40 mil-
lion without compromising sales performance.

people for capturing the most lucrative business, and fund opportunities to reinvest in growth.

Optimized sales-incentive spend. The average spend-optimization benefit (as a percent of sales or revenue) enjoyed by companies that launch sales-incentive-improvement programs is about 6 to 10 percent.[7] Often, the improvement opportunities are even greater for business-to-business (B2B) and business-to-business-to-consumer (B2B2C) companies.

Case Study: High-Tech

A leading high-tech company adopted a cloud-based recurring-revenue model. However, this change revealed areas for improvement in the company's approach to sales coverage and incentives. Perhaps most telling, many people were receiving sales credit on a typical deal. The company reengineered its sales incentive program following an analysis of its coverage model, sales-credit rules, and governance in the context of key sales engagement scenarios. Over the course of three years, incentive spend decreased from 5.5 percent of revenue to less than 5 percent, while top-line performance improved by 60 percent.

On the marketing side, research by Accenture and the Promotion Optimization Institute[8] ascribed a wide range of benefits to marketing-incentive program leaders. For example, trade promotion optimization programs can provide return-on-sales improvements of 2 to 4 percent. More than half of the survey's respondents believe higher profitability resulted from their implementation of formal marketing-incentive programs, while more than one-third cited decreases in time spent. Specific benefits by company size are illustrated in Figure 10.3.

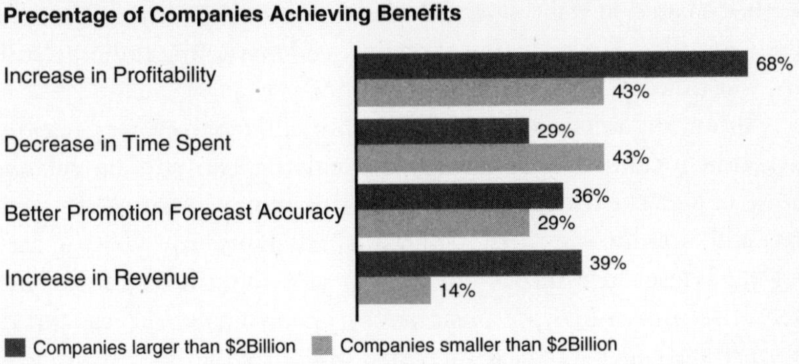

Precentage of Companies Achieving Benefits

Increase in Profitability — 68% / 43%

Decrease in Time Spent — 29% / 43%

Better Promotion Forecast Accuracy — 36% / 29%

Increase in Revenue — 39% / 14%

■ Companies larger than $2Billion   ■ Companies smaller than $2Billion

FIGURE 10.3 Benefits Derived from the Implementation of Formal Marketing-Incentive Programs, by Company Size

Source: Accenture and Promotion Optimization Institute survey, "Charting Your Course to Trade Promotion Optimization," 2011.

In addition, the research conducted by Accenture and POI noted that a variety of less-tangible benefits also accrue to market-incentivization leaders. Compared with other companies, these leaders tend to:

- Spend less time and fewer resources gathering data (thus making more time available for value-added planning and analysis).
- Make better use of trade funds due to greater visibility into ROI.
- Do a better job of focusing spend on promotion-sensitive products/categories.
- More effectively share data and analyses across manufacturer/retailer trading partners.
- Use data and tools more consistently.

Looking at indirect channel marketing incentives through a high-tech industry lens, Accenture's experience suggests that up to one in three dollars spent on channel incentive programs are underutilized. In other words, 33 percent of channel incentive spend is either overpaid due to shortcomings in business processes, data, and technology, or diluted by "double dipping" by channel partners. Worse yet, the balance of the one-third often comprises funds that go completely unutilized—budgeted and approved marketing dollars that fail to be put to work in the market.

Although we've acknowledged that fully optimizing sales and marketing incentive programs is not easy, it can still be relatively simple to get started. Identifying a small-scope initiative, gathering data, and conducting "proof-of-value" analyses can yield a lot of insight. These "prestudies" may help you identify areas for more intense scrutiny, provide insights on your analytical capabilities, demonstrate quick tangible benefits, and provide data from which to develop a broader business case for change. Experienced service providers can help companies focus their efforts and deliver benefits quickly from such focused analysis. They can bring both capacity and focus—boost analytical capacity with relevant domain experience and an understanding to pursue business scenarios that have proven most fruitful for other companies to analyze.

Case Study: Retail

A major U.S. grocer was losing market share. However, the company could not justify spending more on promotions than its competitors; somehow, it had to improve performance within the constraints of its existing promotion budget. The organization subsequently reengineered its processes and developed new metric and decision frameworks. It also conducted detailed ROI analytics focused on the allocation of its retail shelf space and the performance of its in-store promotions to optimize trade promotion spend. Notable results of the initiative included double-digit increases in incremental sales and margin; triple-digit increases in ad sales and ad margin, and a very attractive marketing ROI.

Companies continue to make big investments in sales and marketing incentives and many have made significant progress in knowing where and how much spending is occurring. That's a great start. From there, the high-potential challenge is to improve returns on those investments: identifying what works and what doesn't—both within individual programs and across the collective incentive spend portfolio, and launching sales- or marketing-incentive programs whose laser-tight focus is on driving profitable growth and improving ROI.

SECTION

III

Building the Better Network—Positioning for Success and Effectiveness

When designing, building, and using the capabilities discussed in Section II, organizations must consider the existing skills and requirements of not simply their direct resources, or even the indirect resources, but of all parties engaged in the Agile Selling ecosystem. This goes beyond design and implementation to how these capabilities are governed and where they "sit" in the organization's management structure and system. Importantly, governance structures must be defined by how well they support the successful operation of the entire ecosystem, not simply a company's owned resources; therefore, tighter integration and partnerships with all the other resources or stakeholders is required. This is especially true of what we call the joint initiative (JI) model, in which two or more companies invest in a stand-alone business entity to collaboratively develop, sell, and deliver new solutions to mutual customers' problems—in a way that the individual companies' offers could not do on their own.

The JI model and others like it can be especially helpful to companies looking to penetrate two markets that are rife with complexity and uncertainty: the small- and medium-size business (SMB) market and geographic markets outside of their established, familiar territories.

The vast number of SMBs, their diverse needs, and their unique buying behaviors are all factors that combine to produce an enormously complex test of a B2B company looking to grow in this market. Getting the offerings right, the channel coverage right, and the sales and marketing programs right can be enormously difficult. Among the keys to doing so is a foundation built on segmentation and predictive modeling that can help a company tailor offerings to SMB prospects' needs, as well as deploy a multichannel SMB customer engagement model that incorporates field sales, channel partners, inside sales, teleweb, and other approaches.

When looking to expand globally, it doesn't matter if a company is going from a developed market to emerging markets, or vice versa. Both can be helped immensely by gaining local insight and accessing more sophisticated capabilities via alliances or partnerships with firms already established in those markets—rather than taking the costly, time-consuming, and potentially risky route of creating capabilities from scratch. Companies from developed markets looking to expand into emerging ones can learn from how other companies successfully identified partners to help them adapt their offers and capabilities to local needs, tastes, and cultures. Conversely, companies based in emerging markets seeking to expand into developed markets should identify partners that can bring complementary capabilities that can help them quickly broaden their reach.

In pursuing the SMB and global markets, social media is also a critical enabler of Agile Selling. Social media tools and logic can help B2B companies overcome many of their current sales organization limitations—most notably, functional silos and outdated technologies that impede teaming and information sharing. In fact, social media can help companies create sales forces and processes that are more collaborative and responsive to customers' needs, improve sales force productivity, and increase their ability to identify and close the right deals.

Section III brings greater clarity to these issues while highlighting a number of stories of how companies have succeeded in "building a better network."

11

Joint Initiatives

A Step Change for Sales Collaboration

Mike Heald, Paul Neumann,
and Golnar Pooya

Chapter Summary

- Companies need a holistic and fresh approach to building sales networks. The traditional model is plagued with historical inefficiency and baggage.
- Building a Joint Initiative (JI) is one model for how to reach new markets through new collaboration.
- There are five critical steps in launching a JI and five organizational elements that must be jointly defined.
- Making a JI successful takes senior executive commitment from each involved company and requires a bold challenge to the conventional model.

For many years, companies have used alliances to help them boost their reach and share in key markets and segments. These traditional partnerships are "sell with" arrangements: Teams from the respective companies work together as opportunities arise to jointly sell their respective products and/or joint solutions.

However, as companies in search of growth opportunities plow new ground—emerging markets, the lucrative small- and medium-size business (SMB) segment, and service and solution offerings, to name the most prominent—the JI framework is one potential approach that can enable companies to achieve their objectives.

Emerging and SMB markets, for example, require their own products and services, as well as different selling and pricing strategies. Furthermore, in these new markets and segments, there is far less customer data available that companies can leverage to refine their strategies. Moreover, selling through traditional channels in new markets poses risks—with traditional networks, companies may not have adequate control of the customer experience or even their brand identity. The changing customer expectations stemming mostly from new technologies and trends are further straining the existing selling models.

Traditional selling networks can be too focused on what has worked in mature markets and often do not offer the tailored approach necessary to reach the new markets and segments that comprise today's growth agendas. More and more, the math simply doesn't work: A provider sells to a channel partner; the channel partner represents hundreds of other vendors and may only provide standard sales and market data while the customer is rapidly changing below everyone's radar.

For these reasons, companies should consider Agile Selling to help meet their current corporate growth strategies. A key tenet of Agile Selling is that the selling model—and the offerings—must leverage a market's ecosystem: the community of goods and services that meet the needs of a specific set of customers. To leverage that system, companies will need to sell in cooperation with partners, suppliers, vendors, and co-developers via collaborative models that are highly flexible, adaptable, and responsive. One example of this increased level of collaboration is the joint initiative (JI) concept.

In this chapter, we explore the JI concept in detail, including some considerations and key steps in building a successful JI.

What Is the Joint Initiative Framework?

A JI is a transformation of a traditional go-to-market relationship, whereby two or more "partners" jointly invest to develop differentiated solutions that they bring to market together. A JI has dedicated sales and service teams and integrated operations that pursue aligned business objectives of the two or more participating partners. JIs can be successful both as ongoing JI relationships and when they evolve into a stand-alone line of business for the respective parties, which, through highly strategic teaming, can generate multiples of the revenue that the traditional go-to-market arrangement does. In short, a JI is a highly visible example of Agile Selling in action.

Accenture is one company that has embraced the concept of Agile Selling through JI relationships. Accenture's go-to-market strategy is to provide an independent stance with regard to its technology partners, though customers are increasingly demanding more definitive advice on an integrated solution stack, both with specific technology partners and tailored to their needs. Customers expect companies such as Accenture to provide integrated solutions that can enhance the customer experience and help mitigate risk—an approach that is significantly different from simply bundling technologies together to sell to customers.

As part of the company's growth strategy, Accenture has launched JIs with several key technology companies to jump start significant growth of all the businesses involved. Importantly, these JIs are designed expressly to meet the needs of all involved partners who see value in creating tighter integration with each other.

The JI concept can provide more discipline and focus than most other traditional go-to-market approaches typically have done. It brings a start-up, stand-alone business mentality to the relationship—a fully functioning, discrete "organization" inside an already successful company. The JI can be a catalyst for building solutions and approaching markets in a strategic, calculated, and measurable way.

A JI should have a formal organization structure with explicitly defined roles and duties. Parties investing in these JIs intend to leverage each others' strengths, such as better access to new sales channels, technology superiority, and functional expertise. As noted in

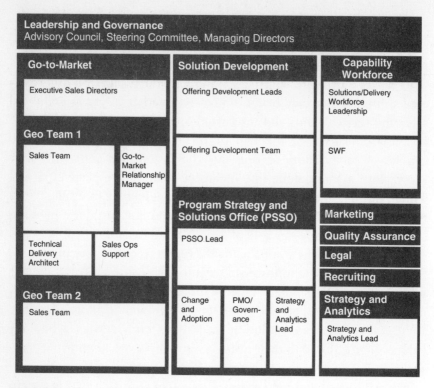

FIGURE 11.1 Illustrative JI Operational Structure

Figure 11.1, there are five key elements of the organization structure, each of which includes representatives from participating organizations. These elements are leadership and governance, go-to-market capabilities, solution development, capability workforce, and program strategy and solutions offices (PSSO).

Leadership and Governance

A JI needs people who are "in charge"—those who provide strategic direction and are the ultimate decision makers. In a typical JI, leadership and governance includes three distinct groups:

1. An advisory council, made up of executive sponsors from the parent organizations, which sets the strategic direction for the JI and is the final decision-making body for the entity.

2. A steering committee, which provides strategic and tactical oversight for the JI and monitors the entity's progress toward its objectives.

3. Managing directors, who manage the JI's day-to-day performance, address all operational concerns, serve as the first level of escalation, and are solely measured based on the success of the JI.

An important function of these leadership groups is to ensure that all stakeholders are focused on the vision and longer-term benefits and that the initiative does not easily sacrifice the longer-term objectives for shorter-term benefits. Most companies are driven by 90-day, quarterly performance pressures that can hamper their ability to implement strategies that are essential to long-term growth and relevance in the marketplace. Although accelerated time to value is important given the significance of the investments that go into these relationships, it is critical to keep an eye on long-term strategic objectives. With the typical JIs lasting between three and five years, leadership must foster a balance between quick wins and long-term priorities.

We discuss the specific roles and responsibilities of these three groups, as well as governance, in the upcoming section on launching a JI.

Solution Development

Unlike a traditional go-to-market relationship, which generally goes to market with standard solutions already existing in the respective companies (most of the time, just a bundle of the two companies' products and services), a JI is based on designing and developing truly differentiated solutions that draw on the strengths, experience, and skills of each partner. A key responsibility of the solution development group is to create a solution road map that leverages the parent companies' market intelligence and demand data. The solution road map should align with the target markets the parties have agreed to mutually pursue based on their respective corporate strategies and strengths. This road map should remain flexible and agile to incorporate changing market demand, and as such should be defined and refined over time by engaging key stakeholders from all parties.

Go-to-Market Team and Capability Workforce

The JI's dedicated sales team includes professionals from all JI partners who are charged with taking the jointly developed solutions to
the market. This group comprises several different roles, with sales
directors and field salespeople accounting for the bulk of individuals in
the group. The go-to-market team is responsible for executing on the
sales strategy developed through analytics (performed by the Program
Strategy and Solutions Office [PSSO], described below) and approved
by the governing bodies of the JI. The delivery workforce is the engine
responsible for implementing the new joint solutions.

Program Strategy and Solutions Offices (PSSO)

A JI has many "moving parts" that must be managed on a day-to-day
basis. That's why a key function of any JI is the PSSO, which is responsible for ensuring that the organizations collaborate effectively while
minimizing the impact on administrative resources and maintaining
the run-rate business.

The PSSO is the "nerve center" between the partner companies,
overseeing JI strategy, program management, daily and ongoing
governance, data analytics, pipeline management, reporting and
opportunity mapping, and change management. Figure 11.2 provides
more details on the activities for which the program management office
is responsible.

In addition to these five groups, a JI often includes a number of
support resources. These include professionals from disciplines such
as marketing quality assurance, legal, finance, and recruiting. In most
cases, these professionals are not a formal part of the JI structure but,
rather, contribute their expertise on an as-needed basis.

Launching a Joint Initiative

Although all JIs are different and their dynamics depend on the
companies involved, there are five key steps to take when launching
one: defining and structuring the relationship; developing a business
case; creating a mobilization plan, long-term road map and governance
charter; developing a joint sales playbook and target account list; and
getting the right people in the right roles with the right incentives.

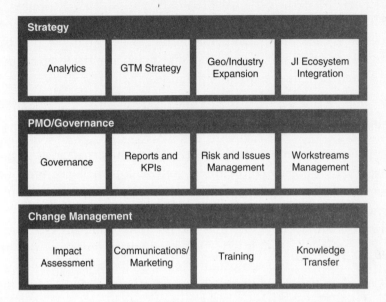

FIGURE 11.2   Key Activities Managed by the JI Program Office

Define and Structure the Relationship

When defining and structuring the relationship, companies can benefit from understanding how the JI will advance specific business objectives. To make that call, each company should explore deeply whether a JI conceptually would offer benefits that other approaches wouldn't and, if so, what those benefits would be. For instance, would it create a stronger pipeline than the company could build on its own? Provide access to important new markets and segments? Improve sales organization performance through combined resources and market intelligence? Enhance the company's brand image? Improve the company's product portfolio?

A key element of this exploration is to evaluate all potential partners the JI could include—both firms the company currently works with and those it could work with. One framework for evaluating these potential anchors of a JI considers complementary products or services, potential customer reaction, alignment of strategic objectives, and sales execution synergy.

When Accenture set up its JIs, it wanted to launch something with significant market impact—which Accenture knew would take considerable time and money. Thus, the company needed to judge whether the other parties had similar commitments in terms of the resources needed and timelines for key milestones. Defining and structuring these relationships can often take many months to position for successful and agile execution in the market.

Develop a Business Case

Companies must ensure that they have the same broad goals in mind before they make any commitment to a JI. But they also must have an understanding of more specific goals, such as sales targets, to build an accurate business case for the JI. Building an effective business case includes details about JI offerings and how each company contributes. It's not enough to simply say, "We're going to build two offerings together." Rather, the companies should explore the specific type of offering they will build together, the high-level design or specification of the offerings, the market for the offerings, and the key market demands the offerings will address.

These discussions will vary by the companies involved. For instance, some technology vendors may be very focused on specific products and how those products could be sold more effectively through a different commercial arrangement. Others might not care about particular offers, but rather, would find the JI attractive because it would help them move toward a more profitable, solution-based selling model that integrates their products.

Although each company will require a business case that has been validated by empowered stakeholders, the partners must work to merge their business cases and create a business case that focuses on the success of the JI. It is only when the companies' business cases are aligned that the JI can be successful. The business case should pursue a long-term vision while incorporating quick wins.

Create a Mobilization Plan, Long-Term Road Map, and Governance Charter

Another key step in launching a JI is planning for a mobilization phase, which is typically around 90 days, to lay the groundwork necessary to support and foster the true collaboration critical to JI success. Without this step, it is likely people will revert to current ways of working and compromise the desired impact of the JI.

The mobilization plan needs to look at both short-term actions to get all parties working together and toward the future by developing the long-term road map for the JI itself. This road map can be a clear plan for how the relationship is intended to evolve over time and should address a variety of critical questions, including:

- How will the customer experience be enhanced? What is the role of each company in defining and delivering the customer experience?
- What is the desired go-to-market strategy? How does each company maintain its own brand recognition?
- What are the first-, second-, and fifth-year sales goals?
- What are potential JI obstacles and mitigating actions?

A critical accompaniment to the long-term road map is the governance document. A typical governance document has two principal, vital responsibilities: It defines reporting mechanisms and the metrics that will gauge the performance of sales, product development, and marketing; and it defines the roles and responsibilities of the JI's governing bodies mentioned earlier in the chapter. Figure 11.3 depicts one example of the governance structure, responsibilities, and meeting frequency of each group.

Developing a Joint Sales Playbook and Target Account List

One of the most important items to have in place when a JI is launched is a joint sales playbook that harmonizes the companies' different selling motions into a common model. The joint sales playbook can not only define the sales channels and joint sales process the JI will use, but also identify the target accounts, align the sales goals and timelines for the JI, and define the incentive model for the JI.

In other words, the sales playbook details how the two companies operationalize the JI and integrate it within their respective

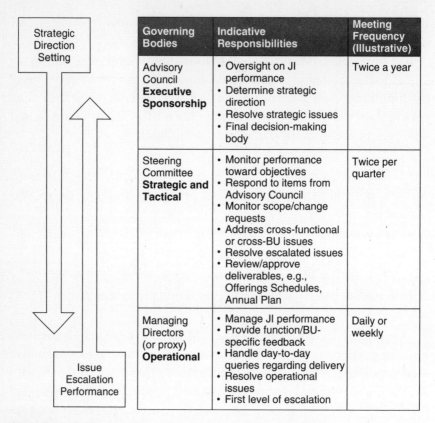

	Governing Bodies	Indicative Responsibilities	Meeting Frequency (Illustrative)
Strategic Direction Setting	Advisory Council **Executive Sponsorship**	• Oversight on JI performance • Determine strategic direction • Resolve strategic issues • Final decision-making body	Twice a year
	Steering Committee **Strategic and Tactical**	• Monitor performance toward objectives • Respond to items from Advisory Council • Monitor scope/change requests • Address cross-functional or cross-BU issues • Resolve escalated issues • Review/approve deliverables, e.g., Offerings Schedules, Annual Plan	Twice per quarter
Issue Escalation Performance	Managing Directors (or proxy) **Operational**	• Manage JI performance • Provide function/BU-specific feedback • Handle day-to-day queries regarding delivery • Resolve operational issues • First level of escalation	Daily or weekly

FIGURE 11.3 JI Governance Roles and Responsibilities

businesses—which is important because each sales team is coming from a different organization with its own culture, sales process, and incentive model. Defining how the teams will work together before any salespeople begin selling the new joint solutions can help create accountability and avoid confusion.

Some of the key questions companies will have to answer when developing their joint sales playbook are the following:

- What are the stages of the joint selling process?
- What sales scenarios do we foresee?
- What are typical roles needed on a JI sales team?

- How will the JI assign an account lead to each opportunity?
- How will the JI leverage existing accounts from each partner?

Partner companies also need to create a consolidated target account list. A JI may have thousands of potential accounts but potentially cannot support thousands of salespeople. Sales analytics is an important capability to help JI salespeople zero in on the most powerful opportunities to pursue. Analytical models can mine structured and unstructured data from each JI partner to address critical questions such as:

- Which JI accounts have the highest probability of a sale?
- Which offers are the best fit for each account and which features align with its needs?
- What are the best cross- and up-sell offers?
- What scenario models can inform next year's sales plan?
- How can the JI improve the effectiveness and efficiency of its sales force?

Getting the Right People in the Right Roles with the Right Incentives

Any successful business needs the right people in the right roles. This is no less true for a JI. The first talent-related decision to be made involves identifying the leader of the JI. The leader has to be, first and foremost, a business operator—someone who has experience managing and running a business. He or she will be expected to not only oversee all aspects of the JI's operations (including solution development, go-to-market activities, and delivery), but also must be savvy enough to interact effectively with C-level executives at the participating companies when necessary. In short, when choosing a JI leader, companies must acknowledge the difference between delivering a project and running something that more closely resembles a business unit.

The JI also needs the right managers, salespeople, and delivery professionals. And just like any successful companies, a JI needs a formal process for bringing people on board—including how they are recruited and interviewed, and what initial training they receive—as well as for meeting ongoing talent development needs. (We discuss the talent dimension of new selling relationships in Chapter 18.)

Arguably one of the thorniest issues is determining how incentives will be allocated and (equally important) shared. As discussed in Chapter 10, having the right incentive structure is vital to an effective sales force. In the case of a JI, it can be critical to design incentives so that the salespeople are not losing any compensation potential by working on the new endeavor as opposed to their existing book of business. It is also important to show salespeople that, by working with the JI team, they will enjoy better opportunities.

Factors for Success

Having developed multiple JIs over the past decade, Accenture has had the opportunity to see first hand what works and what doesn't. From that experience, we see several factors as critical to the establishment of a successful JI.

Set Clear Expectations with Partners Up Front

Not every partner is suitable for a JI. A JI is fundamentally different from a traditional alliance relationship, and that must be openly communicated with prospective participants up front. For instance, complex legal requirements often require considerable lead time to address. It is also important to set expectations that creating a JI with one partner may naturally place limitations on the company's freedom to work with that partner's competitors. This is to ensure that the legitimate purposes of, and investments in, the JI won't be undermined.

Where a company is considering a combination of partners for a single JI it is also important to sequence the conversations. Getting the first key partner on board can make it easier to identify and secure others.

Secure Active Commitment of Senior Executives

In most cases, given the size of the investment needed to get a JI off the ground, executives at the highest levels of the prospective partner organizations must be involved in business-case conversations. Importantly, senior executive involvement should not end with the signing of the agreement. For the JI model to work, it needs ongoing support and involvement from those executives—for example, by having C-level people from the parent companies sitting together on an advisory council, meeting on a regular basis and providing strategic direction for the JI.

Emphasize Agility

For many companies, a product roadmap regularly evolves, addressing factors such as changing customer preferences and technology advances. When companies work together to define an integrated product road map the need for constant change can be amplified. Maintaining flexibility and agility in developing that integrated product roadmap is essential to success with a JI. Feedback from the field is constant and it isn't always obvious at the outset where things are going to go —where a product or service with a lengthy development cycle is going to fit, how it will evolve, or what markets will ultimately embrace it. Remaining flexible is key.

Create a Formal Capability for Managing Change

JIs involve significant change for participating companies. This change often touches many functions in each company, and can often include transforming an existing and sometimes lengthy relationship between two companies. When this is the case, a change is needed in the mindset and culture of the two organizations to work now more collaboratively and in a different way.

A structured approach to managing change with a JI is recommended to understand the impacts to each audience, define actions to stimulate adoption of new behaviors, and engage senior executives in advocating the change. The PSSO often takes responsibility for this capability and the ongoing transformation in culture and behavior.

Insist on Regular Leadership Cadence

Regular meetings of steering committees and sponsors help ensure that people involved in the JI don't get second thoughts or lose patience, and remain focused on the strategic goals the companies have set for the JI. A starting point is to determine appropriate meeting frequencies for the Advisory Council, the Steering Comittee, and the JI Managing Directors, respectively.

Conclusion

Companies can benefit from continuously adapting and refining their sales approaches to succeed in today's dynamic market. Traditional, rigid go-to-market relationships are becoming less effective in helping companies expand reach into newer markets. Increasingly, there is a need for companies to seek new partnering relationships, build tighter linkage between organizations, and dedicate joint resources to adapt quickly to changes in customers' needs and market conditions.

The JI model just discussed can be a major step in that direction. By blending sales, solution development, and delivery, companies can greatly enhance their ability to jointly create and bring to market compelling new solutions to capitalize on opportunities in growing markets. Structured and managed effectively, a JI can be a key differentiator and a substantial growth engine for companies in virtually any industry.

But the JI model is only the beginning of such a shift. We expect to see companies in the near future taking JIs to the next level, tying together already-successful JIs into synergistic "superstacks" comprising the best companies in key markets, all working together to meet the ever-changing needs of customers. As alluded to in Chapter 5, the beginnings of such superstacks already can be seen in the high-tech industry. However, they are likely to also emerge in other sectors as more and more companies determine that "going it alone" could, in some cases, be a recipe for being left behind.

12

A New Look at an Old Problem

Selling to Small- and Medium-Size Businesses

Ron Ref and Lan Guan

Chapter Summary

- Segmented knowledge is critical; repackaging enterprise solutions for small business has minimal impact.
- Vertical, customized solutions and the proper expectation are key.
- Companies need to build "pathways" or route to market models that can efficiently serve the SMB markets.
- Top-line and bottom-line considerations are key in the route to market model.

It's no secret that much of the growth in the economy and job creation in recent years can be attributed to the vibrant growth among small- and medium-size businesses (SMB). Taken together, the nearly 6 million U.S.-based small firms with fewer than 100 workers employ a total of almost 43 million people.[1] Another 23 million people work for companies with 100 to 1,000 employees. And these small- and medium-size firms spend a lot of money: According to research firm IDC, worldwide SMB spending on information technology alone is expected to top US$610 billion by 2014.[2]

With the SMB market expected to grow significantly in the next decade, it is no wonder B2B companies are eager to find the most effective approaches for tapping this fast-growing but fragmented market. Because this market is so highly competitive and difficult to penetrate for B2B firms, it is a natural for the application of an Agile Selling approach.

To successfully tap the diverse SMB market, companies should utilize market data and customer segmentation to target their approach, as well as work with an extensive network of selling partners to bring their offers to prospective customers. In doing so, companies must be sure to not only create a value proposition for the SMBs, but also provide value or incentive for the indirect channel that will sell their products or services to SMBs.

This chapter takes a close look at how companies are using elements of Agile Selling to help them enter and capture share of the promising SMB market.

Big Opportunity

The small- and medium-size business market is being targeted by companies large and small. Many large corporations, among them General Electric, IBM®, Microsoft, Sharp®, and Xerox®, are investing heavily in marketing and selling to the SMB community, tailoring their business models, products, and services to win this new and expanding business. Some big players are making a splash in the SMB market:

- GE Capital, General Electric's financing unit, has launched a major marketing initiative to pursue mid-size companies (with sales of $10 million to $1 billion) around the world that need financing.[3]
- IBM has adopted the marketing slogan, "Midsized businesses are the engines of a smarter planet," and has developed a suite of offerings designed specifically for the midsize market.[4]

- Xerox has targeted the SMB market as a $44 billion opportunity, including $17 billion in North America. Roughly 70 percent of the company's North American equipment installations came through channel partners, which generated 40 percent of equipment revenue. Xerox has 500 independent agents in the United States fielding a sales force of 2,300 representatives. These agents sell the entire line of Xerox offerings to SMBs throughout the continent.[5]

A big reason these large corporations are investing significant resources in marketing and selling to SMBs is the widespread recognition that this is where the growth in the U.S. economy is taking place. As the nation and the world begin to emerge from the prolonged downturn, the SMB market is widely seen as one of the few robust growth opportunities for organizations seeking to expand their sales and revenues over the short term.

Certainly the economic figures support this view. Mid-size companies in the United States alone have been a major source of new jobs. Companies with sales of $1 billion or more eliminated a net 3.7 million jobs during the recession, but mid-market companies with sales of $10 million to $1 billion added 2.2 million jobs. In 2011 alone, U.S. mid-market companies added 940,000 jobs, compared to 630,000 new jobs added by S&P 500 companies.[6]

Why Many SMB-Targeted Sales and Marketing Efforts Fall Short

Although the SMB market is highly attractive it's also a challenging nut to crack. Several large firms have put significant resources behind this market, including creating a function focused on it, but efforts have been challenged. There are four areas where companies typically fall short:

1. Taking a one-size-fits-all approach.
2. Insufficiently investing in technology and data management.

3. Missing the mark on product and service offerings.
4. Failing to get full leverage from the indirect channel.

Taking a One-Size-Fits-All Approach

Often, traditional marketing and sales programs fall short when applied to the SMB opportunity because they simply fail to take into account the market's complexity and the difficulty involved in meeting its diverse needs. In fact, the SMB market's highly heterogeneous makeup dictates that marketers and sales forces just cannot treat it with a one-size-fits-all approach.

The SMB market encompasses multiple segments with varied buying habits and preferences. It is a far more diverse market than the large company/enterprise market. For one thing, the sheer number of prospective SMB customers is vastly greater than the number of large companies in the United States alone, for example. The millions of companies in the small-company segment (with fewer than 100 employees) of the SMB market often exhibit buying behaviors similar to consumers. At the opposite end of the SMB spectrum is the large mid-market, comprising companies with sales of $500 million to $1 billion. This group often buys much like the large company enterprise market. But many SMBs tend to act like a blend of both consumers and enterprise units, which makes them challenging to reach via conventional marketing approaches and channels. Furthermore, when targeting decision makers, the relative size of the organization doesn't mean there is a small number of decision makers. For instance, a company with $5 million in sales may have half a dozen or more influencers and decision makers, while a $100 million firm may have fewer. These different business needs and buying preferences add complexities to the marketing strategy.

These are just a few examples of the diversity within the SMB segment, but they shed light on why many companies realize it's a pretty complex puzzle to solve. How do they optimize coverage, making sure that the right resources are representing the right products? How do they determine the right market segmentation approach and target the right accounts? How do they effectively distribute leads once they are in hand to the right nodes of the sales network?

A one-size-fits-all approach is insufficient given the complexity of this market.

Insufficiently Investing in Technology and Data Management

Another common shortcoming of many SMB programs is their failure to invest in the necessary technology and data management to support effective sales and marketing strategies. This shortfall is manifested by poor-quality leads, leads that don't get distributed in a timely manner or to the right resources, and leads that simply evaporate, never moving further through the sales pipeline—all of which are a drag on efficiency and lead to unprofitable sales economics. If B2B companies are serious about succeeding in their SMB marketing efforts, they should invest in data management and advanced analytic capabilities to support effective and efficient sales initiatives.

Data is clearly a challenge for companies pursuing the SMB market, both in the data's completeness and its accuracy. Without good SMB data, a company will find it difficult, if not impossible, to effectively segment the market and apply the appropriate marketing and sales techniques to generate demand.

But as many companies have discovered, it can be difficult to obtain data on SMB firms. More than three fourths of SMBs in the United States are privately owned and thus aren't required to publicly report their financial results. This contrasts with the large-company segment in which approximately two-thirds of the 2,000 U.S. companies with revenue of $2 billion or more are publicly owned. Further complicating matters, SMBs tend to be reluctant to provide data to either research firms or their suppliers. Demonstrating an attitude shared by the consumer segment, some are reluctant to reveal information due to security and privacy concerns or a fear that they will be opening themselves up to unwanted solicitations.

When data *is* available for SMBs, it can be incomplete, inconsistent, or inaccurate and usually requires both cleansing and enrichment. Typically, companies must integrate multiple data sets—often 6 to 10 different data sets must be combined—to obtain a full picture of the SMB customer. Moreover, when data is assembled from multiple data sets it typically isn't normalized. For example, how a customer is described in one database may be different from the way it's described in another. In addition to data normalization issues, there are referential integrity issues to address and data cleansing to be done, including missing fields and incomplete or inaccurate data entries. This data-quality shortcoming poses a stumbling block of sorts, making it difficult to develop deep insight about customers' propensity for buying as well as their potential for profit. It also makes it difficult to predict which potential companies to target and how to qualify and convert them into profitable customers. The upshot of this lack of available and accurate market data is that firms typically have to spend considerable money and time to clean and enrich their SMB customer data.

The relatively high rate of churn among SMB businesses, specifically in the lower end of the market, adds to data management issues. Small companies are, on average, far more likely to fail than mid-market or large companies. This high rate of churn adds one more complication for B2B marketers trying to develop SMB databases that are clean and accurate.

On the positive side, with the rise of public social media sites such as Facebook, Twitter, and LinkedIn, B2B companies now have a strong channel through which to track what SMB companies are saying about them, their competitors, and their needs. Social media present a major source of valuable SMB customer input for B2B companies that know how to tune in and leverage this largely untapped trove of sales intelligence.

Missing the Mark on Product and Service Offerings

A third reason companies' SMB sales efforts fall short is if products and services are not designed from the ground up to meet the specific needs of the SMB market. Most companies develop new products and services for either consumers or large enterprises. Some have taken their existing enterprise or consumer offerings and "shoehorned" them into the SMB market. The result, not surprisingly, is not positive. SMBs by and large have specific segmented needs that are not answered by products and services designed for other markets. Consequently, products or service offerings are most successful when tailored to the SMB market segment or subsegments.

Take, for example, the high-tech industry that historically has focused on consumers or enterprise solutions. Until recently, the SMB market has tended to be an afterthought, with products for this segment simply being "versions" of other offerings. Similarly, in the financial services industry, huge marketing efforts have been focused on the needs of both consumers and large corporations, with the mid-market and SMBs tending to receive less attention. And in the consulting and IT services business, many vendors have opted to concentrate on serving the needs of large multinational corporations, with little attention given to SMBs, especially those at the lower end of the market. In many instances, these smaller SMBs have received their IT services and consulting help from smaller, similar-size SMBs offering these capabilities and specialties.

Savvy SMB marketers have found that they must tailor their products and pricing to meet the needs and financial capabilities of the small- and mid-size business. When a B2B company tailors its offering to the SMB market and provides unique value, the results can be impressive. For example, a 100 percent cloud-based IT solution may be appropriate and affordable to a business with 50 employees, whereas the large enterprise with 5,000 workers may decide that a hybrid solution of in-house data center and the cloud would serve its needs more effectively.

Failing to Get Full Leverage from the Indirect Channel

Small- and medium-size businesses translate to a relatively small dollar amount per sale relative to bigger customers in virtually any industry. The smaller revenue per sale makes it difficult to apportion significant sales and marketing resources to sell to any one SMB, and mandates that companies take a more efficient and effective approach to covering this market. Indirect channels (including distributors, resellers, sales agents, and other intermediaries depending on the industry) can serve as the conduit to the SMB market, offering B2B companies local geographic coverage and the mechanism to effectively scale demand generation.

But the SMB economics are not necessarily any more attractive to channel partners than they are to the B2B companies. Hence, B2B companies that get full leverage from their channel partners work diligently to create a value proposition for channel partners that incentivizes them to go after SMB on their behalf. These value propositions take various forms, some of which include sharing of costs and responsibilities. Enterprise firms take the cost to market and sell to the SMB out of the channel partners' operating structure and create a scalable, shared capability across their entire indirect channel ecosystem. Enterprise firms also brand the value of their indirect channel with the end customers they serve.

As an example, a high-tech company realized that, despite its strong desire to capture greater share of the SMB market, its channel partners viewed the SMB market as not nearly as profitable as the large-company market they also served. The partners wanted to know from the supplier how to make the SMB market more profitable, and thus more attractive to pursue. They suggested that the company infuse marketing dollars to generate demand, taking that burden off the books of the channel partner. Critical to generating demand or creating leads was the quality of those leads. The company leveraged analytics when generating leads, thereby significantly increasing the lead pool's "probability of close." The partners would then pursue the leads once generated. After all, the high-tech company could generate demand more effectively and efficiently than its partners by using its global scale, market intelligence, branding expertise, and demand-generation tools. Conversely, the channel partners had the local network to most efficiently pursue leads. This approach was financially attractive for both parties.

In some industries, customers require implementation help or other services related to the B2B company's products, and these are provided by third parties. By necessity, the B2B companies' relationships with their indirect channel partners expand in complexity when they rely on their channel partners to provide high-quality services such as certified installation, training, and after-sale service in addition to product sales. Because of the sheer volume of SMBs, finding the means to provide profitable value-added services to this market can be challenging. A certification program for channel partners can be an important component of the SMB value proposition for resellers as well as a means of demand generation for B2B companies.

If the company can make its "installation certification" valuable in the minds of SMBs, it serves as both a push and a pull for demand. By marketing the certification, the company and its partners can push demand. It is also a pull in the market for channel partners as SMBs seek out certified installers as a proxy for quality. This requires marketing investment on the part of the B2B firm and special branding of that certification, but it can prove to be a valuable proposition.

B2B companies also depend on indirect channel partners for many other roles, all of which contribute to the channel's effectiveness for the company. For example, they depend on partners to establish a local marketing presence, sales capability, and services. A strategy that demonstrates commitment to the channel moves B2B companies a long way toward their goal of capturing their share of the SMB market.

In the end, the reasons that SMB sales and marketing efforts fall short can generally be fit into one or more of these categories: They fail to tailor their efforts or their offerings to the distinctive characteristics of the SMB segment; they have insufficient data management and advanced analytics capabilities to make insightful sales and marketing decisions; or they don't fully optimize their use of indirect channel or third-party capabilities to economically and effectively cover this huge market.

How to Approach the SMB Market

The tremendous numbers of companies, their diverse needs, and the unique buying behaviors of different businesses are all factors that combine to produce an enormously complex test of a B2B company's abilities. The way to overcome the challenge is to develop and follow a strategic plan to get the offerings right, the channel coverage right, and the sales and marketing programs right.

For example, to one integrated communication provider, the company's medium business segment is a complex, highly fragmented market of 175,000 customers, ranging from regional medical practitioner offices to multisite high-tech companies. Too few customers were actively managed, channel coverage overlapped, and lead lists were inaccurate and created too slowly. The company developed a strategy to target the medium-size organization. One of the main goals of the initiative was to create a 360-degree view of the customer. Armed with this customer-centric view, the company was able to identify mainstream and premium (highly profitable) customers and segment them. Customer segmentation, in turn, allowed the company to tailor its products and services and the channels it used to market and sell them. The implementation of its SMB strategy has resulted in more effective marketing campaigns, a much higher sales conversion rate, and ultimately significant SMB growth. (For more on this company's experience, see the case study sidebar on page 231.)

From a more granular view, B2B companies should begin by establishing a strong commitment to the SMB market from executive leadership at the top of their firm. Without this commitment, they often lack the organizational fortitude to build the SMB business model and the capabilities they need to succeed. Once established, they should develop a plan for market segmentation to be able to create micro segments of the market and perform predictive modeling. They also should build an offering strategy that articulates the SMB segment needs and their implications for the B2B firm's product/service offering and pricing, with offerings tailored to the needs of that segment. Next, they should create a multichannel SMB customer engagement model utilizing a variety of approaches, including direct sales, channel partners, inside sales, indirect channels, teleweb, and others. They should consider the new or enhanced capabilities required to execute the SMB strategy and synchronize their marketing and sales organizations by creating globally standardized operating procedures. And to boost their capabilities, they should invest in a customer data management and analytics function that gives the marketing and sales functions a common data set and customer models (Figure 12.1). We discuss each of these areas in more detail below.

Market Segmentation

The SMB market segmentation analysis is used to develop distinct SMB customer profiles, a clear understanding of customer needs, and

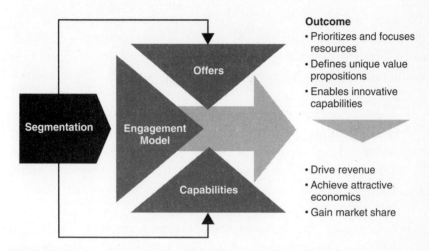

FIGURE 12.1 B2B Model for Targeting the SMB Market

alignment with the sales approach, channel strategy, and overall sales tactics. B2B companies can use customer analytics to discern how customer needs vary, which is important when segmenting SMBs into distinct groups. Those customer segments will then have their own offerings, engagement models, and requisite capabilities.

The most commonly deployed segmentation strategy considers total booked revenue. Leading companies evolve their SMB segmentation as their strategies get more specialized based on measurable and quantifiable criteria that offer both increased value and actionable approaches.

For instance, a company could create customer segments based on customer wallet share and total customer spending in the category, differentiating between premium relationships (where the company had high wallet share and the customer spent a large amount on the category) at one level and mass market relationships (low share and low spend) at the other. Such a segmentation can improve the company's understanding of customer complexity and enable the company to clearly delineate where the direct sales force and the third-party partners would focus resources, minimizing overlap, and enhancing the effectiveness of each.

Multichannel Operating Assessment and Engagement Model Design

The engagement model design is important to successfully reaching the SMB customer segments and addresses how companies efficiently and effectively market and sell to the SMB customer. A holistic solution would examine both the customer and channel partner engagement.

- From a customer perspective, a broad range of channels might be used to engage customers with different preferences for buying. Within this diverse set of channels, enterprises should migrate customers to the lowest-cost channel that meets customer needs. Companies can consider a combination of low-cost channels including teleweb and web.
- Companies then consider how these channels are leveraged with their indirect channel partners so they can optimize SMB engagement for the partners. Different engagement models are accounted for in the partner program aligning to the appropriate support level.

The holistic solution focuses on a mutual win-win *economic* incentive where the partner can make an attractive return on SMB business and the vendor can offer differentiated engagement that maximizes his return. The engagement model is designed toward efficient alignment of vendor and channel activity focusing on no redundancy, smooth lead handoffs, and leveraged tools.

Assessing and planning the appropriate engagement levels requires working with partners to secure the appropriate sponsorship for the SMB engagement model and committing the operational resources to pursue the SMB segment.

Online Experience Design and Enablement

Most SMBs use the web as a primary vehicle in purchase decisions. At the same time, suppliers are working to drive efficiency through low human touch engagement while still providing superior experience and service. An online experience design can provide the means to richly engage SMB customers online while doing so efficiently. B2B companies targeting the SMB market must provide a branded online experience (in websites, dedicated portals, and more) to respond to many SMBs' natural inclination to gather more information online, and to efficiently engage with SMB customers via the online channel and distribute leads back to the appropriate channel partner. To do so, leading enterprises perform an industry analysis of those capabilities that are driving differentiation for them and build the experience around highlighting and supporting that differentiation. They also quickly test and execute against the changing needs of the market to ensure that the branded online experience they are offering is tailored to meet the target segment's needs.

Offering Design

The offering strategy articulates the combination of price, product, and service that make a compelling value proposition for the customer needs of each SMB segment. Generally, the products or services should represent a simplified SKU structure and product portfolio and offer pragmatic solutions focused on solving business problems.

From a pricing perspective, leading companies are combining a multipronged pricing strategy with low-touch approaches to compete effectively in the SMB market (see Chapter 8). Pricing should support identifying and targeting desirable customers while avoiding nondesirable ones. At the same time, companies should be able to leverage pricing flexibility in nonprice-sensitive items while driving strong price impression in others.

The Targeted Marketing Engine (TME)

We have found that technology is critical to support the full SMB go-to-market model we have described earlier. We call this capability a "targeted marketing engine" (TME). It is an SMB customer-centric data analytic platform capable of performing ad hoc analysis, predictive modeling, and campaign development. The TME is the core technology for any effective and efficient marketing campaign aimed at

SMBs, enabling B2B marketing managers to drill deeply into customer needs, mining a database of thousands or even hundreds of thousands of SMB customers. It can facilitate customer data collection and cleansing, and application of customer analytics, enabling companies to quickly identify those customer attributes that matter most. It then enables marketers to segment these customers and determine the optimal sales coverage, which customers to pursue, and how many sales reps to assign, as well as how to tailor product offers and product pricing to each customer segment. The TME is what makes it possible and efficient to do micromarketing to the vast SMB market. By aligning the efforts of statisticians, data management experts, and marketing professionals through a TME, B2B companies can deliver improved campaign execution, greater lead conversions, and increased win rates.

Charting the Course to SMB Success

The small- and medium-size business market represents a vast, expanding, and profitable market opportunity for B2B companies, but due to its complex, fragmented, and highly competitive nature, it poses special challenges to the unwary. Numerous companies have tried and failed to penetrate the SMB market, largely because they relied too much on business models optimized for marketing and selling to enterprise customers.

By contrast, B2B companies that apply an Agile Selling strategy tailored to the needs of a highly fragmented SMB market universe are far more apt to succeed. Agile Selling can help companies increase win rates through targeted marketing; improve market coverage through an integrated multichannel approach (telephone, online, partners); and create a scalable, low-touch online experience. The payoff for these companies is greater market share, increased revenue, and heightened customer and partner loyalty in the highly attractive but tough-to-penetrate SMB segment.

Case Study: How a Communications Company Succeeded in the SMB Market

A multibillion-dollar telecommunications services firm, with millions of business customers (ranging from small companies to large multibillion-dollar enterprises), knew that mid-size businesses represented a key market segment. In fact, this segment represents about one-tenth of the firm's customers, spanning a wide variety of organizations, from physicians' offices to large high-tech firms.

At one point, the company faced a significant challenge from cable providers and new Internet Protocol (IP) businesses that were competing in this mid-market segment. This intense level of competition caused challenges in the company's sales channel. Among the problems, too few customers were being actively managed, overlapping channel coverage meant that customers were called by more than one of the company's units, and lists of leads were often inaccurate and developed too late to head off the competition.

One source of these problems was that the company had acquired numerous businesses over the years, and each had continued using its own information systems. In many cases, these isolated information systems weren't integrated with one another. As a result, the company decided it needed to overhaul its sales and marketing programs, integrating them within a single system. In doing so, the company developed a strategy to target the medium-size organization. One of the main goals of the initiative was to create a 360-degree view of the customer, including where it was headquartered and where branch offices

(*continued*)

Case Study: How a Communications Company Succeeded in the SMB Market (*Continued*)

were located; the corporate structure; number of employees; and the number and kind of services they used. This was a much richer set of information on each customer than in the past and became the core of the company's targeted marketing engine.

Armed with this customer-centric view, the company was able to identify mainstream and premium (highly profitable) customers and segment them. Customer segmentation, in turn, allowed the company to tailor its products and services and the channels it used to market and sell them. Larger customers with more complex needs (and in-house IT resources) now work with the company's field reps, while smaller customers use its call center reps. This streamlining of how different customer groups are handled enabled the company to reduce by half the number of customers served by each sales rep. In addition, sales reps have customer data on their desktop computers, and reps in the field have desktop tools with pertinent customer data.

The company was able to obtain a 360-degree view of the customer by combining hundreds of data elements from internal information systems that were used to support the SMB sector in the past. This overall view of the customer allows marketers and sales reps to better understand each customer's product usage, such as when they added or dropped certain products. Moreover, the company's analytics team can run extensive analysis, such as creating an industry-wide view of sales, or learning whether the number of sales visits affects the level of sales.

Two years later, the company's medium-size business unit turned in a great year, with revenue up significantly from 24 months prior. The company ran four times as many marketing campaigns than in the past, which positively impacted revenue. Marketing campaigns that used to take a month to create can now be devised in a single day. In addition, the micro-segmented marketing campaigns resulted in 25 percent greater revenue than the non-targeted sales campaigns. And the company's sales close rates jumped by more than 250 percent. At the same time, the company posted a two-thirds reduction in the time it takes to identify leads, from three weeks down to one week. Finally, the accuracy of the sales lead list has jumped as well.

13

Using Social Media to Engage Buyers, Empower Sellers, and Reinvent the Sales Process

Kari Kaario and Jason Breed

Chapter Summary

- The demand for more complex solutions is, understandably, forcing sales organizations to rethink how they operate and engage with customers.
- Existing sales models impede the flow of information and collaboration among salespeople and other potentially relevant players, compromising the sales force's effectiveness and responsiveness.
- Social media logic and tools can be applied to the sales force to help salespeople target the right prospects, get access to key information quickly when crafting a solution, and share results and insights with the larger organization.

Special acknowledgment to Tom Sjöberg for his contributions to this chapter.

As sales-enabling technologies have evolved over the years, B2B companies have witnessed a significant shift in their customers' expectations. Customers increasingly want to simplify the buying experience and are looking for a company or group of companies to provide a single solution that meets their needs.

This change in customer mind-set has put pressure on many companies—especially those in the machine-building, construction, and technology industries, as well as other businesses that are dependent on an installed base—to make the transition from providing products to selling more comprehensive and multifaceted solutions that combine machinery and hardware, software and services. With this shift comes the need for a cross-functional sales effort in which people from across the organization (and possibly between organizations) are involved. It also calls for the elimination of departmental silos so that knowledge can flow freely across the enterprise and be accessed by those professionals who need it to shape deals, identify customer needs, and satisfy customers' unique and ever more stringent solution requirements.

The demand for more complex solutions is, understandably, forcing sales organizations to rethink how they operate and engage with customers. In this new environment, step-by-step, linear sales and management processes (carried out by professionals with clearly defined roles and responsibilities) must give way to more dynamic, just-in-time interactions that, together, solve customer problems. And hierarchical organizational structures, which are typically slow to react to market demands, must become highly networked and streamlined. In short, the new B2B sales imperative calls for new methods of internal collaboration.

That call has not gone unheeded. For several years, Accenture has sponsored a global survey conducted by research firm CSO Insights, which assesses thousands of companies' current sales performance, challenges facing sales teams, the reasons those problems exist, and what organizations are doing to resolve them. In the 2011 study, enhancing team communications and improving access to information were seen as the most important ways to improve sales effectiveness (cited by 39.6 and 38.3 percent of respondents, respectively).[1]

The Sales Force Is Struggling to Respond

Unfortunately, such initiatives seemed to fall short. When asked to cite the sales management area most in need of improvement, the effective sharing of best practices across the sales force came out on top (noted by 56 percent of respondents).[2] Why the struggle to share and collaborate?

Part of the Problem Is Organizational

Companies are usually organized functionally, which creates silos and prevents them from collaborating for the benefit of the customer.

Sales teams still are largely linear and hierarchical in nature, with systems optimized more for reporting rather than selling. Selling complex solutions requires a team at every phase of the sales process. Sometimes these teams are virtual and they might even be placed in different parts of the world. To build, offer, and deliver a solution requires cooperation among sales, marketing, customer service, product development, finance, human resources, and even other stakeholders.

Similarly, traditional aspects of linear information flow as the basis of collaborating does little to eliminate the "silo syndrome," which is manifested by insular thinking and an unwillingness or inability on the part of employees to interact with other groups. In that scenario, people move information and decisions vertically. As mentioned earlier, today's solution sales require the involvement of the entire organization. To facilitate the selling of multifaceted solutions and meet customers' expectations for responsiveness, companies must knock down the departmental barriers once and for all and jettison the cumbersome, fragmented approaches to collaboration that have propped them up.

Another Part of the Problem Is Technological

In addition to having an organization structure that doesn't easily accommodate collaboration, most B2B sales organizations either have not fully embraced collaborative technologies or are not using them to their full benefit. For instance, the 2011 CSO Insights study explored the issue of sales force collaboration and found that although 70.4 percent of respondents said they were using collaboration tools, only slightly more than half believed that these tools were helping the sales force share best practices.[3]

Even if they have formal collaboration tools, many companies still rely on more traditional methods of communicating with peers such as e-mail, meetings, and phone calls—all of which are proving to be inadequate and quite limiting as they rely solely on individual networks. These outmoded ways of interacting often result in fragmented, lost, or incomplete information. Details from phone conversations can be forgotten and e-mail can go unanswered, leading to significant knowledge gaps and the inability to reuse information or promote organizational learning. Excessive e-mailing and phone calls also can lead to information overload, which causes the overall effectiveness of communications to decline. E-mail continues to confine the sales team to a relatively myopic group of specialists and people who can help (you can't include someone if you don't actually send them the e-mail), which does nothing to break the internal silos within an organization. And beyond being difficult to search, e-mail focuses sales teams on the artifacts of what happened. In short, many companies still spend considerable time on one-to-one and one-to-many communication (phone and e-mail) with overlapping and unproductive use of time and resources.

Another technological obstacle to better sales performance are the sales force automation and customer relationship management systems that traditionally have supported companies' sales processes. Most of these systems require a lot of input data from the user (i.e., salespeople) and most of the functionality is targeted for the benefit of sales management. As a result, salespeople spend an increasing amount of time on administrative work and less time interfacing with customers.

And where's the IT function in all of this? Like sales, struggling to keep pace. In most companies, traditional IT projects take too long to design and build sales-support applications that help salespeople to keep up with customers' fast-changing needs.

How Social Media Can Improve the Situation

Social media tools and logic offer significant promise in helping B2B companies overcome their current limitations and create sales forces and processes that are more collaborative and responsive to customers' needs. Consider a simple example that compares the way a salesperson would typically pursue a new company that his firm has never done business with and how social media tools and logic could vastly improve the approach.

In the traditional approach, the salesperson first looks for information about the prospect, either by searching the company client database or his or her own contacts (which could be stored at a personal level, such as on his or her own hard drive). Often, salespeople find the data in the corporate customer database to be inaccurate or even missing, so they then try to uncover customer data by contacting the company using the information on the company's webpage. After several attempts at e-mailing or phoning various people at the target company, the salespeople finally connect with a person and schedule a meeting with her—although at this point, there's no guarantee the person is the right person to meet with.

Nonetheless, the salesperson begins to prepare for the meeting by sending a number of e-mails to colleagues within his or her company and holding multiple meetings (which take days to organize) to gather information on the prospect (some of which ultimately ends up being outdated, at a very high level, or limited to what's publicly available). The information the salesperson gathers remains in his or her personal files, unusable for others in the organization who could benefit—including several other teams in the company who, unbeknown to the salesperson, also happen to be working on a proposal for the target company.

When the salesperson arrives at the target company's office for his meeting, he signs in at the reception desk. After exchanging basic information on each other's company, the prospect begins a detailed and complex conversation about her company's needs. At several points during this conversation, she asks the salesperson highly technical questions that he admits he can't answer. He notes the questions and promises he will get back to her with the answers after he returns to his office and confers with his company's experts.

After the meeting wraps up, the salesperson returns to the office. He knows he needs to update the client database with his notes from the meeting, but gets sidetracked by other issues. His handwritten meeting notes remain in the salesperson's personal notebook and, at best, might be distributed to the group of people who helped him prepare for the meeting. But any insights he gained from the meeting remain hidden to the broader organization—including the salesperson's manager, who needs such information to remain in tune with what her team member is doing and what the company's pipeline and sales prospects look like.

Compare the preceding to an illustrative (and hypothetical) social media-enabled scenario, in which the preceding process would unfold in a much different and more effective way. The salesperson uses LinkedIn as a customer database from which he quickly identifies relevant customer contacts in the target company, confident that the contact information is correct because it is updated by the contacts themselves. Using the "get introduced" function of LinkedIn, he leverages a mutual business contact or former coworker to set up a meeting with the new contact. To prepare for the meeting, the salesperson uses the logic of Facebook to inform others throughout his company about the customer visit and gathers the latest insights about the particular customer and its market situation (using publicly-posted information). He also monitors Twitter to see what the contact he's meeting with, as well as others in the prospect organization, are discussing relative to their business needs and solutions they are considering.

Once at the meeting, he uses the logic of Foursquare® to "check in" at the customer's site (to let people at the home office know whom he's meeting with). Instead of getting stumped by difficult questions from his prospect during the meeting, the salesperson quickly gets answers from available colleagues back at headquarters using apps on their mobile devices. When the meeting is over, the salesperson leverages the logic of Chatter® to quickly communicate to his colleagues the outcome of the meeting and any insights about the prospect he gained (information that is automatically distributed to all relevant parties in the salesperson's company and remains part of the prospect's record in the company's database, easily accessed and searchable for future use).

The preceding example, while hypothetical, could become reality with currently available social media tools. It clearly shows how laborious and time consuming the traditional sales process is, and how companies can apply the capabilities offered by social media technologies currently available to radically improve that process and sales professionals' effectiveness. In fact, as early as five years ago, an article in *Harvard Business Review*® argued that salespeople with a nuanced understanding of social networks can outshine their competitors because they are able to provide information when others demand it and access information when they, in turn, need it. This point forms the basis of what has since been termed *social sales*.

Our own research and experience supports that article's contention. We have found that top sales forces across all industries achieve an optimal balance of data, technology, process, and talent. Social sales provides a low-cost mechanism by which companies can not only achieve the balance of skills they need, but also find a balance between technology and talent supported processes. This, in turn, helps organizations improve their sales force productivity across the sales life cycle, from identifying prospects to winning the deal (Figure 13.1).

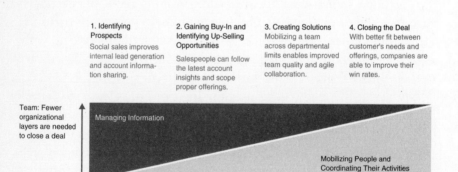

FIGURE 13.1 How Social Sales Helps Organizations Improve Their Sales Force Productivity across the Sales Life Cycle

How Social Sales Works

A social sales capability involves using social networking platforms such as Tibbr®, Yammer®, Jive Software®, Socialcast®, or Chatter® to establish internal communities that spark new levels of collaboration and information sharing. Because community participants are employees with common interests and complementary expertise, the quality of content shared is more often of a higher standard.

Importantly, social sales does not adhere to a traditional corporate hierarchy. Instead, it dismantles functional boundaries and enables workers to lend their expertise to a team dedicated to resolving important sales issues and addressing complex customer requirements (Figure 13.2). In the area of solution shaping, for example, social sales networks allow the necessary activities to be undertaken by communities of people, who bring a wide range of offerings to the table. Furthermore, sales managers can give feedback on a proposed solution within just a matter of minutes.

In solution shaping—or, for that matter, any other phase of the sales cycle—social sales shifts the emphasis from individual task completion to shared outcome creation. This makes social sales a

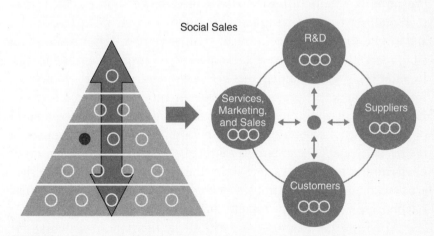

FIGURE 13.2   Social Sales Dismantles the Traditional Corporate Hierarchy

particularly valuable capability for organizations with comprehensive product and service offerings that address a complex set of business requirements. For such B2B businesses, social sales helps ensure that the right mix of professionals is always at hand to tackle the most difficult sales challenges. When one issue is resolved, the resources gravitate to the next. Similarly, organizations with highly mobile sales forces and globally dispersed pockets of know-how can use social networking platforms as an effective and cost-efficient way to ensure that their distributed expertise is accessible and is used appropriately to influence sales success. Even organizations that do not operate in a global or complex sales environment can benefit from social sales. For them, part of the advantage lies in creating an atmosphere of collaboration and active engagement. Not only does such an environment boost employee morale and job satisfaction, it also can help to attract younger workers, who are typically heavy consumers of social media in their personal lives and for whom the adoption and use of networking technologies is second nature.

At the top of the sales funnel, social selling can supply a much more profound impact than traditional lead purchases, magazine advertising, and even "smiling and dialing." With social media, companies have an opportunity to be recognized by customers and prospects as a thought leader or as a place to get curated content on their industry. As an example, with steady content flow, trackbacks, and low bounce rates, a well-executed blog can have better results than a big marketing budget ever did, especially in terms of earned media. In addition, social channels can help salespeople get early indicators from customers and prospects on their intentions, and become more relevant by focusing on the timing of the buyer experience instead of the timing of sales leadership. By monitoring prospects via social media, salespeople can start to better understand much more about the customer's needs—such as when they are ready to buy, when they are researching new solutions, when competitors are deepening their relationship with these customers, and much more.

For instance, many buyers will query their social networks for leads on a few vendors or to test product ratings; salespeople just have to listen to these conversations for the right indicators. Similarly, if a salesperson's customer is getting new connections to a competitor on

LinkedIn, he can bet that his string of wins at that customer could be quickly coming to an end unless immediate action is taken. Periodic purchases to append customer records should be complemented by more real-time information that social technologies are capable of generating, while—as with all uses of relevant data—respecting applicable privacy laws.

In short, advances in collaboration that are now enabled by social media tools are empowering companies to move from selling the product they want to produce to selling the complex solutions customers demand.

Consider the example of a global communications and high-tech company, whose sales executives have recognized that becoming a solution-driven enterprise would require better collaboration and easier access to sales-related content. Like many other B2B operators, the company's existing content was scattered and difficult to find. Its sales professionals had no easy way to share best practices or contribute to a global body of knowledge. Similarly, they lacked a direct feedback mechanism that allowed them to comment on sales assets.

The company designed and implemented a social networking capability, based on the Salesforce.com Chatter platform. The solution created a vibrant digital community comprising more than 3,000 sales and marketing professionals. It delivered three key benefits:

1. More customer-facing time, based on better access to relevant information needed in daily sales work and improved reuse of existing sales and marketing collateral created by others.
2. Improved sales performance, based on the improved quality of market and customer intelligence, sales and marketing materials, and sales training programs.
3. Improved engagement among employees, brought about by a deeper sense of belonging to a global sales community and the ability to take advantage of enhanced peer-to-peer networking and collaboration.

By adopting this cutting-edge social sales capability, the company continued its transition from being a device manufacturer to a solution-oriented company—and along the way, gained the reputation as an innovator in workforce collaboration.

Engaging Buyers, Empowering Sellers, and Reinventing Sales Processes

In considering further how social sales can help B2B companies respond to their sales challenges, we find it can be especially useful in helping salespeople achieve three major goals:

1. Engaging buyers with relevant content.
2. Empowering sellers by supporting better team selling.
3. Reinventing sales processes through analytics-driven customer insights.

Engaging Buyers

Individuals are extending their use of social networks to communicate with companies for whom they work or with whom they do business. It's not surprising that B2C companies—especially those in the consumer products space—have been particularly bold in their use of social media platforms to engage with customers. For them, social media's ability to engage directly and cost-effectively with communities of customers is simply irresistible.

B2C businesses use networking technologies to enable customers to "follow" their favorite brands on popular social sites, take part in real-time discussions about product preferences and experiences, and even contribute to the design of new products and services. Such activities are components of "social CRM" strategies, which companies are developing to reinvent their relationships with customers.

Although some B2B buyers are embracing social channels to make better purchase decisions, B2B sales organizations have been slower to embrace the advantages of social networking. That is primarily due to the fact that their products and services are typically not geared to satisfy mass markets of individual customers. Rather, their offerings are usually customized to meet the needs of select business customers for whom the B2C social networking model holds less interest. That said, savvy B2B companies are beginning to recognize that social networking can add tremendous value to their efforts to more effectively engage their target customers. (Ironically, it is the complexity and highly specialized nature of their product and service offerings that make social networking so appealing.) This is especially important given the initiative B2B customers are taking to use the web to learn more about a subject, identify best-in-class vendors, and get examples of others companies with similar challenges. Social media is empowering these buyers with more information than ever before, which can lead to unprepared sellers encountering situations where they are "outgunned" by buyers who know more than the sellers do about a product or service they offer.

Social sales also can help B2B companies create digital peer-to-peer support groups, in which their customers participate to help each other address challenges that the company's products are uniquely positioned to address. Such groups reduce the incidences of customer calls to the company, which significantly reduces customer service operational costs.

Dell is one of the foremost users of social media across its enterprise. It is especially adept at leveraging social tools to engage with its customers. From its pioneering IdeaStorm crowd-sourcing website for product development, to its @DellOutlet Twitter account through which it posts product offers and answers customer questions, to its sophisticated "command center" that enables the company to monitor, react to, and be proactive participants in online conversations their customers are having, Dell's forays in social media have helped set the bar for how enterprises can use social media to build and sustain strong buyer relationships.[4]

Empowering Sellers

Recent technical advances also have altered the context in which sales occur. Traditional boundaries are dissolving. From an organizational perspective, sales departments now work more fluidly with marketing, R&D, and customer service to better understand customers' needs. Extranets and Web 2.0 platforms have shaken up the standards by which collaboration and communication take place, allowing previously siloed functions to work together to create a more compelling value proposition for the customer and an altogether more satisfying customer experience. In this new sales environment, many more employees become "touch points" to the marketplace. This means that many more employees—not just the sales team—can enhance (or harm) the organization's reputation and its likelihood of sales success.[5]

Social sales can build on those advancements in many ways to further empower the sales force. Adoption of mobile devices such as the iPad could help strengthen these advancements. For instance, it can put the most relevant information at the fingertips of the sales organization when they need it, thus boosting productivity and effectiveness in many ways. Social media tools speed up the access to needed information while in the field. Mobile solutions enable the sales force to seamlessly and quickly update vital data—which is critical given that meetings are becoming increasingly more complex, and having information immediately at hand can spell the difference between a lost sale and a win. Such solutions also enable a salesperson at a customer site to send a fast "tweet" to or engage in a live chat with a colleague, solution team member, or other expert who can answer important, complex questions a customer might raise. Furthermore, having updated sales and product presentations on their mobile devices or tablets helps ensure that all salespeople are delivering a consistent message.

Toshiba America Business Systems (TABS®) provides an example of how a company can use social sales concepts to empower sellers. The company was looking for a way to improve the way it communicates with its dealer network, as the established vehicles of e-mail, voice, and the company's intranet portal were proving to be too static to keep pace with TABS's dynamic market. TABS implemented a new social media tool based on the Jive platform that serves as a place where dealers can go for all sorts of product information and best practices as well as collaborate with TABS product experts. The exchange has been a huge hit, thus far helping TABS's sales reps and dealers shave two months off the time to achieve its sales goals and increasing sales revenue attainment by 30 percent.[6]

Reinventing the Sales Process

Social media tools and logic also are introducing new opportunities to rethink the process of selling, especially at the enterprise level.

In general, social sales capabilities make the entire sales process run more efficiently and unleash new levels of sales force productivity. These capabilities enable leadership to measure the entire sales process rather than just the artifact, which creates a new class of insights-driven decision points and ultimately more predictability. Visibility into the sales process becomes instantaneous. Content becomes easier to find, reducing duplication of efforts and time-to-market decreases as employees can seamlessly connect with and respond to one another from anywhere, at any time. As communication and collaboration become more streamlined, less time is needed for back-office tasks and salespeople can spend more time with customers. And as just mentioned, the use of collaborative mobile applications enhances this benefit further by allowing salespeople to get support from their peer group throughout the sales process, thereby further diminishing the need for phone calls and e-mail.

Additionally, the sharing of information via social networking applications allows the organization to acquire knowledge that has historically been located on people's notepads and not captured within traditional customer relationship management (CRM) systems. Contributing ideas becomes as simple as updating one's status and sharing it with the relevant audience. The value of this shared information grows cumulatively as community members access and comment on feedback contributed by others. Innovation is accelerated as people, knowledgeable on a certain topic, come together for a common purpose. The power of a company's collective network is much more powerful than the independent networks of each employee.

Social sales also makes it much easier for companies to conduct deeper analysis of sales activities to identify what's working and where improvement is warranted. By having more effective, systematic coverage of all customer-facing activities (phone calls, Tweets, customer visits and their outcomes, proposals, and other critical customer interactions), a company can apply advanced analytics to the performance of the entire sales process.

From a technology perspective, tools such as Jive Software® and Salesforce.com can overcome the limitations of traditional sales force applications and systems-development methodologies, thus further enhancing sales processes. Such tools can be implemented in a few months, bringing with them an ecosystem of new sales applications to be used as they are needed. Starting with targeted functionality and then adding more to the solution based on the feedback from the user is one of the most critical success factors of any tools implementation project.

Applying Social Sales to the Traditional Sales Funnel

For a clearer picture of how social sales can benefit an organization, let's look at how a company could apply various social media tools and concepts to the traditional sales funnel (Figure 13.3).

The role of the sales funnel is twofold. First, it should guide sales management to focus sales efforts on right opportunities. Second, it should provide data for sales forecasting. Traditionally, sales management has been responsible for both. Bringing social sales into the picture changes the way we traditionally have thought about funnel management.

The content of the sales funnel is traditionally open to sales management only. We think that it should be opened for a wider audience

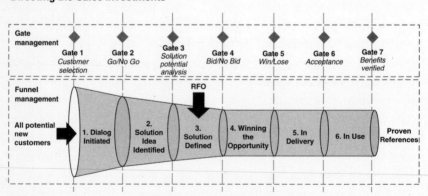

FIGURE 13.3   The Traditional Sales Funnel

Source: Kari Kaario, *Transformation Kaleidoscope: The Missing Link for Successful Sales Strategy*, Helsinki, 2009, ISBN 978-951-0-35362-2.

as well. Sharing best practices, identifying similar customer situations, and finding suitable solutions from other customers will become easier both if opportunities are visible to a wider audience, and if people participating in the sales process can enhance both customer insight and solution characteristics.

At the beginning of the funnel, sales efforts are focused on customers with the most potential in both the short and long term. Using social sales will help a salesperson initiate contacts to the right people at the customer. Salespeople can be recommended by the right people in the customer's personal network and initial contacts can be initiated through social media tools such as LinkedIn. Participation in and contribution to the right discussion groups can help salespeople position themselves and provide the initial contact to other people in the discussion group, including customer representatives. It is easier for a customer to engage in a dialog through social media than answer an e-mail (not to mention via the telephone).

All sales and customer service people should be trained and motivated to enhance customer information using social sales tools. While in contact with customers, they are exposed to customer needs that could be fulfilled by other parts of the organization. Collaborating with other people working with the same customer about an opportunity will speed up lead generation and also change the role of marketing. This requires a cultural shift in the sales organization. Besides taking care of one's own role in the sales process, frontline people should be motivated to identify new opportunities outside their own scope and communicate about them to the rest of the customer team. Gathering and enhancing customer insight will become the task of the whole customer-facing organization.

Once the solution is identified, social sales will help the sales organization in many other ways. Content from other similar cases can be reused more easily. Analyzing winning proposals will help salespeople to learn from other sales teams and use similar approaches with their own customers. And social sales tools will help the sales team by distilling publicly available customer information and putting it in front of the sales team.

Social sales also can be especially beneficial in helping to enhance a company's win rate, which is one of the most important metrics of funnel management. A company can improve its win rate by winning more and losing fewer bids—which, in turn, requires pursuing a greater number of bids that the company has a *higher likelihood of winning*. Here's where social sales comes in. Using a similar feature to Facebook's "Like" action, a company can solicit input on specific opportunities from a wider group of people who are knowledgeable about those opportunities and the proposed solutions. By "liking" certain opportunities, these individuals can indicate deals they think the company is well positioned to win (and, by extension, those they think the company probably will lose). By factoring that input into their "go/no go" and "bid/no bid" decisions—focusing its efforts on the opportunities with the greatest number of "likes"—a company can go after higher-probability deals while minimizing its investments in pursuits it has less of a chance of winning (and on which they are likely to get no return) (Figure 13.4). In other words, a company could replace its traditional "probability to win percentage" with a prioritization of opportunities that is based on collective liking or disliking by knowledgeable parties.

Giving the decision power to a wider audience would ensure motivation and commitment of the organization to a given opportunity. It would make resource mobilization for proposal preparation easier and

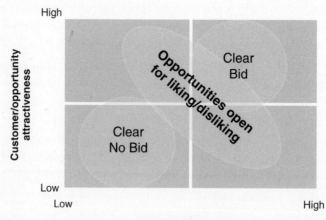

FIGURE 13.4 Social Sales Can Enhance a Company's Win Rate

should also enhance the win rate. Opportunities would be prioritized by using collective knowledge of a larger pool of people. Using this approach would also give sales organizations opportunities to later analyze the decisions they made. Based on such an analysis, one could determine which certain people tend to have better judgment—by tying their participation to deals ultimately won.

One could take this thinking a bit further. Consider a social media index tool (think Klout Score) that measures influence based on a person's ability to drive action (like on social channels)—including the true reach of their message, ability to amplify a message, and value of the person's network. These types of influence indexes could be a part of the social sales methodology.

After applying this method for prioritizing opportunities, social sales influence indexes could be assigned to people who have contributed to the go/no go decisions by liking or disliking specific opportunities. People whose participation correlates most strongly with win rates would earn a higher social sales influence index than those who have liked a higher proportion of opportunities the company ultimately failed to win. Over time, the company could begin to give the opinions of people with a higher index figure greater weight in opportunity prioritization decisions.

Using social sales influence scores in this way would have profound impacts on the sales culture. Sales management would not automatically be able to make what they thought were the best decisions about which opportunities to focus on and invest in, and the account manager or executive would have less complete authority to make all bid/no bid decisions. Instead, the entire customer-facing organization would be much more empowered and motivated to participate in the sales process and proposal preparations.

Making the Transition to "Social Selling"

Despite the promise, social sales has to dramatically improve saleseffectiveness—transitioning from an e-mail-buried enterprise working in siloes to an openly sharing enterprise with reduced hierarchies may be more challenging that it appears. In fact, during

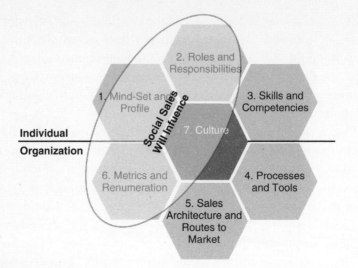

FIGURE 13.5   Four Organizational Dimensions That Social Selling Will Impact

Source: Kari Kaario, *Transformation Kaleidoscope: The Missing Link for Successful Sales Strategy*, Helsinki, 2009, ISBN 978–951–0-35362–2.

the transition, a company likely will have to juggle three different ways of working: the traditional approach, the new way, and a gray middle-ground mix of both. How well a company makes the shift will depend on its success in managing the impact of social sales on four key areas of the company and its sales force (Figure 13.5).

Culture

Social sales cannot be an isolated initiative brought forward by middle management or the marketing department. The message that "social will be the way we do business" must come from the very top of the organization. Leadership has to integrate social messages into their ways of leading their enterprise and communicating to their teams. Leaders have to utilize new social sales tools and be highly visible in their company's social platforms using their own words and personality. Delegating this responsibility would indicate lack of commitment from their side.

Once leadership has committed to social sales, they can set a clear and crystalized vision for their company that is empowered by social tools and methods. They can support the transformation, which will embed social ways of working in every aspect of how business is conducted. One way to demonstrate their support is to make sure that the social sales initiative receives a sufficient level of investments. Leadership has to state, as well, that the change will not happen overnight, but will gradually become the dominant way of doing business, so social sales is not just a fad that will fade in few months. There also is a need for a long-term road map that will illustrate how the transformation will be executed and provide people with time to adjust to the change.

Mind-Set and Profile

People naturally like to share information and work in team environments. This is one of the reasons Facebook has been such a huge success among its users. However, even if people are increasingly using social media in their personal lives, mind-sets of many people in the corporate world will need to change. The biggest challenge is to change the *me only* attitude that lives strongly in many sales organizations. If leadership is truly committed to creating a *we* attitude, it needs to understand that it will have to allow people time to digest the changes and gradually accept and support the initiative. As is the case with other change efforts, people who are initially against a social sales initiative may ultimately become the biggest advocates.

Roles and Responsibilities

A salesperson is no longer just the person who meets the customer. When sales becomes truly a team effort, there is a need for new roles—for example, coaches, peer group members, content creators, content reviewers, information sharers, and "social listeners." These new roles will not minimize the importance of the current salesperson role or responsibilities. They simply make the sales process more efficient. It will also mean that the salesperson will start counting more on real-time back office support and interaction throughout the sales process. Support, thus, must be available when needed. For instance, when a salesperson in a customer meeting pings the home office that he needs help with a specific customer question, the recipients of that post had better be able and willing to respond immediately. The days of taking hours or days to respond to e-mail are fast disappearing—a notion that is given credence by the increasing number of organizations that have expressed plans to stop using e-mail entirely and move to chat-based capabilities or social group pages.

Metrics

If social is the standard way of working, then a company needs new metrics that can gauge whether that new way of working is taking hold in the organization.

This means that it has to make sure that it measures the right things such as level of collaboration. If the company does not integrate these new metrics into its established KPIs, support for the initiative will evaporate because people tend to do what they are measured on.

For instance, in the past, salespeople were rewarded based on individual credit: the amount of sales they generated. In a social sales environment, people could be rewarded based on their composite "value" score, which is derived by using a complex algorithm that considers such things as how a salesperson affected his team's sales efforts; how much content a salesperson generated for a deal and how much her peer group appreciated the input; and how strongly the salesperson's input contributed to the win. Sales bonuses would be paid out of a pool and would be available to not only the salesperson who closes the deal, but to the entire internal value chain that participated: from initiating an opportunity to creating the right type of proposal to convincing the prospect to buy. Individual bonuses could be based on a simple formula such as dollar amount available for a won deal times each person's weighted "value" score among all people who participated in the particular deal. Such a calculation will automatically steer resources toward bids that have the highest probability to win and away from deals the company is unlikely to win. This will have a profound impact on ways companies manage sales funnels today.

Pitfalls That May Cause Social Sales to Fail

The ubiquity of social media, and the fact that hundreds of millions of people are using such tools as Twitter, Facebook, and LinkedIn, may make it seem like adopting social sales will be easy. It won't be, and there are many potential obstacles a company must be wary of. We have identified five major pitfalls that could cause social sales initiative to fail within a company.

The first is lack of leadership support. Without a leader firmly behind the initiative, it won't get funded and it will never gain the momentum among the "troops" it needs to become firmly embedded in the company's culture and standard way of working.

The second is a company's assuming that what has worked for someone else will work automatically for it as well. It won't. A company must paint a clear vision of what social sales means in the context of its own organization and people.

The third is a failure to integrate the social sales platform with the company's existing CRM and other key corporate systems. A platform such as Yammer or an alternative, implemented as a stand-alone tool, will not likely deliver on the full promise of social sales and may remain the domain of only a few enthusiasts.

The fourth, as alluded to in the previous section, is failure to incorporate the appropriate new metrics and reward structures that will encourage adoption of a social sales philosophy. Without these, people will simply continue working as they did before and the social sales initiative will not survive.

The fifth potential pitfall is inattention to change management, especially among top executives. If a company underestimates the change management effort necessary, or delegates responsibility for change management too low in the organization, there is a high risk that execution will fail. Just because people use social media in their personal lives doesn't mean they will embrace it in their professional ones.

Expanding Far beyond Corporate Boundaries

Considering the many benefits of social sales, it's only a matter of time before forward-thinking B2B organizations move to extend their collaborative social networks outside their home turf (Figure 13.6). Whereas social sales currently enables many-to-many communications within communities, the future social sales environment will connect a larger ecosystem—one in which collaborative networks that extend the value chain beyond the sales organization to areas such as R&D and communities are broadened to incorporate a given company's supplier, partner, and even customer networks.

When a company succeeds in creating an internal collaborative social sales culture and supporting platforms, it can start thinking how to take this ideology even further. First, it can consider opening up parts of its collaboration tools to suppliers, partners, and vendors. In doing so, the company could improve enterprise-value chain management and an understanding of what is important to its partners. Second, the company can start thinking how the end consumer or customer can be taken into consideration. One early idea that has been proven successful is mystarbucks.com, one of the first crowdsourcing sites that has helped Starbucks® to develop more products and service concepts.

R&D Marketing
Knowledge-sharing teams have members from different departments and skill areas

Sales Efficiency Solution Selling
Information that assists in creating matching solutions for clients is available on demand at the right time

Reaching Out to the Suppliers and Customers
Stakeholders can communicate directly to people across the organization

Internal   External

FIGURE 13.6 Extending Social Sales to the External Network

Better engagement and collaboration among stakeholders can improve capabilities and the results of the R&D process and marketing campaigns. Ultimately, better information leads to improved revenues with lower cost.

Key Points to Consider in Adopting Social Sales

Based on our experience working with companies on social sales initiatives, here is a summary of some of the key points companies should keep in mind during adoption.

Strategy and Vision

- Clearly define the problem statement and the issues to be solved.
- Define the short- and long-term vision for how the company would expect end users to act once the social sales model is in place.

Process

- Identify the areas or processes that the company expects to primarily support the social sales model (e.g., customer, market, and competitor insight).
- Define the expected use cases highlighting how the company would like the end users to behave in the future.
- Identify "content owners" or people who will be responsible for feeding relevant content and assets to the social sales community.
- Define the key metrics and dashboards the company will use to gauge user adoption and activity of the community.

(continued)

Key Points to Consider in Adopting Social Sales (*Continued*)

Organization

- Clearly communicate the problem statement, vision, and expected benefits the company is trying to achieve with the social sales model.
- Explain basic concepts of social media and clearly communicate the expected behavior to the end users.
- Ensure that leadership is committed to using the social sales model daily and use it as their primary way of selling.
- Find someone to own the community—a person who will create content for the community, support users, and moderate discussions.
- Identify local champions who "lead by example" and encourage others to use the new social sales model.
- Monitor key metrics and organize frequent follow-up calls and meetings to gather feedback from the sales community.

Technology

- Ensure that the selected platform complies with the business requirements and defined use cases.
- Make it easy for end users by enabling single sign-on so that it will be easy for users to access the solution.
- Implement desktop and mobile clients as soon as possible to enhance user adoption.

The Future and What to Do Now

Before companies pursue the development of a social sales capability, they should be mindful of the implications such a move may have on their sales organizations. As a first step, we recommend that organizations gauge their readiness across three dimensions.

The first is organizational readiness. As mentioned previously, social sales tools allow personnel to focus their energies on creating valuable outcomes for customers, rather than simply carrying out functional tasks or discrete process steps. To take full advantage of this shift in priorities, organizations should answer the following questions:

- Do we have a vision for social sales and what we hope it will accomplish?
- Are we prepared to introduce nonlinear structures that encourage cross-functional teamwork?
- How will we monitor and measure the success of our social sales program?
- Will social sales be actively supported by our senior leadership team?
- Which resources will manage the social sales program, establish and monitor usage policies, own/edit content, and keep conversations on track?

The second area to consider is sales team readiness. Here, sales executives should determine whether their sales team is prepared to not only adopt new behaviors, but also to embrace the notion of being part of an ecosystem where specific roles are less important than fluidity and adaptability. This involves answering questions such as these:

- What programs and communications strategies will best facilitate the necessary transition of our organizational mind-set from task completion to outcome creation?
- How can we ensure that our employees have the right social media skills? Can we use more networked employees to bring our other employees along?
- What role should incentives and rewards play in encouraging the active collaboration that a social sales program requires?

The third area of consideration is technology readiness. Among the many advantages of social sales technologies is their relative ease of deployment. Networking platforms are fully scalable and can be set up inexpensively and quickly—either as stand-alone systems or integrated with existing CRM applications. For this reason, many B2B businesses may see little danger in piloting a community network. Yet, issues can arise. Companies that spend up-front time thinking about the technical implications of their social sales capability will ultimately be in a better position to respond and adapt. To make sure that they are prepared, companies should answer the following questions:

- How will we evaluate and select the right social media tools that best meet our needs? Will we focus on pure-play social media applications such as Yammer? Or will we explore options now available from established technology and service providers such as Salesforce.com, Microsoft, and SAP? How much (if any) customization will be required?
- How should we integrate our social sales platform with existing CRM systems? What are the advantages—or the risks—of doing so?
- Are we prepared to establish system requirements, usage protocols, and standards?
- Who should sponsor a social sales program? The CEO? The CSO? The CIO? All?

In our experience, businesses that understand what is involved in social sales deployment and are able to answer the questions posed earlier are better positioned to reap the benefits of collaboration.

Conclusion

The ubiquity of social media, coupled with the emergence of new networking technologies, is pushing organizations in all industries to rethink how they communicate, collaborate, and engage with their key stakeholders. One opportunity that holds great promise—especially for organizations struggling to keep pace with the fast-changing sales environment—is social sales.

By drawing on the networking capabilities of social media platforms, sales organizations can build highly collaborative, cross-functional communities of expertise. They can dramatically improve sales force productivity. They can more easily attract a new generation of technically savvy and socially networked employees. And they can strengthen (or, in some cases, build) solution-based business capabilities that their customers now demand.

Companies that move quickly to build their social sales capabilities will achieve first-mover advantage and enjoy several characteristics their competitors can't replicate: The ability to produce, share, and use the right knowledge at the right time; the ability to deliver highly specialized, comprehensive solutions that their customers crave; and the ability to unleash a collaborative spirit that enables high performance.

14

Around the Block or Around the World

How to Enter New, Global Markets

Christian Requena, Golnar Pooya, Grant Hatch, Pieter Becker, and Tomas Kandl

Chapter Summary

- New markets have specific needs, and companies will not be successful without a localized and adaptive approach.
- Any successful market entry strategy is based on an understanding of cultural and behavioral norms and how a company's product relates to those norms.
- Local partners can provide valuable capabilities, both in helping to adapt offers to local tastes and in providing capabilities that can enable a company to scale its presence and reach quickly and with less risk.

Global expansion is not a new phenomenon. Businesses in search of growth and new opportunities have been looking outside their established borders for thousands of years. And when they've gone exploring new horizons, businesses always have found various challenges along the way that threatened to thwart their efforts. Those that managed to find a way to overcome those challenges were rewarded. However, the instances of enterprises that failed far exceeded the number of success stories.

Today is no exception. Whether a company is going from developed to emerging markets, or the reverse, it's much harder than it looks.

Indeed, everyone is trying to play by the rulebook in expanding to developed markets (especially in China, India, and other Asia-Pacific countries). But nonetheless there are myriad examples of large, influential companies that have experienced high-profile failures when attempting to penetrate emerging markets. These companies made huge investments in establishing a presence in such countries as China, India, and Russia and, in return, had very little progress to show for their efforts.

Similarly, as emerging markets have grown in strength and influence, a number of companies based in those areas have begun to seek growth in developed markets. However, making such a move can be just as daunting and frustrating. For every success such as China's Huawei®, Brazil's Embraer®, and India's Tata®, there are dozens if not hundreds of instances in which companies have either failed outright or are struggling to gain ground.

But that's not to say that there aren't success stories. A number of companies in developed markets have figured out how to approach emerging markets and are reaping the benefits. And several companies in emerging markets are experiencing significant success as they expand into well-established developed markets.

In studying these companies, we have found that, regardless of which direction a company is going, making effective use of partners is a major factor in their success. For both developed-market and emerging-market companies that want to ramp up rapidly in each other's regions, gaining local insight and more sophisticated capabilities often requires "selling through someone else" working through alliances or partnerships with firms already established in those markets rather than creating capabilities from scratch, which generally takes too long, costs too much, and can be very risky. In particular, companies from developed markets looking to expand into emerging ones identified partners that helped them adapt their offers and capabilities to local needs, tastes, and cultures. Companies based in emerging markets looking to expand into developed markets generally created relationships with partners that could bring them the relevant capabilities for broadening their reach.

In the remainder of this chapter, we explore in more detail the issues surrounding some of the most robust and highly promising emerging markets—inland China, India, Africa, and the Middle East—and how some companies have been able to build a strong and profitable presence in those regions by creating an Agile Selling operation built on a combination of internal capabilities and relationships with key local partners.

China's Inland Provinces: Staking Out a Position in One of the Biggest Consumer Markets on Earth[1]

China is a huge and diverse country. Its urban areas along the eastern coast are as modern and glitzy as any metropolis in the world. Contrast this with its inland region, often referred to as China's Tier 3–5 markets, that has many smaller, underdeveloped markets. Yet, it is these inland provinces—with their vast collection of farms, villages, and towns—that have captured the attention of multinational corporations and local companies alike. Business interest in the more remote parts of China is driven by several factors, including the growing demand for products and services in these areas, and a disposable income growth rate among residents that outpaces the rate in urban areas by more than 3 percent.[2]

As more and more companies recognize that sales growth and business expansion in China will require more than focusing solely on the fiercely competitive urban markets, they are expanding their growth strategies to encompass the Tier 3–5 markets. There, as in large cities, consumers are worth fighting for. And there, as in large cities, strategic planning and flawless execution are critical components of success.

Businesses looking to penetrate lower-tier cities and remote areas can benefit from building Agile Selling capabilities that enable them to maximize the opportunities presented by China's inland provinces. Accenture's research and experience suggest that six steps are particularly important.

Engage Local Government and Social Communities as Partners

The government in China has always played a large role in the success of local and multinational companies operating in the country. With the ambitious targets outlined in the 12th Five-Year Program, the government's influence on and involvement in business affairs will become even more pronounced.

Having appropriate, lawful, and positive relationships with government officials can help businesses obtain licenses to operate, overcome policy hurdles, and gain access to scarce resources. For instance, the Chinese government launched a four-year program to increase the penetration of consumer electronics in inland areas. Chinese consumer electronics giants such as Lenovo® and Haier® and leading electronics retailers such as Suning® are reportedly using this initiative, which offers a 13 percent subsidy on a range of modern electronic products, to penetrate more rural markets.[3]

Consumer products giant Procter & Gamble (P&G) is one example of a multinational that drew support from government entities to more effectively penetrate the inland market. In April 2007, P&G signed an agreement with China's commerce ministry, committing itself to invest in improving its rural sales networks, expand new sales sites, and train more than 10,000 local sales agents to improve rural employment. P&G also agreed to mobilize local nongovernmental organizations (NGOs) to distribute free products. For its part, the government promised to connect P&G with thousands of local sales sites in the central six provinces, crack down on the sales of fake P&G products, boost the rural area's consumption, and stimulate the rural economy.[4]

The P&G example confirms that if companies are to build and retain public trust and confidence in rural regions, they must demonstrate that they are genuinely interested in helping solve some of the major issues affecting socioeconomic development. For instance, there is no point in businesses waiting for governments to figure out how to fix the region's infrastructure deficiencies; they must make many of those investments themselves. A core point is that businesses have a moral and ethical responsibility to the communities in which they work. In Tier 3–5 market areas, they can make major contributions to education, health, and welfare, and, as was the case with P&G, employment. The efforts must not be viewed simply as philanthropy. They should be about harnessing business capabilities and seizing favorable opportunities to drive profitable growth and positive social change.

Because inland consumers are unfamiliar with many commercial products, they often look to trusted sources such as friends and family members for advice when making purchasing decisions. Many companies have developed innovative communication pathways, often borrowing from social marketing models to use word-of-mouth channels to promote their products and services. Their social networks—which can often be built in partnership with NGOs, self-help groups (SHGs), microfinance institutions (MFIs), and local rural populations—have a business and social purpose. For example, combined MFI-SHG social networks in India have access to 50 million consumers over whom they also exert influence. This makes the MFI-SHG network a powerful distribution and retail channel that combines reach, proximity to the consumer, and access to finance.[5] It is an example of a high-impact, multipurpose channel that not only captures and identifies consumer needs and preferences, influences purchasing decisions, and helps lower overall distribution costs, but also ultimately grows the market. There's no reason a collaborative network like this couldn't enjoy similar success in rural China.

Introduce Innovation to the Fourth "P" (Product)

Given the diverse cultures, habits, and purchasing behaviors in China's inland areas, companies must offer products at an appropriate price to meet the unique demands. Proper pricing is critical to boosting sales value and volume.

Companies have several options when it comes to setting the right price points. They can, for example, offer low-priced products from the beginning, with a range of less expensive variants. Or they may opt to sell products as discrete units rather than in multiunit packs. Some consumer goods companies, both local and multinational, provide products ranging from food to shampoos in smaller packaging sizes to increase category penetration. Alternatively, they may practice value engineering and lower the input costs by using alternative sources for raw materials or packaging.

Besides pricing, package size, and source materials, companies can leverage the high visibility of their brand portfolios, as well as their ability to customize product displays to not only differentiate their products, but also to attract more consumer views. Because such displays attract more interest, store owners are usually happy to place them in highly visible areas. Businesses can also generate interest in their products by "going green." Chinese consumers, in particular, are very attracted to green innovations and would consider making a choice based on a product's ecofriendly characteristics or biodegradable packaging.

Finally, and perhaps most importantly, is a company's ability to create new categories of products designed specifically for consumers in more rural areas. This calls for a deep understanding of what those consumers want and need (an understanding that's often provided by key local partners). It also requires companies to pay attention. When it learned that villagers were using its washing machines to wash vegetables, one company created washing machines specifically for that purpose. It also modified its machines to produce less noise and keep rats out—two factors inland region consumers said were important to them.[6]

These examples show that there are plenty of innovative ways that companies can make their products more appealing to inland region customers and more responsive to their day-to-day needs.

Build Up Sales Skills in New Territories

A key challenge for companies looking to extend their reach into inland China involves a lack of trained sales people and fewer qualified resources to fill local sales jobs. This capability gap requires innovative talent-creation models.

Some companies prefer to assign and train dedicated sales teams to Tier 3–5 markets. Establishing an in-house team dedicated to inland region sales requires strong leadership involvement. Top managers can convey the seriousness of their organization's rural commitment by personally serving stints in the inland regions. The top-down message conveyed is that professional growth lies in helping to drive smaller market growth. At the same time, companies looking to build their Tier 3–5 market sales forces must do so with care and attention. Different skills and competencies are needed, such as cultural sensitivity and adaptability. Employees must be willing to live in less urban areas and be able to empathize with local customers and understand their needs. They also require knowledge of the local language, the ability to manage sales across several product lines, and the creativity and enthusiasm to carry out their responsibilities in often adverse circumstances.

In terms of creating an effective sales capability, the creation of a standard sales process with well-defined and specific business activities is critical. So is a clear articulation of responsibilities, with reasonable key performance indicators. With these elements in place, it is possible for less-qualified, local new hires to become effective salespeople. Moreover, using monitoring tools to track and assess sales activities and business intelligence tools to help formulate quick and accurate responses to sales opportunities can help team leaders monitor sales progress and ensure the sales team's compliance with standard processes. Finally, long-term Tier 3–5 market sales team training in the areas of talent creation, planning, and management—both at the top and the bottom rungs of the skills pyramid—will be extremely important to establishing a sustainable talent acquisition and development capability. (We explore the talent aspects of sales organizations in more detail in Chapter 18.)

For companies less inclined to invest significantly in developing their own sales networks, store owners in inland China can serve as the existing sales agents. This is feasible, because these individuals have already accumulated basic sales skills and experiences, and they tend to be the closest and most trusted sales advisors for consumers in these areas. Businesses that apply this approach should support the store owners as much as possible to help them achieve their sales targets. This should involve monitoring and tracking the store owner's sales resource utilization and the effectiveness of his or her sales promotion activities. By offering this sort of guidance, businesses can be more confident that the store owners will act as dedicated (albeit third-party) sales agents. For instance, a local milk powder manufacturer helps rural store owners in Guizhou optimize their products, displays and also track and execute their trade promotions in Tier 3–5 areas to boost store sales. Conversely, a beer manufacturer in the same province failed to track the utilization of refrigerators it had provided to local store owners. Those assets often sat empty, or worse, were used to cool competitors' products, making the initial investment meaningless.[7]

Invest in Supply Chain and Distribution Infrastructure

Given the big weakness in distribution and logistics in rural China, investments in supply chain and distribution infrastructures can prove helpful to companies looking to gain long-term competitive advantage. Indeed, companies know that better transportation, warehousing, infrastructure, and storage can boost returns over the long term for all participants in the supply chain. However, they must also be realistic. Given the immaturity of the inland market, profitability there is likely to be based on low margins and high volume.

To achieve high-volume sales in inland areas, companies need to focus on building their infrastructures properly from the start, with the right sourcing and procurement features, and with supply chain linkages and structures that will act as growth multipliers over time. These efforts might involve replacing the middlemen who had acted as procurement agents, increasing the presence of subdistributors, or establishing company-owned outlets in large villages with heavy consumer traffic. Developing a hub-and-spoke distribution model is another option—for instance, having a manufacturer transport its products to hubs, or large distributors, and from the hubs to the spokes, or smaller distributors in inland areas. These small distributors then pass along products to village retailers.

A less ambitious (and expensive) approach to improving inland supply chains involves collaborating with noncompeting local players.

These entities usually already have well-formed distribution infrastructures. Identifying and mapping key stakeholders, and building trusted relationships with these local players—whether through joint ventures, alliances, or other arrangements—can help companies reduce their cost to serve and simultaneously extend their reach, strengthen their capabilities, and accelerate their speed to market.

Finally, an innovative, flexible, and efficient supply chain and logistics management and monitoring platform is vital for success. This platform can ensure the local execution of supply chain activities and, at the same time, optimize the existing distribution infrastructures and supply chain and logistics capabilities. Because mobile penetration in rural China has reached 90 percent,[8] investing in supply chain and logistics management solutions that are deployed on mobile devices can be a quick-win option.

Fuel Growth with High-Quality and Timely Data

Regardless of the tactic—or combination of tactics—they use to engage with customers, companies will need to base their inland market strategy on deep knowledge of the markets they seek to enter. Customer segmentation, while difficult, is necessary to develop this knowledge—even if in just a single province or region. Thoroughly examining those segments' value through business intelligence and customer analytics tools can generate insights that enable companies to more effectively tailor their business model to fit the inland market.

Companies that prepare carefully and act on a solid understanding of a local area will be able to bring a tailored and innovative approach to their chosen slice of the market. Importantly, they can actually use those insights to shape their larger inland customer strategy. The winners will be able to learn about—and act on—the nuances of local markets by applying economic data analysis to various interaction scenarios. And they will gather and analyze key data before acquiring local distribution networks or setting up new retail outlets. For them, having a clear way of segmenting customers, and knowing the priorities and behavioral patterns of each segment, will be a key differentiator and critical asset that will help them win the war for the inland customer.

Find New Roads to Customers

In the vast and fragmented inland China, the tactics used in cities to engage customers—such as holding product introduction meetings, or assigning marketing people to call or visit consumers—don't apply. They are difficult and expensive to execute and exhaust companies' investments and resources for questionable returns. Instead, companies looking to penetrate inland China should focus on developing localized interactions that effectively and efficiently bring providers and consumers closer together. These interactions can take several forms.

Rural consumers tend to rely heavily on their acquaintances when it comes to their purchasing behaviors, so companies should consider leveraging local store owners and related industry players to build up an offline localized interaction network. Such networks are appealing to consumers because participants are their friends or elders in the villages. Haier established such a network to link its 6,000 Goodaymart-branded franchise stores and form relationships with tens of thousands of village store owners and local repairmen.[9]

An aggressive way for companies to build relationships is by leveraging online channels to form connections with large numbers of customers and potential customers. A host of companies have launched such a tactic in areas much like rural China. One example is Ching's Secret®. This Chinese cuisine manufacturer in India has attracted 100,000 fans on its Facebook page in one year.[10] In China, there are also multinational companies trying to build interactions with target consumers via the Internet. Social media channels such as Facebook and Twitter can be especially powerful tools for building strong relationships with prospective customers.

Another way to forge paths to consumers is by using real roads. Delivery vans and sales vehicles can be used as mobile channels to reach the interior regions. Nokia makes contact with its customers in remote villages through its "Care-on-Wheels" program. With this program, Nokia provides after-sales service, and supplements its rapidly growing distribution network in rural India, all while building customer loyalty.[11]

Regardless of the type of company looking to penetrate China's inland areas, the most successful ones have this in common: They understand that their success is based on the art of winning customers. With fierce competition for consumers raging in China's cities, coupled with the fast pace of urbanization, inland China is the new consumer battleground. Intelligent investment in internal talent, tools, and processes, coupled with the judicious use of relationships with local talent and resources, can help companies tap into the enormous growth opportunities inland China offers.

Africa: A Growing Middle Class Offers Substantial Opportunities for Growth

Until recently, any conversation about emerging markets was dominated by talk of Brazil, Russia, India, and China (BRIC) and select other emerging economies. However, after decades of poor performance, Africa has worked its way into the global dialogue on economic opportunity and growth.

Many news outlets—including Bloomberg,[12] Reuters,[13] Newsweek,[14] and Time[15]—have reported that the next big growth story is Africa. In fact, the growth of Africa's gross domestic product (GDP) between 2002 and 2008 makes it the second-fastest growing region in the world. Indeed, according to the World Bank, nine African countries have higher GDP per capita than China and 16 higher than India.[16] And the continent's growing consumer wealth—driven largely by a burgeoning middle class—makes Africa an increasingly attractive market for all types of goods and services.

How can companies create an Agile Selling approach that can enable them to tap into this massive potential? Several actions are key.

Understand the Target Market

The first step toward participating in the African opportunity is developing a deep understanding of the market, competitors, and consumers. Due to a large informal economy and the prevalence of cash transactions, accurate and representative data on consumer spending is sparse.

How can companies bridge this gap? They must get creative, tapping into local networks to gather insights, partnering with academia and companies that possess usable customer data provided such use is legitimate (banks and telcos, for example), and designing market-facing pilot "experiments" with risk mitigation mechanisms (such as "seed loans" to test methods for accelerating future expansion). They need to be prepared to walk the local markets and gain insights from talking to street vendors, watching consumers, and building a qualitative model of how the market operates. This approach is different from that used to understand a developed market with large volumes of quantifiable data. Together, such strategies can help companies gain the insights they need to craft differentiated, relevant offers for the African segments they are targeting.

CfC Stanbic®, a division of Johannesburg-based Standard Bank Group®, provides an example of how this is done. One of the key aspects of doing business in Africa is the predominance of individual, self-employed vendors. For instance, Nairobi alone has approximately 100,000 such businesses. For banks such as CfC Stanbic, the challenge is loaning money to the most promising of these entrepreneurs, many of whom have little or no credit history.

To tap into this opportunity while reducing its loan default risk, CfC Stanbic used a tool that enabled portable psychometric testing of potential loan recipients, rapidly assessing their risk tolerance, ethics and honesty, intelligence, and business skills. CfC Stanbic also deployed a mobile workforce to complement its local banking branches, and further mitigated risk by using "seed loans" with "graduation plans," which allowed the bank's business with a given customer to grow as the customer's credibility was established.[17]

Develop the Right Value Proposition

With a solid understanding of the opportunity, companies seeking to do business in Africa must deliver a relevant, differentiated offering tailored to their target consumers—as they must do in any geography.

African consumers have unique requirements that companies must take into account. For example, price remains the key consideration for the majority of African consumers, and all offerings should take this into consideration. In addition, community and family are strong elements of African culture, so companies should ensure that branding and promotional efforts resonate with these values—for example, through corporate social responsibility and sustainable development programs. Distinct segments of African consumers have unique needs and preferences that companies must incorporate into their value propositions.

Consumer goods giant Unilever has excelled in understanding and meeting the unique needs of African consumers. The company has had to find a profitable way to make its products available and affordable to all Africans, including the poorest. To achieve this goal, Unilever created the "small unit packs/low unit price" concept: for example, selling small sachets of detergent or salt. This strategy has allowed Unilever to deliver the volumes required to support expansion while capturing the loyalty of lower-income customers. The strategy also has prevented the margin-eroding resale of its bulk products in smaller portions.

Unilever collaborates closely with local wholesalers that supply Africa's informal market while providing the company with market insights and customer feedback. Unilever has embedded corporate social responsibility in its strategy to further boost the brand's relevance with Africans.[18]

Enter the Market with Minimal Risk

Although Africa has shown tremendous improvements as a consumer market in recent years, many barriers to entry, ranging from a lack of infrastructure and local talent, to burdensome regulations and bureaucracy remain. To choose the right strategy for overcoming these hurdles, companies must assess risk and then decide whether to go it alone or enter via an acquisition or a partnership.

Each approach has its pros and cons: Going it alone can result in the biggest payoff if entry is successful, but also is the riskiest choice for companies that lack local market knowledge, access to distribution channels, or political connections. Conversely, entering Africa via an acquisition can be expensive and time consuming, but can provide immediate access to existing networks and distribution channels and the opportunity to gain deep market insights that can be scaled. Partnering provides a faster way of gaining access to local market knowledge and distribution channels, but selecting the right partner requires careful appraisal of ownership, control, pricing, and local partner capabilities.

Ultimately, the right strategy must reflect the company's goals and priorities, the state of local market development and regulation, and the specific nature of the entry barriers to be overcome.

Reach Customers Effectively

Given that more than 60 percent of Africans live in rural areas and have limited access to transportation, simply covering "the last mile" to reach the final consumer can be extremely costly and difficult.[19] Poor roads and limited infrastructure can make delivering products or services to consumers a daunting task. Companies must build strong sales and distribution networks by leveraging a mix of third-party, wholesale, and direct-distribution models. The route to market, in our view, is the greatest obstacle that companies must overcome to build a successful business in any African market.

This is especially the case with less-affluent consumers, whom companies can reach most effectively by employing locals to act as agents, or by partnering with local organizations that have links into the rural market.

Johannesburg-based MTN® is a seasoned veteran of doing business with rural consumers, with operations in 21 markets across Africa and the Middle East (plus Afghanistan). To boost its market share among rural, low-income Africans, MTN has created services tailored to their needs through a network of local agents, established kiosks in rural areas, and motorbikes given to agents to reach the most remote areas. MTN also has implemented lower denominations when selling airtime, reflecting the low and unpredictable income of many Africans. Through such innovative distribution and promotional activities, MTN has been able to capture a significant proportion of the lower-income consumers, which is a critical entry point to the African market.[20]

Another South African company, Tiger Brands Ltd®, also has found strategic partnering to be critical to expanding across the continent. According to Mike Conway, managing executive for Tiger Brands' international division, distribution is a key factor to the company's success. "There are often no formal distribution systems in developing Africa regions and developing your own can be extremely costly," he explains. "Competition from existing local players also is a major challenge. We have adopted a strategy to first investigate what local distribution channels exist and then to try and partner and tap into these existing networks. You will often find that local players have wide networks into Africa with strong existing relationships."

Ensure Demand through Marketing and Promotion

Companies used to stimulating demand through Western-style marketing and promotional approaches must adjust their strategies—and their expectations—for the African market.

Traditional media, namely television and radio, does not always reach all market segments, particularly people living in rural areas or urban slums. In much of Africa, weak infrastructure limits access to electricity, telephones, and the Internet, making access to media—whether TV, websites, or social media—erratic. Although tailoring messages and offerings to specific market segments is critical to success, most companies will struggle to obtain useful market insights on Africa's largely informal markets.

Companies must identify strong local partners through which they can access informal markets and obtain information they can use to refine their offerings and messages. Companies also must spend their marketing budget wisely, being mindful that TV, radio, and print campaigns will not have the same impact as they would in developed markets. In particular, when attempting to reach lower-income segments, companies must ensure that their promotions and marketing are focused on the community and are visible in the market through relevant media such as radio and competitions.

East African Breweries Limited (EABL®) has tailored its marketing approach to become East Africa's leading branded alcohol beverage company. Tusker Lager, one of its beers and the biggest brand in East Africa, was initially perceived as old-fashioned by younger consumers. While EABL was determined to rectify this perception, the company had a limited marketing budget, and knew that the impact of traditional TV- or radio-based advertising would be limited within East Africa. To maximize the return on its marketing resources, EABL focused on a single, high-impact platform that would resonate with younger consumers: Project Fame, a reality show focused on regional talent. To overcome limited access to TVs, EABL sponsored "viewing bars" where the show was screened in conjunction with promotions on EABL drinks. Competitions were held to boost audience engagement. EABL provided training and branded material to retailers to ensure that the brand was delivered successfully to target consumers and leveraged mobile and Internet technology: The company generated more than 1 million SMS votes and web traffic of approximately 70,000 hits per week.[21]

Until recently, doing business in Africa had been hampered by an unstable political and economic environment, a lack of infrastructure, and widespread poverty. At the same time, the predominance of informal markets and cash transactions in Africa had prevented companies from uncovering the types of consumer insights that have helped companies penetrate other markets. But now, the African continent is open for business. The business environment is improving, infrastructure is being strengthened albeit slowly, and growing numbers of consumers now are earning more and looking to purchase products and services that support their aspirations.

As the African opportunity becomes more attractive, companies can use an Agile Selling approach to tap into the African opportunity in ways that meet the needs of customers while protecting their margins and growing their revenue.

Middle East: Forging the Right Mix of Business Arrangements across the Region

Doing business in the Middle East carries its own set of opportunities and challenges. Given the growing population and the high GDP per capita in most countries in the Middle East, in addition to the demographics of the region, the Middle East is an important region in which companies can drive long-term growth. With the region's age distribution profile (specifically, a large portion of the population below the age of 25)[22], and a culture of being extremely brand loyal, companies must establish a presence that allows them to reap the longer-term benefits of an established brand.

However, although it's a lucrative market, the region poses many business challenges for companies trying to penetrate the region. The business challenges that must be addressed are mostly regulatory and cultural. For example, in the majority of countries in the region, 100 percent foreign ownership is not allowed, which means companies expanding into the region have to work with local partners. Additionally, there are significant cultural differences across the region that can have a big impact on how a company can do business.

Companies seeking to enter the region typically face three initial decisions: where to establish their regional headquarters, whom to sell through, and how to structure their business in the region.

For most companies, the location of choice for headquarters operations has been the United Arab Emirates because of the country's more liberal commercial regulations, the government's strong pro-business attitude, existence of large and established free-trade zones, favorable tax policies, and large expatriate population just to name a few.

Whom to partner with and how to structure the business are, however, more difficult strategic decisions that should be evaluated in light of the company's long-term objectives.

From a partner standpoint, foreign companies often find that they could benefit by teaming up with the local government or one of the large family businesses that exert significant power and influence over the local economies. With the governments owning the majority of infrastructure and industries, foreign companies often find it necessary to establish some level of partnership with governmental and quasi-governmental organizations. In some countries, especially those in the Gulf Corporation Council (GCC), a few family business conglomerates also control a large proportion of the local economies.

While historically restrictive regulatory regimes obligated foreign companies to find a partner, and the family businesses with their strong ties to royal families seemed to be the most obvious partners, today companies are finding they can realize significant value by partnering with these families. These family business conglomerates, through their partnerships with other multinational companies over the years, have developed capabilities that will prove valuable to new foreign partners.

Regardless of the partner selected, a powerful local partner in the Middle East can help foreign companies address some of the local challenges they will encounter entering the region.

In addition to finding the right partner, choosing the most appropriate legal structure for the business is a significant decision. Depending on the industry, the level of involvement a foreign company seeks in its Middle Eastern business, and the company's long-term growth strategy for the region, the legal structure and the operating strategy chosen will vary. Furthermore, legal structures in some of the countries in the region have only very recently been defined, while in others, they have long been established. For example, in the UAE, foreign entry is only a phenomenon of the past few decades, while in countries such as Iran and Egypt, foreign companies have had a presence for much longer.

The differences in legal structures and culture from country to country mean foreign companies should not approach the Middle East with a single, generalized strategy for the entire region.

Finally, in the consumer market, another challenge that foreign brands face is localizing their products for the market. This is yet another area in which a strong local partner can be beneficial. In sum, while the Middle East is often generalized, it is important to understand that regulations and cultural implications can vary, often substantially, from country to country. Although establishing a hub in the region is a first step and often the easiest decision, companies should develop a country-specific strategy that enables them to choose the best partner to sell through and with, and accordingly set up the right legal structure for their business in the region.

Conclusion

As companies continue their ever-present pursuit of growth, they will encounter challenges—especially when looking to expand into markets that are unfamiliar to the ones they are used to serving. Different customer needs, cultures, customs, and ways of doing business—not to mention varying levels of infrastructure sophistication and access to key customer segments—can make it difficult for companies to establish a foothold and grow in a new market. Companies generally find that offers and capabilities that have worked well in their "home" markets often don't translate to new markets.

The practices we explore in this chapter can help companies overcome the inherent challenges in global expansion—especially those involved in penetrating the attractive and fast-growing but difficult emerging markets. Enterprises that craft the right mix of internal and external resources to help them understand and tailor their offers and capabilities to the local target markets will be better positioned to capitalize on the opportunities those new markets can afford them.

SECTION

IV

Beyond the "Pilot" Phase: The Core Components of the Agile Selling Enterprise—Positioning for Efficiency

Thus far in our book we have discussed why companies need to embrace the elements of the Agile Selling model, what that model looks like in practice, and some of the core capabilities necessary to getting the model off the ground. In Section IV, we explore the core infrastructure needed to sustain the critical relationships with customers, channel partners, and other entities that are critical to Agile Selling.

It is somewhat ironic that many of the things that are disrupting companies' sales efforts and pursuit of profitable growth are also the "cure"—especially mobile technologies and cloud computing. More than any other tools, mobile and cloud solutions hold massive promise for helping companies create the Agile Selling organization—one that can rapidly respond to new market demands, quickly drive new products through the R&D pipeline, share information to interact with customers and partners in real time, and satisfy customers' unique needs. Mobile and cloud solutions are fueling the development of highly flexible and collaborative business processes that are ideal for today's new selling ecosystem.

The IT organization plays a critical role in the development of such processes and, indeed, in the selection and implementation of key supporting technologies and infrastructure. And that's why, as they move forward, companies must ensure that the sales and IT organizations are on the same page. Without tight coordination between the two, technology can fall far short of helping the sales organization—both internal and external—respond as quickly and nimbly as the market demands. In fact, both the CSO and CIO must be intimately involved across all segments of the sales organization and agree on how the sales technology infrastructure and supporting applications must evolve over time as business needs change.

Companies must also choose the right method of implementing new agile technologies—a decision that's influenced by two main factors. One factor is what we call "business penetration," or the extent to which sales, channel partners, and other customer-facing entities and activities need to change to accommodate the technologies. The other is "process intensity," or how much the new application affects key business processes. Assessing the situation using these two dimensions will help companies determine whether they should opt for a "plug and play," trial, proof of value, or iterative transformation approach.

From a mobility perspective, there's been an explosion of mobile device use among sales forces. And for good reason. Mobile devices enable salespeople to inject speed, responsiveness, and easier access to vital information into the sales cycle, with the end result being more deals closed, more quickly. However, in most organizations, salespeople are making their own decisions about which technologies to use and how and when to use them, which opens the door to a whole host of potential problems—consistency, standardization, optimization, and security—for the larger enterprise. These challenges are especially problematic when a company sells through multiple channels. Thus, it's critical for IT organizations to help build more strategic and standardized mobility-technology programs and strategies without exerting so much control and so many restrictions that it compromises their effectiveness.

15

The CIO Sales Agenda

How to Build an Advanced Sales and Distribution IT Infrastructure

Robert Wollan, Paul Daugherty, and Saj Usman

Chapter Summary

- The CSO and CIO agendas are converging, but dealing with environmental and business changes are pushing them farther apart.
- Ambitious plans to respond to market complexity at the right speed is exposing operational complexity from years of layering on sales tools.
- CIOs today are taking on exponentially more complex issues as they deal with aging legacy applications and hardware that are slow, but not "obsolete enough" to make replacement justifiable from a cost standpoint.

Special acknowledgment to the Accenture High Performance IT Research team for their contributions to this chapter.

- CIOs have an opportunity to play a significant role in the move to Agile Selling by adopting a more agile IT operating model and contributing their expertise to sales network enablement.

As we discussed in Chapter 1, advancements in technology have failed to deliver any measurable improvement in sales organization performance since the advent of sales force automation tools two decades ago. We underscored the fact that "dueling complexities" of the chief sales officer and chief information officer have played a major role in that failure, typically preventing the sales and IT organizations from more effectively aligning their agendas in the pursuit of growth. Such misalignment simply must be overcome for any company to successfully make the transition to an Agile Selling model.

In this chapter, we explore in more detail the operational complexities the typical IT organization confronts, discuss how the IT organization must evolve to rise above these challenges to be better positioned to support an Agile Selling model, and highlight some ways the CIO can play a more prominent role in a company's extended sales ecosystem.

IT and the Battle of Operational Complexity

We have spent considerable time to this point in the book discussing the complexity the sales organization confronts on a daily basis and how that complexity challenges the current sales operating models in most companies. However, the IT organization faces its own challenges to address unprecedented operational complexity across the entire enterprise. Some of the most significant of these challenges are:

- *Supporting new business models:* Today's complex new business models are rapidly outpacing the capabilities of many existing technologies. CIOs are trying to adapt the existing IT infrastructure and applications to whole new ways of doing business— not just in the sales arena, but also in finance, marketing, manufacturing, and logistics. Doing so is akin to the proverbial "changing the tires while the car is speeding down the highway."

- *Fostering speed to online*: The online channel offers immense promise to improve many aspects of a company's business—something that leading companies have recognized. According to Accenture's High Performance IT research,[1] for example, high performers have web-enabled 42 percent more of their customer interactions and 93 percent more of their supplier interactions. Yet most companies still struggle to fully adopt online solutions that can strengthen customer and channel partner relationships.

- *Imbuing enterprise agility:* CIOs are confronted by the reality that legacy technologies are too rigid, heterogeneous, and often outdated as a result of decades of patchwork maintenance, merger and acquisition (M&A), inadequate governance, and many other factors. Making matters worse, ongoing pressure to reduce operating costs has stymied many IT organizations' efforts to upgrade their core applications (although many companies are approaching the tipping point at which it becomes more cost effective to replace these systems than continuing to pump more money into maintaining them).

- *Accommodating social media and mobile:* These technologies offer substantial promise on so many levels. However, as we discuss in Chapter 16, many companies are having difficulty keeping pace with not only the innovations in these tools, but also user demand for them in their work environments. In fact, in our experience, most companies still don't have robust, relevant strategies for how social media and mobile tools are deployed across the company.

- *Avoiding being "disintermediated":* Frustrated with IT's sluggishness and inability to respond to their needs, business users increasingly are buying technology solutions directly—especially cloud solutions, which require minimal technical expertise on the part of the end users to get up and running. For instance, chief marketing officers are expected to outpace chief information officers in direct technology spending within the next five years.[2] Less involvement from IT in the purchase and deployment of technology solutions introduces a whole host of issues for enterprises—not the least of which involve standardization and security.

- *Managing "big data":* The promise of "big data" is tantalizing, and companies are rushing to determine how they can leverage big data to unlock new growth opportunities. Along the way, they have come to realize that to be truly effective and impactful, big data analysis efforts must be coordinated and centralized—and have determined the CIO is the person for the job. Managing and capitalizing on the power of big data is neither easy nor straightforward, and requires significant IT attention and resources (both of which are in short supply in many companies).

- *Winning the battle for technology talent:* Just as CSOs struggle to recruit and retain the right sales talent, CIOs face their own talent crisis. They find it increasingly difficult to strike the right balance between having the skills needed to maintain legacy applications and bringing in or developing new skills necessary to support emerging tools and technologies (especially mobile and social media) that are rapidly becoming critical elements of the business technology landscape. To more strongly support the business's need for agility, CIOs must have the right people on board.

Clearly, CIOs face huge challenges—challenges they must address if they are to become a more valued partner in the sales organization's drive toward Agile Selling.

The Need for an IT Evolution

Bringing CSOs and CIOs closer together starts with an evolution of the traditional IT operating model.

Many IT organizations have evolved from discrete, project-oriented technology providers to multisourced, multilocation services businesses. IT operations are increasingly characterized by a smaller but more dispersed workforce, complemented by multiple sourcing partners that deliver a variety of capabilities. For the most part, CIOs have managed this evolution as efficiently as possible. However, as many businesses centralize governance and control to support global operations, the increased organizational complexity has placed new demands on how CIOs manage and run the IT function. Increasingly, IT organizations are expected to be flexible, responsive, and innovative in supporting the business growth agenda—all while continuing to aggressively manage costs. CIOs must balance these sometimes conflicting agendas in the context of disruptive technology trends such as cloud computing, mobility, and the growing desire of employees to bring their own technology into the enterprise. Each of these trends pushes IT organizations farther away from the historic model of an integrated, in-house line function.

Unfortunately, the very sourcing models that helped CIOs improve IT's efficiency and cost structure may now be hampering the flexibility that many IT organizations need to deliver cloud-based and other emerging services to the business. The ability to strategically use sourcing relationships to provide value to the business is one of the key differentiators between high performance businesses and those that are simply trying to keep up. For example, Accenture High Performance IT research shows that high-performance companies provide IT services via a standard, services-based catalog at twice the rate of other IT organizations.

During the downturn, many organizations emphasized running IT as cost-effectively as possible. Now, as businesses revisit investments in growth initiatives, attention turns to agility and innovation. How can IT organizations achieve excellence in these areas? Managing an increasingly complex, global "shared services" model—characterized by the integration of historically independent business functions such as finance, procurement, and marketing—requires a rethinking of everything from core IT architecture to IT skills. Fortunately, CIOs have many tools to help them improve the IT organization's flexibility and effectively support the business growth agenda.

Four Steps to Improve the Global IT Operating Model

Accenture High Performance IT research shows that 67 percent of CIOs want to position IT as a strategic asset that will help the business grow through the use of innovative technology, products, or processes. Unfortunately, many IT operating models that were built around cost management during the downturn cannot sufficiently support the new growth-oriented agenda. Adding to the challenge, uncertainty about future growth is forcing many businesses to hedge their bets about where and how to invest, with the expectation that they will have to respond rapidly to unanticipated market or customer shifts. It is this market uncertainty that convinced a multinational energy company to adopt a new IT organization model that can respond more quickly to varying scenarios—and, in some cases, lead business innovation instead of following.

As the energy company is discovering, increasing an IT organization's agility while simultaneously balancing efficiency with the need to innovate requires changes to four key organizational elements. First, the IT architecture must evolve to support new and more diverse business models and processes. Second, the IT sourcing model must incorporate an increasing array of in-house and third-party solutions as businesses embrace the cloud and other emerging technologies. Third, the IT workforce must adopt new skills—ranging from technical expertise to relationship building—to support the new model. Finally, CIOs will need disciplined governance policies to establish priorities for innovation and manage both internal and external stakeholders in the new IT operating model.

Evolving the IT Architecture

Today's IT architecture is made up of an increasingly diverse mix of standardized software and service components, from open-source platforms to cloud services, many of which must be integrated with legacy systems. Supporting this heterogeneous footprint is not easy; Accenture High Performance IT research found that one out of five CIOs admits he or she is struggling to modernize application architecture. The challenge is heightened by the need to design and develop applications and tools for multiple communication and collaboration channels. Consider how the rise of smartphones in the enterprise requires new mobile-enabled "apps" and functionality layered on existing architectures, or how changes in the ways that customers research products online require a shift to corporate websites that are more content-oriented than transactional or promotional.

Competing in this complex environment requires agile IT architectures that can scale up or down to accommodate business needs. Traditional approaches—consolidating around one of the major enterprise software platforms, and building supply side capability that the business may or may not leverage—are quickly becoming outdated as IT organizations seek more flexible IT sourcing models.

Accenture High Performance IT research, for example, shows that high-performance businesses are three times more likely to prioritize regular refreshes of their application architecture than are other organizations. Although many companies are hindered by legacy environments, high performers have mapped out transition plans that take into account short- and medium-term business needs and then match the right architecture components to those needs.

The global energy company cited earlier is in the early stages of its IT architecture transformation. A major first step was recognizing the challenge of being a truly global business. A clearer view of the drivers of business success is helping the IT organization to design an architecture that is less rigid and more diverse than in the past, with an emphasis on cloud and other emerging technologies. A large European retailer has embarked on a similar transformation journey. The company has spent the past three years consolidating the IT architectures of its three main retail businesses—grocery, pharmacy, and liquor—to increase supply chain and other operational efficiencies. Although the architectural transition is still under way, the IT organization has already achieved significant improvements in scalability, flexibility, and cost control. (We explore how to develop a more flexible IT architecture in Chapter 17.)

Building Flexibility in IT Sourcing Models

With the IT architecture agenda in place, IT organizations can fine-tune their sourcing model, not simply to improve cost efficiencies but also to use external capabilities more effectively to drive innovation and growth. Unfortunately, many of the sourcing partnerships that CIOs established in the past decade may not be the best relationships to support the business's growth agenda. The first wave of outsourcing was established largely to address cost and improve IT's ability to operate more efficiently. In many ways, this early outsourcing model centered on plugging in capacity and new capabilities as needed to replace or augment more costly or less efficient in-house capabilities. For the most part, organizations have moved beyond this early approach to outsourcing, but they may now find themselves restricted by partnerships that were built from a cost-management perspective.

Enterprises have evolved from buying capacity to buying services, often involving multiple vendors, solutions, and skill sets. An Asia Pacific financial services company, for example, has restructured all of its IT activities into a services catalog that enables IT to quickly deliver emerging technologies or additional capacity to its business units. Proactively managing these services in support of business initiatives has enabled the IT organization to operate more efficiently and respond more rapidly to business needs.

As this company has demonstrated, the next generation of outsourcing is all about matching the growth agenda with the most appropriate IT sourcing options. CIOs must be proactive in the IT/business planning process. Close alignment with the business will help CIOs identify the best types of IT sourcing relationships as well as the in-house skills required to support these relationships. In a multi-source model, the capabilities of both the internal organization and the sourcing partners will change.

Information technology organizations require in-house personnel who are as skilled at managing partnerships as they are at writing code. Managing suppliers requires a specific type of knowledge, and managing the business/IT interface—not just as an order taker but as an active participant in business process development—requires different skills as well. Information technology is in a unique position to develop processes that align business users with the third-party services that best address their needs.

Adapting the IT Workforce

The emergence of new sourcing models, including cloud services, is reshaping the IT workforce. In the past, IT organizations focused primarily on internal enterprise software and developed specialized knowledge and skills to support this environment. Now, with many of those resources provided through managed services, IT organizations may lack expertise about the applications they are running. Shared services models are forcing CIOs to take a fresh approach to their workforce.

Some CIOs are moving more quickly than others. Accenture research shows that high-performance businesses are seven times more likely than other IT organizations to have invested in new technology skills development and three times more likely to be addressing skills development for application and technology architectures and information management. One large financial services provider in Europe discovered an IT skills gap as it reorganized around three core platforms: SAP, Microsoft, and business intelligence. The IT organization retained its top performers, eliminated roles that were no longer core to the new structure, and moved to an IT sourcing model with strategic partners for each platform. This strategic sourcing model enables IT to scale quickly to meet business demand, while retaining the knowledge the IT workforce is developing in support of these platforms.

CIOs should not underestimate the complexity of this type of cultural change. All participants in the IT ecosystem—including internal staff, external vendors, and even business users who interface with IT—must adapt their skills to accommodate new global models for technology services. But there is a significant potential upside to the new IT operating model: It can help the CIO make proactive choices about which competencies to build in-house.

Running IT as a Business

As IT workforce competencies evolve, CIOs will need to adapt their own skills as well. Many CIOs are in the midst of a transition from managing a technology organization to managing a business, in which their primary mission is building relationships and helping senior leadership drive the business agenda as a partner, not a provider. A seat at the table is a cliché, but it is precisely what the CIO requires to foster innovation and prove IT's value to the business. The CIO has historically been charged with keeping the lights on while controlling costs. In the new world, with a broader set of technology options available to serve the business, the CIO must become more adept at matching those options to current and future business needs. With its deep technology expertise, the IT organization remains a catalyst of innovation, but the CIO must be able to show the business how to capitalize on that innovation.

IT governance models should also adapt to accommodate the changing relationship between IT and its sourcing partners. High-performance IT organizations are adept at ensuring that service providers conform to the security and performance expectations of IT and the business. For example, three-quarters of high performers in Accenture's 2010 High Performance IT research said they employ sophisticated metrics and processes to track the effectiveness of application outsourcing providers, compared with 36 percent of other IT organizations in the survey.

Achieving maximum return on investments in cloud and other external services requires high levels of both stewardship and accountability. A clearly defined IT governance model and service catalog will also help business users follow a consistent process for procuring services, without having to sacrifice the flexibility they need—and now expect—to quickly deploy or scale new services and functionality.

New IT operating models are also likely to require revised security and compliance policies that account for the integration and interoperability of third-party services. In particular, IT organizations will have to ensure that customer information or other sensitive data maintain the same high-level protections within third-party services as they do behind the enterprise firewall. IT governance models that are aligned with business needs can make it easier for CIOs to secure future investment in strategic initiatives. Nearly 9 in 10 high-performance IT organizations say they develop a business case for most new IT initiatives, and they are eight times more likely than other companies to measure the benefits realized from these IT projects, Accenture High Performance IT research shows. At one large energy services provider, business cases for new IT projects are developed jointly by IT and the business sponsor. ROI is categorized in two ways: "tangible" (will the investment deliver calculable returns to the general ledger or payroll?) or intangible. This process has helped raise the realization rate—the actual harvesting of business benefits in the project business case—to 98 percent.

The CIO's Role in Agile Selling

The changes just discussed can go a long way toward helping CIOs create a more nimble and flexible IT operating model and, subsequently, provide greater value to the sales organization. But their contributions don't have to stop there. CIOs also have an opportunity to play a more significant role in the extended ecosystem that is the hallmark of the Agile Selling model. They can help boost the effectiveness of a company's channel partners and encourage them to sell more of the company's products.

For example, they can play an instrumental role in providing robust training to partners on the company's products and selling processes. Although all channel partners need training that helps them understand the basics, in an Agile Selling model, a company goes far beyond simple training courses to provide partners with comprehensive learning programs—such as what Avaya has done, as mentioned in Chapter 2. But those learning programs don't happen by accident. They require a top-notch IT infrastructure and applications to be effective. By teaming with the sales organization to design and deliver leading-edge learning programs, IT can help make both the *sales* force and the *selling* force more effective.

CIOs also can provide valuable assistance in the area of sales performance analytics and coaching. For instance, a company could offer (where permissible and where data may be properly exchanged) its most important partners significant analytics support in exchange for downstream customer and sales data, going so far as to actually run analytics operations on partners' own sales forces to generate insights that help partners improve their marketing, leads management, compensation, incentives, and other related activities. American Express®, for example, has long provided retail merchants with advanced analytics on credit card transactions and cardholder information to optimize store sales.

A third way that CIOs could actively help the company equip and optimize its partners is by creating a de facto CSIO role—or "Chief Sales Information Officer." This role may even be played by the CIO directly. The CSIO could provide specific technology expertise to the sales organization to ensure that sales and its network are taking full advantage of the right technologies and tools. The CSIO could help in two distinct ways.

Assessing the Data and Technology Capabilities of the Existing Partner Network to Identify and Eliminate Waste and Bottlenecks

Companies often have many different types of network partners: franchisees, independent agents, distributors, and resellers. Some are larger, more influential, or more strategic than others. Some are simply low-cost ways to maintain a presence in a specific market that can't support a large investment in a sales force. For instance, large hardware and software companies often run massive partner networks, ranging from large, strategic, multinational consulting firm partners such as Accenture, to small shops that meet the specific router needs of a town or city.

The CSIO could have clear accountability for helping to create a network whose performance can be optimized by providing advanced technology and data support, isolating partners that have the ability to take advantage of that support, identifying areas in which partners are not taking advantage of what's available to them, and uncovering ways in which the company could help existing network partners beef up their data and IT capabilities.

Evaluating Prospective Partners' Data and Technology Aptitude and Capabilities

The CSIO also could play an integral role in the assessment of potential channel partners to provide the deep technology expertise necessary when evaluating prospective partners' IT capabilities. Today, the use of such expertise in partner evaluation is rare. Most CIOs find that they are excluded from partner evaluations, but then must figure out how to support the relationship technologically once the decision is made. This scenario is neither efficient nor effective, and only adds to the burden CIOs must manage. By getting involved early in the partner evaluation process, the CSIO could identify which partners would be better equipped technologically to support the company's sales efforts, as well as how much time and money might be needed to integrate those partners' systems with the company's own. Such insights could prevent a company from making a potentially costly move by bringing aboard a partner that needs far more attention and work to enable and support than it's ultimately worth.

In both cases, the CSIO could employ a framework that helps a company prioritize its technology investment in channel partners to get the greatest return. This framework would assess the availability and maturity of the data, process, and technology in the internal and partner networks today; identify potential changes that could be made to those capabilities to raise the maturity level; and calculate the overall return on investments in such changes (in the form of improvements in specific sales performance metrics).

Conclusion

As the sales organization moves toward the Agile Selling model, CIOs have an opportunity to position their IT organizations as strategic partners that can help make that transition successful—and, in the process, become a more active contributor to the company's growth agenda. To be successful, the IT organization requires a new type of operating model, one that is global in scope and offers the right mix of services and skills that can adapt quickly as business needs change. Such an agile operating model will provide a foundation for IT's own evolution in a rapidly changing business environment, serve as a foundation for the CIO to play a more active role in enabling the entire selling ecosystem, and help close the gap between the sales and IT agendas that has existed for far too long.

16

Tablets, Smartphones, and Apps

The Importance of a Clear, Standardized Mobility Strategy

*Yusuf Tayob, Terri Rinella,
and Aidan Quilligan*

Chapter Summary

- Early adopters have exposed the most common new issues from the mobility explosion, and also which investments are paying off.
- It's different this time: Mobility rollouts to salespeople (including tablets and smartphones) should have less adoption issues than the previous two decades, but only if it is a trade of value with the field.
- This is more than just for frontline salespeople. The convergence of cloud, mobility, web, and social media has created a new opportunity to roll out new solutions to others.

The use of mobile technology is nothing short of staggering. Consider these comparisons: There are 1 billion cars and trucks in the world and 3 billion credit cards. But, there are 6 billion mobile phones, of which 1 billion are smartphones. And, while the world population is roughly 7 billion, there are more than 9 billion connected devices in use globally.[1]

With numbers like these, the business implications of mobile technology (and the need for proactive, cohesive mobility strategies) shouldn't be surprising—especially because more and more employees are using their own devices for work-related functions. However, increased usage is not the only reason companies need a mobility strategy. Coordinated use of tablets, smartphones, and apps can also help salespeople work more efficiently, make better account-management choices, shorten sales cycles, and create better and more tightly tailored customer experiences. Outside of your enterprise, standardized use of mobile technology makes it easier for selling partners to interface with you anywhere and at any time, access up-to-date information about your products and services, and readily promote your capabilities and information. A partner whose mobility capabilities are well-aligned with your own may also be more inclined to work with you first.

As Gary W. Loveman of the Harvard Business School aptly observed: "Gains come not because of technology, but because it supports breakthrough ideas in business process."[2] This axiom serves true with mobility; deploying tablets alone will not improve sales execution, which Accenture defines as the planning, design, and implementation of selling methods, sales, and sales supporting processes, enabled with appropriate selling tools. Determining where mobility fits into the overall sales execution approach is a critical component for achieving measurable results.

Therefore, you must pick a strategy before it picks you. When it comes to mobile technology, companies cannot wait for consumer trends and pockets of employee usage patterns to dictate how mobile tools are deployed across the company. Instead, organizations need a proactive strategy—clear but not overly dictatorial—that can help ensure a profitable, shared experience between sales representatives and their customers. This chapter looks at the role mobile technology can play in an Agile Selling model, and how companies can build mobility strategies that help sales forces—both internal and external—improve their performance.

New Tools, New Potential, New Challenges

Everywhere you look, sales professionals are formulating *their* own mobile strategies—not just deciding which mobile tools should support their selling efforts, but making specific decisions about how those devices are used. These efforts are obviously well intentioned: Reps are just trying to sell as much as possible, as fast as possible. However, employee-directed mobile-technology decisions are invariably based on personal views and preferences. So it's nearly certain these choices will not (in the aggregate) produce maximum benefit for the organization. The more likely results include:

IT headaches and challenges: Salespeople are using their personal devices for work functions. So IT is pressured to handle the management of devices and applications and contend with the security risks of this "bring your own device" trend.

Oversight barriers: The longer ungoverned usage remains in force, the tougher it becomes for companies to monitor, guide, and improve mobility-related sales behaviors.

Process standardization challenges: As technology adoption rates rise, companies find it harder to implement organization-wide sales approaches, such as account planning, pipeline, and forecast management and activity reporting.

Compromised information sharing: With mobile devices, salespeople can talk to each other voice-to-voice and e-mail-to-e-mail. But consistently tabulating, analyzing, summarizing, and exchanging data is more difficult in a highly diverse, user-defined mobile technology environment, without integrated data.

Too many paths to the same end: With easy access to small, independent, mobile sales applications, representatives may download their own sales productivity tools, thus creating a chaotic assemblage of apps across the organization. From a B2C perspective, this varied selection of apps may also result in inconsistent brand and marketing messaging to the end customer.

Legal and information-security problems: Corporate security, data rights, and total cost of ownership are rarely considered when employees make their own mobile technology decisions. With customer data accessed and stored on mobile devices at the edge of the network, organizations are at risk if unsecured phones or tablets are lost, stolen, or used improperly.

Unfocused skills and expectations: As sales representatives spend more time with various tools and applications outside the work environment, they may expect employers to provide the devices with which they (the employees) are most familiar. This can wreak havoc on procurement, technology support, and overall efficiency.

Compromised potential: Uncoordinated use of technology limits a company's ability to optimize any one tool.

All of the above challenges are amplified when a company sells through multiple channels. After all, more channels generally means less control, more coordination problems, and increased risk. Which is why most sales organizations' mobility strategies should make interaction and integration with strategic partners and other allied organizations a primary consideration.

In sum, the difference between mobile technology's current (ad hoc) and ideal (strategic and standardized) situations is similar to the distinction chemists make between mixtures and compounds: Various contributors to a mixture coexist in the same container without creating a distinct, potentially valuable entity. In a compound, ingredients unite to form a singular substance with new characteristics and new potential. When it comes to mobile technology—and mobility strategies—companies need compounds, not mixtures.

Social Media: Consider the Similarities

There are many similarities between companies' mobile technology issues and those associated with social media—another widely embraced consumer-centric medium over which most organizations have an uncomfortably low level of control. For example, nearly two-thirds of respondents to a 2011 Accenture survey stated that social media is an "extremely important" or "very important" channel for interacting with customers, prospects, partners, and other stakeholders. But like mobile technology, most organizations have been slow to act: Only 8 percent of B2B companies currently consider themselves heavy users of social media. In addition, research results suggest companies' limited involvement with social media is closely linked to the uneasiness they feel about making good investment decisions. Even though many have identified specific social media goals, only one-quarter of respondents expressed great confidence in their company's social media investments; nearly 20 percent have little or no confidence in those investments.

So like mobile technology, executives understand social media's potential value, but they continue to play an awkward waiting game. Not many have set up active policies concerning employees' use of Facebook or Twitter, just as few companies have established specific hardware, software, or brands as company-wide standards for mobile-device use. For neither technology have most organizations considered specific sales-optimization opportunities; salespeople pretty much do what they think is best. And few performance benchmarks exist for either area, which makes it difficult to define, much less measure, optimal behaviors.

Not surprisingly, there are many similarities to fixing the problem. Not unlike mobile technology, the most important component of a social media program is a robust strategy that aligns with, and supports, companies' larger business objectives. Likewise, it's vital to position social media—or mobile technology—as part of a holistic customer strategy whose success in a sales context requires flexibility, innovation, and the avoidance of user (salesperson) disempowerment.

How Are Companies Responding to Their Mobile Technology Challenges?

Despite the earlier mentioned pitfalls, most sales organizations are sitting on the sidelines—unready to make hard decisions about mobile technology standardization and strategy development. This is a key finding drawn from a recent sales performance optimization study sponsored by Accenture.[3] From that study, researchers determined that more than 90 percent of firms are using (or starting to use) tablet devices in their sales organizations—a 50 percent jump in only one year (Figure 16.1). However, more than half the members of that group do not have a formal program for tablet usage (Figure 16.2).

To be fair, Accenture research shows that CIOs are working to establish mobile technology goals. When asked what mobile capabilities they plan to implement, a majority mentioned streamlining operations with enhanced order, asset, and inventory tracking. Cited next most frequently was accelerating the sales cycle by improving access to back-end systems and data.[4]

These are viable goals. But in our experience, many sales executives are more concerned about sales reps making their numbers than about technology consistency and standardization. These priorities may also be appropriate, but the stark reality is that both missions are critical. However, CIOs are probably more cautious about mobile

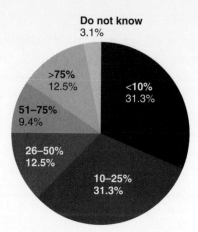

FIGURE 16.1 What Percentage of Your Sales Force is Currently Using Tablet Devices to Support Their Activities?

Source: CSO Insights, Sales Performance Optimization Research, 2012.

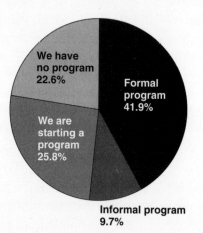

FIGURE 16.2 Which Statement Best Describes Your Company's Policy toward Tablet Device Usage in Sales?

Source: CSO Insights, Sales Performance Optimization Research, 2012.

device mandates because they are hesitant to simply order salespeople to use (or not use) a particular tool or application. This is a critical point: Because force-feeding usage standards can backfire, companies will need to accommodate, embrace, and optimize rather than dictate.

They will have to establish boundaries and guidelines that abet standardization, but do not set down unenforceable rules or discourage innovation. In short, they need a clear, flexible strategy.

In the remainder of this chapter, we examine ways to develop more strategic and standardized mobility-technology programs without being excessively (and unproductively) heavy-handed.

Strategy-Development Cornerstones

The business case for a proactive, standardized mobility strategy is solid: increased efficiency, tighter relationships, more productive interactions, shorter sales cycles, and fewer security gaps. These benefits apply equally to external as well as internal sales forces. However, formal mobility strategies are a particular boon to companies' relationships with external sales partners: streamlining interaction, minimizing incompatibility and maximizing the exchange of ideas and information.

To achieve these ends, a variety of objectives should always be kept top of mind. For example, any mobility strategy for the sales force should align with the organization's overarching enterprise-mobility strategy. Most companies' CIOs are currently working to imbue multiple enterprise functions with mobile technologies. Mobility strategies developed for the sales organization must align with these corporate and IT strategies.

It's also important to plan for the need for continuous innovation and evolution. Twenty-five years ago, it wasn't unusual for a businessperson to travel with a 30-pound "laptop." Today, smartphones and tablets are de rigueur. Tomorrow, who knows? And when it comes to apps, the pace of innovation is staggering. The point is that mobile technology hardware and software (as well as our definition of what is "mobile") is constantly changing, and companies must be flexible enough to keep up. That requires a commitment to allocating funds, resources, and capacity over an extended period of time.

Another vital mobility tenet is to not lose sight of the user and how he or she (1) uses mobile tools and (2) will respond to tighter, more-defined guidelines (see sidebar, "Why Sales Reps Push Back and What to Do about It"). Toward this end, it's vital that any mobility strategy helps create a distinctive user experience. For every use of a smart-phone or tablet, a salesperson must get something back—something that helps him or her sell more effectively. The idea is to position mobility not simply as another tool, but as an unparalleled genera-tor of better performance and higher rewards. Along the same lines, any mobility strategy must emphasize ease of use. For example, device-management policies and data-refresh regimes must be as unobtrusive and intuitive as possible. The "holy grail" is complete transparency.

Emphasizing those features and functions that make mobile devices unique is a related way to maximize user acceptance. Mobile devices make many compulsory tasks easier and more fluid. Appoint-ment scheduling, customer contacts, and account data management are just a few examples. But simply replicating on a mobile device what salespeople formerly did on some other tool (e.g., a laptop) is far too limiting. Instead, companies can strengthen their standardization and strategy-development efforts by focusing most heavily on capabilities that set mobile devices apart. By promoting and enhancing features like location-based services, simple-to-use form factors, brilliant user interfaces, integrated photography, and rapid or automatic synching with corporate IT, companies play to salespeople's selling strengths and potentially elevate their enthusiasm for higher levels of standardization and governance.

Several companies are exploring ways to make sales representa-tives' conversations more interactive and engaging by using tablets. For instance, the tablet's instant-on capabilities make it easier for sales rep-resentatives to quickly launch presentations. In addition, as highlighted in Chapter 5, tablets can drive the development of on-site, interac-tive, and customized content. A salesperson and prospect might work together to build a quote or proposal in real time or view the customer's order history during a meeting. Every company and every industry will emphasize different things, but the need to maximize mobile devices' unique value—to continue making them novel, interesting, and fun, as well as valuable—is universal.

Most important of all may be the need to encourage user creativ-ity. Today's mobile devices have a high "cool factor." Salespeople like using them and are excited to see what their new toys can do. However, the buzz won't last indefinitely—particularly if people's ability to experiment is stifled by corporate strictures. Sooner or later, in fact, smartphones and tablets could become just another burdensome tool whose cool factor is drowned in a sea of protocol. The point is this: Overarching mobility strategies are definitely needed to glean maximum value; but companies must find ways to let salespeople's ingenuity flourish. Should this fail to happen, user adoption may never reach a high enough level, and valuable input—employee-generated ideas about using smartphones and tablets to maximize sales effectiveness—will be drastically curtailed.

Framing a Mobility Strategy

Clear-cut mobility strategies—whose missions include widespread standardization and enterprise-wide governance—can be achieved without heavy-handed dictums. It's less about high levels of control than about high levels of consistency, innovation, and buy-in. To begin bringing shape to those strategies, consider the following high-level activities.

Take Stock of the Role Mobility Plays (and Could Play) in Your Sales Organization

Most of your people are already using mobile devices, so the key is not utilization but rather value and coordination. If the organization's use of the devices is already improving sales performance, how much further could you go with better, more standardized use of mobile technology? Involve representatives in the brainstorming of opportunities and desired features and functions of the mobile applications to help garner buy-in from the start.

Decide Who Will Lead

Should the effort be sales-led or CIO-led? Mobility policies relating to sales cannot be defined without direct involvement of sales leadership, channel leadership, and a group of end users. In some cases, however, IT will have to take the lead. In this case, it's doubly important to capture consistent, high-quality input from the sales organization—including feature/function insights and feedback from individual users.

Establish Target Benefits

What, specifically, do you hope to gain from a strategy of increased standardization and tighter governance? Sales organizations should have a solid, data-driven understanding of which mobile capabilities are game breakers, which ones are simply nice to have, and how various capabilities will deliver value across the enterprise and to individual sales representatives.

Determine How Mobile Technology Fits into the Overall Sales Execution Approach

A sales organization's mobile technology approach will need to integrate with its overall sales execution approach (including planning, design, and implementation of selling methods, sales, and sales support processes). It must add value to the process, not simply replace what the sales executive would otherwise do on less mobile technology.

Identify and Enforce the "Nonnegotiable" Aspects of Your Mobility Strategy

Some elements of a mobility strategy are simply not up for debate. These must be identified early. Take safety and security of client data: Because anything less than "total protection" is not acceptable, security and data encryption are usually nonnegotiable points. Fortunately, the existence of some nonnegotiables can help frame the strategy and embed the organization's values.

Decide How to Integrate Mobile Tools with Existing CRM Applications and Processes

Mobile device initiatives will generally fail to meet expectations if the tools are deployed without focusing on their integration with current customer relationship management CRM systems. Insufficient integration can result in lower utilization, which can limit the value gained and turn the sales force away from future efforts.

Develop a Roadmap That Sales Force Automation Vendors Can Use to Help Develop Solutions

In some cases, an off-the-shelf solution will meet the core needs of the sales force and play well with other tools. However, there will likely be differences in timing, as well as role- or function-specific needs for which companies will have to build custom applications. In these cases, organizations should factor integration efforts into the solution plan, define the basic steps, and reach consensus about which people should be involved in the implementation.

Pilot and Experiment to Learn Lessons

Mobile technology development and implementation should be highly iterative, with constant feedback available about what works and what doesn't. Rapid piloting and quick assessment/assimilation of lessons learned can speed up the identification of successful approaches and accelerate the attainment of real business benefit.

The answers to the following questions help form the foundation of the mobility strategy:

- What are the high-value mobile applications for representatives and what is the priority for implementation?
- Who will own the device(s)?
- Will we control the devices' apps or let salespeople maintain control?
- Will we build or buy key apps?
- To what platforms and technologies should we give priority?
- How will we integrate new devices with existing sales technology?
- Without compromising our standardization efforts, what can we do to encourage user innovation?
- Are our organization's brand, culture, and market positioning reflected in our use of mobile technology?

- How frequently should we expect to deliver new capabilities?
- How will we maximize consistency in the use of apps?
- How will we make sure that everyone is up to speed and trained?
- Does our strategy enable and accommodate future implementations of mobile technology?

Of the preceding questions, one of the fundamental issues that sales leaders and CIOs wrestle with is how to handle the "bring your own device" decision within the strategy. Many companies recognize the difficulties associated with compelling or preventing the use of a specific device. In fact, an Accenture Institute for High Performance survey[5] in late 2011 found that despite employers' concerns around data security and IT protocol, nearly one in four (23 percent) employees worldwide regularly use personal consumer devices and applications for work-related activities. As a result, many companies are pursuing hybrid approaches that involve both company-owned and independently acquired devices. Each company should determine its best approach given its culture, security requirements, industry, and other factors. Toward this end, several vendors offer mobile device and application-management solutions that can help companies overcome the challenges associated with employees bringing their own device to the workplace.

Why Sales Reps Push Back and What to Do about It

In a 2012 *Harvard Business Review* post[6], business author and thought leader Tammy Erickson offered some reasons as to why organizations may fail to get employees to adopt social media tools:

- "We are ordered to use this equipment rather than invited."
- "Little of what we actually get paid to do (or believe we get paid to do) requires information or input from most other people on the network."

- "Participation feels like dropping pearls into a black hole. There is often no sense of getting something in return for sharing an idea or suggestion."
- "We have no control over who sees our information and little idea what they are doing with it."
- "An encyclopedic manual is needed to get started."
- "Software is generic and requires a workaround to do the specific things we really want and need to do."

These concerns directly reflect the larger issue on which this chapter focuses: A great many organizations are enamored with mobile technology. They want to embrace the new thing—even before they've created a solid reason for doing so, and before developing the discipline they need to make the move pay off. Sales representatives, on the other hand, may recognize the tools' potential value but feel their creativity—and the technologies' value—are quelled by an endless wave of rules set down by the sales organization. People may also perceive that tool-usage guidelines are taking away their autonomy or that the directives are increasing their workload without adding any value. When implementing mobile sales tools, organizations can avoid these pitfalls by providing and communicating value directly to sales representatives at every interaction point.

Delivering Results through Sales Innovations—Exploiting the "Cutting Edge" of Mobility

The good news is that companies that have created proactive mobility strategies for sales have found several predictable areas to exploit that are both attractive to their teams (which drives better adoption) and deliver incremental business (i.e., better results). Some of the most common areas a company should explore first are:

- *Improved representative effectiveness*: One leading company is considering leveraging location-based services to notify sales representatives when they are near an account where they owe a follow-up. Driving more timely and consistent follow-through can lift the performance of the sales teams, increase customer satisfaction, and help to improve sales.

- *New levels of flexibility*: A leading global pharmaceutical company is redesigning its traditional sales tools for tablet devices to create new levels of role and geographic flexibility. By disaggregating the individual functions into smaller, bite-size functions, the company can use one common sales force automation platform to deploy different combinations of sales force tools to different types of sales representatives across the globe.

- *Locating nearby opportunities*: Companies are taking advantage of location-based services on Apple iPads to show nearby opportunities and unclaimed leads. With this information in hand, representatives can take advantage of downtime between sales calls to prospect qualified leads that are in close proximity.

- *Remote presence*: Several high-tech companies are exploiting the connectivity and rich media capabilities of tablets by implementing live video conferencing to enable their sales representatives to bring remote subject matter specialists directly into the customer conversation. In this case, mobility is making it possible for the sales representative to deliver answers at the point of need and minimize follow-up work.

- *Richer customer dialogue*: A number of companies are exploring ways to make sales representatives' conversations more interactive and engaging by using a tablet's touch screen capabilities to deliver content. For example, the instant-on capabilities of the Apple iPad make it easier for sales representatives to launch quickly into customer presentations. In addition, tablets can deliver rich, interactive media based on customers' preferences as they select content that is directly relevant to them. This might include collaboratively building a customer's quote or proposal in real time, or viewing a customer's order history to answer questions during the meeting.

- *Real-time order placement*: An organization is complementing its enterprise systems by building a front-facing ordering application for the iPad. The application leverages the tablet's usability and combines with on-line and off-line working capabilities, allowing sales reps to place customer orders immediately during the sale. This accelerates the order-to-delivery process, makes order confirmations available more quickly, and helps the seller realize revenue more rapidly

Case Study—Delivering Results through Sales Innovations
Salesforce.com's Approach to Tablet Adoption

Salesforce.com's (SFDC) strategic approach to tablet use and adoption is a great example of emphasizing value, ensuring communication, and considering user and customer. When SFDC announced that all salespeople would receive iPads, the devices had been on the market for only three months. Thus, SFDC capitalized on the excitement its employees would have for this new technology.

SFDC also combined its tablet implementation with a new sales methodology. Before receiving their iPads, people had to receive training on the methodology and the device. Part of the methodology's cornerstone is a consistent, common sales process that articulates all the mobility capabilities needed to execute successfully.

SFDC also built a series of apps and installed them on all issued devices. Every iPad thus came "fully loaded," with the same look and feel, and the ability to communicate the same information in the same format to sales leaders and teams. Each device looks the same—right down to the order in which the apps show

(continued)

Case Study—Delivering Results through Sales Innovations
(Continued)

up on the desktop. SFDC knew that, when it comes to reporting, varied formats and communication mechanisms are almost never beneficial.

Last, SFDC stressed continuous innovation. The company continues to build and disseminate new apps, and to emphasize standardization and consistency. Everyone from vice presidents to new reps uses tablets in the exact same way and understands that ongoing improvement is part of the package.

The net effect is that SFDC maximized buy-in and excitement by perching itself on the leading edge of a new phenomenon—a shiny new toy that everybody wanted and that most people didn't yet have. So even if standardization and tight governance were the rules of the day, salespeople could still be avid proponents. Today, tablets, smartphones, and emerging apps are more or less mainstream entities. But the buzz is nowhere close to wearing off, nor is the potential for new uses, enhancements, and leverage points. To build successful mobility strategies, companies must capture that energy and ensure that it isn't buried by an avalanche of rules and requirements.

Looking Ahead

If the advent of digital technology has taught us anything, it's that innovations we can barely conceive of are always over the horizon. Mobile technologies (tablets, smartphones, and apps) are perfect examples: tools that almost no one envisioned a decade ago are now established parts of people's private and business lives.

However, in a business context—particularly because employers often issue the devices or otherwise subsidize their use—a certain amount of coordination and control is simple common sense. It's like any other business context: Planning and executing a strategy that is results- and customer-focused is good business. However, mobile technologies' concurrent role as consumer devices can't help but change the game. So any strategy a sales organization formulates should acknowledge that consumer-driven experiences and preferences will affect people's business-related use of the same devices. This is why it's essential to formulate strategies that (1) communicate real user value, (2) avoid heavy-handed mandates, and (3) encourage innovation and feedback.

Mobile tools will continue to evolve. More uses and devices will come to the fore. CRM and cloud technologies will become more powerful. Consumer behaviors will go on driving enterprise innovation. These are some of digital technology's great inevitabilities, and companies and sales organizations that are smart about acknowledging and leveraging them should have an inside track for a long time.

17

New Rules for Tools and IT Infrastructure

The Cloud and Agile Tools, Processes, and Systems

Saideep Raj and Beth Boettcher

Chapter Summary

- The "cloud dilemma" is real: It is a hot topic with fantastic promise, but many are not clear on how to get started.
- Promise stems from the convergence of the cloud, mobility, and business analytics—attacking bigger problems, at faster speeds, than the previous generation of solutions.
- Ecosystem-wide collaboration will open doors to vastly different business solutions, and emerging technologies will power that innovation.
- Four different approaches have emerged; picking the path wisely has never been more important to delivering results.
- IT basics still apply to implementations, but overconfidence in today's capabilities without looking for new skills in the IT team spells danger in cloud solutions.

As we discussed in the opening chapters of this book, the market is demanding that businesses operate at an unprecedented pace—rapidly responding to new demands, quickly driving new products through the R&D pipeline, sharing information to interact in real time with customers and partners, and satisfying customers who want their specific need met "now." These market demands are placing significant pressure on businesses to be more nimble and efficient in how they go to market. In this environment, high-performing sales organizations must make more collaborative, rapid, rigorous, and outcome-based decisions and they need the technology support to make this happen. These are all characteristics of the Agile Selling model.

For the first time, the technological confluence of cloud computing, mobile technology, and business analytics software can enable sales organizations to achieve outcomes at the pace required. However, companies must take a careful and coordinated approach because the changes can be substantial. Cloud-based agile processes and systems must be designed and developed the right way or they could result in an inflexibility that prevents the experimentation and speed they offer.

There is no "silver bullet" for how to implement more agile technologies; there are different ways to deploy technology, each suitable for different environments. This chapter discusses how business and IT should work in concert to select and deliver the best approaches that will help support an Agile Selling model that brings the promise of pace to fruition.

The Need to Be Collaborative, Rapid, Rigorous, and Outcome-Based

In the highly complex and rapidly evolving selling ecosystem that is a hallmark of Agile Selling, high-performing sales organizations need the ability to be more collaborative, rapid, rigorous, and outcome-based:

- Collaborative to orchestrate sales activities in a complex ecosystem.
- Rapid to intentionally and strategically respond to quickly changing opportunities and issues.

- Rigorous to bring discipline and science to bear to improve operations and outcomes.
- Outcome-based to make key decisions based on strong business cases, data, and analytics in addition to intuition and judgment.

Collaborative

The drive to increase collaboration across the business has been under way for some time. After all, the more seamlessly sales teams can orchestrate sales activities within their company, the better the sales outcome. But today, this orchestration extends in many more directions. Collaboration requires navigating a complex network of interactions: across business units, across functions, partner to partner, partner to customer, all in an effort to generate demand. It is no longer a world of "we" and "them," but one of "us," as companies integrate activities across multiple channels and partners to create a consistent customer experience, coordinate their go-to-market approach, and, ultimately, increase their sales.

This level of collaboration will require information-sharing between partners and across lines of business at an unprecedented level, using new technologies and skills that most organizations don't yet have. And although it's challenging to get data from new and different sources, there are also many tools that organizations already have—such as e-mail—that possess valuable information companies don't fully utilize. So although collaboration is vital, it continues to be elusive to many organizations.

The sales organization of a financial services company offering insurance, banking, and investment products is tackling the collaboration challenge through a "big data" effort. Royal Bank of Scotland (RBS®) must gather and analyze information across lines of business to be proactive in cross-selling the company's offerings. It is using big data techniques to join together disparate data sources including transactional customer records, demographic data, macroeconomic data, stock-market data, aggregated feeds, and any number of social media sources. It then uses a proprietary tool as well as other tools (such as sentiment analysis and text mining) to analyze and identify a customer's propensity to need new financial products, and to be able to suggest these products in a timely and optimal manner.

Rapid

In many ways and to many companies, the need for sales teams to be "rapid" is intuitive. Organizations must quickly respond to global megatrends such as rapid growth in Asia and South America and an expanding middle class around the world. Accelerating product innovation means that a company has shorter windows of time to sell new products, which means that the sales organization must be armed more frequently with the right selling information to generate returns on big product development costs. Just consider software companies that now issue product releases every three months compared with what was historically an 18- to 36-month cycle. The sales executives who represent this software need frequent education to keep pace with such rapid product releases.

Social media and mobile devices are accelerating the need for sales teams to be rapid in response. Sales teams are pervasively quick and tactical as they try to respond to new business opportunities, social media chatter, and customers who are increasingly reachable anytime/anywhere through any mobile device. Successful companies embed processes that foster rapid decision making and tie those processes closely to their technology platform.

Rigorous

Rigor is required to bring a combination of process discipline, the right analytics, and the right decision criteria to bear to make the best decisions. As detailed in Chapter 9, Accenture refers to this as bringing science to the art of selling. Rigor enables sales teams to better determine whom to spend time on influencing, conduct thorough health checks of the sales force, have a sharper sense of what pieces of the marketing mix are working or not working, and much more.

Typically a company that uses rigor in decision making makes optimal technology choices. These choices strike the right balance between transformation and tactical efficiency gains. By applying a more rigorous and standardized approach to how sales organizations are enabled by technology (regardless of the market they serve), companies can employ modular solutions that reduce total cost of ownership and improve efficiency. Although a global organization may not be able to be 100 percent standardized across countries, Accenture experience indicates that sales teams can achieve at least 60 to 80 percent standardization.

Outcome-Based

Accenture research found that between 2008 and 2010, a large proportion of business decisions in surveyed companies were based on judgment rather than business analytics.[1] In fact, weak analytics capabilities—ranging from siloed data, outdated technology, and a lack of analytical talent—are preventing organizations from gaining valuable insight that could lead to better business results. By basing key decisions on insights from data and analytics tools, sales teams can improve their ability to take the right actions at the right time to the right target customer. Such outcome-based decisions result in a more optimized allocation of time and resource and an improved return on investment for the sales organization.

In addition, successful companies ensure that when making technology investments, they focus on the up-front business case. Without this business case, teams face an excessive administrative burden trying to keep measurements on metrics that seem to change considerably.

What Technology Can, and Must, Deliver

Technology is the underpinning of the Agile Selling model, enabling the sales organization to be collaborative, rapid, rigorous, and outcome-based as described above. As such, IT infrastructure and governance models for developing and optimizing technology must advance to deliver the capabilities needed at the pace of change required by evolving sales needs. There are several implications for what technology must be able to deliver for the business.

Provide the Sales Organization with Lower Cost, Higher Value, Faster-to-Implement Tools

Agile sales organizations need tools that can deliver immediate value and flex with changing needs. They need new sales and marketing technologies that don't "break the bank" in the traditional cost buckets of new hardware, software, and training, much of which will be abandoned when a better offering hits the market. The tools must be easy and fast to implement and—because they may only be useful for a limited time until the next innovation comes along—lower cost to purchase and less costly to maintain. Whatever technologies are deployed, they must be accessible from multiple devices—tablets, smartphones, desktop, and otherwise—so any transaction can be completed on any device.

Taking advantage of lower-cost, more-disposable tools will enable businesses to not only get technology in the hands of sales executives, but also in the hands of partners and customers to engage with them in more meaningful ways. Although in the past it was cost-prohibitive to equip customers and partners with technology, today it's both affordable and fast. For example, utilizing software-as-a-service technologies, a company can have a customer portal established within a matter of days.

This approach even raises the question of why a company should develop or purchase software versus using technology that's available to the mass markets to help mine data (within legal boundaries) to achieve a company's business goals. Specifically, think about how a company can use social media to mine critical customer information to conduct contact management, and leverage information about life events to instigate a specific action. For example: If a customer publicly posts a note on Facebook about the new car he bought, how can an insurance provider use that information to offer an insurance quote or to notify a local agent to contact the customer? Or, consider another life event: A customer publicly posts about her new baby. How can a financial advisor help set up a savings/investment account for the newborn?

Provide the Sales Network with Greater Access to Information

Information from all parts of the company *and* outside the company must be integrated and available to support the sales organization's decision making. However, unlike the historical approach of doing this through highly inflexible, integrated systems, this must be accomplished through a nimble technical architecture. The architecture should draw on both structured and unstructured data to provide a single source of customer information that reduces internal confusion over what data is accurate and enables salespeople to sell to more informed, more savvy customers. This information must be available for new analytics tools so the sales organization has the insight to make rapid decisions. This is also enabled by the right IT architecture.

In an Agile Selling organization, it is equally important to share data with channel partners and equip them with more and deeper insights about their markets, customers, and competitive environment. This requires defining what kinds of information will and can legitimately be shared through which means, and also requires developing a level of trust with third parties regarding privacy and how to appropriately exchange information.

Companies could even shift the burden of keeping customer information up to date from their customer relationship management (CRM) systems to their customers. Companies have spent a lot of time and money on building a customer master and maintaining the best customer information. Now with Facebook, LinkedIn, and other social media, customers are updating their information every day. By figuring out how to embrace social media as the "system of record" and integrating that back into their enterprise systems, companies can place the responsibility on the customer to be the single source of truth for customer information. Although there are likely to be few, if any, large enterprises utilizing this approach today, it is certainly a design consideration for forward-thinking companies to contemplate.

Utilize Different Mechanisms for Developing and Deploying Software

As companies implement systems such as software-as-a-service platforms, the new tools no longer align to traditional application development models. New tools require different mechanisms for developing and testing software that enable companies to test as they go, and accomplish the faster implementation the tools profess to offer.

Many leading companies are using a hybrid approach to deploying and testing software, particularly to respond to new market opportunities. For example, pharmaceutical companies are using cloud computing to rapidly distribute sales capabilities to new markets while putting more robust technology in mature markets where they have more established operations. If the companies find the technology or new business process in the new market isn't useful, they can shut it down without having made a huge investment.

What Happens When Business and IT Aren't on the Same Page?

There is tremendous potential for companies to use technology as a competitive weapon in this complicated new selling environment. However, without a coordinated business and IT effort, technology can easily fail to enable sales teams and channel partners to deliver at the pace and agility the market requires. Neither the CSO nor the CIO can tackle technology efforts in isolation. Common CSO and CIO leadership is needed across all segments, and there must be agreement on how the technology road map changes over time.

When IT and the business are working in isolation, they tend to take tactical steps that have incremental value or they attempt to fix problems in an uncoordinated way. Addressing point problems rather than looking at the entire sales value chain (which includes multiple channels to customers) is certainly less expensive. Such small expenditures can often be included in small departmental budgets. But over time, such an approach can result in a proliferation of technology tools that are costly to maintain and nearly impossible to integrate. Change is almost unfeasible, and if not that, then costly and slow.

In the end, a collection of tactical steps doesn't achieve the ultimate goal of turning a sales organization into a powerful, coordinated, integrated selling machine—the type necessary now to attract and retain customers.

When the sales organization or line of business doesn't partner with IT to enable their sales force with tools, they run the risk of developing business-led solutions with a number of issues. Business-led solutions are typically very nimble because they aren't integrated with the rest of the enterprise systems, but they often have data integrity issues for the same reasons. But, also because they are not integrated, independent sales tools don't have "one version of the truth" for customer and other information, decreasing the sales team's confidence in the insights they draw from customer data.

Business-led solutions also typically result in a higher total cost of ownership because they are purchased by individual lines of business, regions, or sales functions instead of being aggregated to create purchasing power. Not only can license costs be higher, there also can be more administrative costs to maintain the solution, run reports, and perform analytics. Furthermore, if solutions are not integrated into critical corporate systems, this typically leads to manual "workarounds" that reduce efficiency. Independent practices also don't promote enterprise-wide best practices, as each line of business or region defines its processes and best practices within the technology and does not share them more broadly for the organization to collectively benefit.

Conversely, solutions that are developed by the IT function run the risk of being technical-led solutions that have decreased adoption. Rather than thinking of the solution as solving a business need, IT may see the solution as a data mapping and migration exercise. If neither the sales rep (IT's customer) nor the end customer (the sales rep's customer) are "front of mind," IT runs the risk of developing solutions that are perceived to increase the administrative burden on the sales reps and diminish the customer experience. As a result, salespeople fail to adopt the solution, staying focused instead on old ways of selling and next month's numbers.

Companies need the proper collaboration, sponsorship, and leadership balance between business and IT to successfully deploy sales technologies and take full advantage of new tools. Without this balance, value (in a variety of forms) is left on the table.

The Promise of Cloud and Agile Delivery Methods

For the first time, the technological confluence of cloud computing, mobile technology, and business analytics software can enable sales organizations to achieve outcomes at the pace required. The cloud and agile tools, processes, and systems give companies the affordable means to be more collaborative, rapid, rigorous, and outcome-based in their decision making.

Consider the era of technology before the mid-2000s. To provide the sales organization with tools, companies implemented enterprise sales force automation and customer relationship management systems that resided on their own in-house servers. Such projects were (and still are) expensive, took a long time to implement, and required lots of training. Furthermore, often by the time they were deployed, the sales processes had changed, organization structures had been updated, or other changes had occurred that diminished the usability of the solution before it was even in use. The amount of information available for salespeople in the field was limited to what could be sent to their laptop computers when downloaded from a hotel room—which was not extensive and certainly not current. The lack of ubiquitous Internet access meant that information was hardly available in real time.

The technological confluence of cloud computing, mobile technology, and business analytics software gives companies the means to redesign how they use tools to enable the sales ecosystem. Cloud computing is dramatically lowering the cost of tapping into software—CRM, social media-based collaborative tools, and once-costly business analytics software. When these applications are made accessible by a public cloud (owned by a third party), companies can pay for such capabilities on an as-used basis (similar to how customers pay for resources actually used such as electricity or cable services) rather than having to make massive investments in their own systems. And when they put such applications in private clouds (meaning, cloud systems that can be used by only one organization's multiple business units), this, too, can lower the cost.

Such cloud-based systems have ushered in the era of "disposable IT"—the ability of companies to test and try new technologies that improve demand-generation without having to make huge bets in terms of technology investments. This, in turn, will enable companies to experiment continually with new technologies to improve sales, which, of course, then will require them to be able to update their processes and people's skills much faster than in the past.

The lower cost and disposability of cloud computing means that companies can now enable the selling ecosystem in ways that were previously not possible. The customer is making purchase decisions and influencing the purchase decisions of others through many mediums. Because tools are affordable, and allow companies to share information in a more dynamic manner, companies can make tools and information available to a much broader audience. Phuong Tram, CIO of DuPont, expanded on this point in 2012: "In the past I could do something [deploy software] for maybe 10,000 users, or maybe I could do something for 100,000 users. But there are a massive number of contractors, partners, customers, and potential customers. No company has been able to do that. That's where cloud computing comes in. Any other way would be cost prohibitive and unsustainable."

Although cloud-based processes and systems offer great promise, they must be designed and developed the right way. Otherwise, they could result in inflexible sales processes and systems that prevent companies from speedily experimenting with and implementing new sales processes and technologies—and, thus, not allow them to achieve the power of pace. If these new solutions are not designed correctly, the sales organization's ability to be nimble is reduced. Companies have to find ways to develop sales applications that don't reduce their ability to alter the solution to support their need to be rapid and collaborative.

Agile software development methods offer the means to reap early benefits from cloud-based solutions. Agile methods are based on iterative and incremental development, where requirements and solutions evolve through collaboration between cross-functional teams.

It promotes adaptive planning and evolutionary development and delivery, and encourages rapid and flexible response to change.

When done right, agile development helps to manage a well-defined scope, and uses highly engaged business users to define use cases and test them in the application, aligning all capabilities to the achievement of desired business outcomes. But if the business can't devote the time and energy, or the approach is applied to architectures that can't be developed in an agile manner, another approach is better.

The waterfall method is how most companies have historically done systems development.

It is a more sequential process for software development that aligns to rigorous IT governance processes, but typically isn't a particularly flexible or fast approach. Traditionally, a waterfall project is executed in meaningful "chunks" over the course of 8 to 12 weeks. New capabilities are delivered in each chunk, business resources are engaged throughout, and integration with other systems happens after processes are tested and validated. However, when the waterfall method is not done right, projects go on for months or quarters before being deployed, requirements are "thrown over the wall" and interpreted by systems resources and "injected" back to the business at a point that it is too costly to change the solution if it is not right.

There are projects where an agile approach is appropriate and projects where a waterfall, or even a blended approach is best. What is most important is to use the *right* approach for the project, neither staying tied to the "old world" of waterfall development nor moving wholesale into agile methodologies.

Determining the Right Approach

There is no "silver bullet" for how to implement more nimble technologies; rather, there are different ways to deploy technology, each suitable for different environments. Thus for each new solution they deploy, companies must think about the right development method as discussed earlier (agile, waterfall, or some blend of the two), and also give careful consideration to the implementation approach and level of integration required. Cloud-based agile processes and systems must be designed and developed the right way or they can result in an inflexibility that prevents the experimentation and speed they offer.

From Accenture's experience, there are two dimensions to consider when determining the right approach for a project (Figure 17.1). The first is "business penetration," an assessment of how much sales, channel partners, and other customer-facing entities and activities need to change. Is the solution intended to experiment with changing a few activities or to standardize a change across the organization? Is change limited to a specific business line, region, or product or does it permeate across the enterprise?

The second dimension to consider is "process intensity," an assessment of how much business processes are impacted by the new application. Changes to sales-related processes and technologies result in either embedded or disposable technology tools. Embedded tools require significant investment, become core to the way the organization sells, and are difficult to remove. Disposable technologies are those that enable the organization to experiment and quickly move on when a new, better technology becomes available.

By bringing these two dimensions together, companies have a framework for assessing the right approach for each cloud-based SaaS

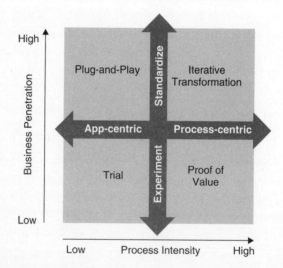

FIGURE 17.1   Framework for Determining the Technology Implementation Approach

technology project. We label those with high business penetration but low process change as "plug-and-play." Those with both low penetration and process change are well positioned for nonintegrated or minimally integrated trials. Projects that have limited business penetration but are embedded in the organization require a proof of value. And those where the stakes are high in terms of business penetration and integration into the process of the organization are transformative in nature and require an iterative approach.

The following is a summary of the key elements of each approach.

Trial

Trial is an implementation method used when the tool is not integrated and is highly disposable. If the trial does not result in the desired outcomes, the company does not proceed with an integrated installation or does a retrial of the solution. Typically, companies that prove the trial then move to a more integrated (plug-and-play or iterative transformation) approach.

A trial is appropriate when there is minimal or inconsistent business penetration throughout the organization. Typically it is a sales function where the specific sales methodology and the enabling tools are being tested.

It is also appropriate when less rigorous processes are needed; for example, if there are opportunities to "test" aspects of a methodology, solve a specific problem in the organization, or for specific gaps in sales skills.

For example, as we mentioned earlier, a company may want to experiment with transferring responsibility for maintaining customer information to the customer through the use of social media. They may believe that they can turn to LinkedIn to get information on an individual customer that will be more complete and current than a traditional database such as Dun & Bradstreet.

Plug-and-Play

A plug-and-play approach is appropriate when there is high penetration of the solution throughout the organization such as a solution that is core to the sales function. Projects in this quadrant offer the opportunity to standardize a process across lines of business and regions of the world, recognizing that regulations can affect how a process is executed in certain countries and industries. A good example of a project in this quadrant is contact management, which is an important process no matter how big the company.

Typically, a company doesn't need a true business case to make such investments. They are known to improve core processes that are critical to effective selling. Furthermore, these new tools usually require integration with other applications (e.g., contact management requires minimal to no duplicate records in the database).

When implemented and integrated correctly, a plug-and-play tool becomes highly embedded and hard to eliminate. Returning to the contact management example, companies will typically implement a process such as contact management on more robust tools and implement more robust data synchronization processes, making it difficult to dispose of the contact management solution over time.

Proof of Value

A good proof-of-value project is one in which there is minimal or inconsistent business penetration throughout the organization, such as a new sales approach or tool to support entering a new market. There are potential opportunities to standardize business practices; however, practices can vary by line of business or geography. For example, when testing a new sales process or entering a new market, a company usually must have technology that will allow an organization to "ebb and flow." Typically, a company would do a pilot to determine what business practices can be standardized prior to full deployment.

As the name suggests, there are opportunities to test aspects of the processes *and* the technology, validating the test against a clear set of business metrics that determine success or failure. Value must be realized in a meaningful amount of time (typically one quarter) and it should be a solid mix of technology, people, and process all marching toward a common strategy. Typically, companies that take a proof-of-value approach do so because there is a strong business case that can be demonstrated. They then move to plug-and-play or iterative transformation to deploy the proven solution more broadly.

Ideally, the test can be done in a stand-alone technical environment. However, it is important to execute the test in such a way that it can be validated that the lack of integration with other solutions was not the cause of success or failure.

Iterative Transformation

Iterative transformation is appropriate when there is high penetration of the system throughout the organization and significant opportunity to standardize processes worldwide. In most instances there is no business case tied to this approach. Typically, companies that go through an iterative transformation do so because there is a known strong business case, or the application has already been trialed in a proof-of-value effort. This is a transformational program that is targeting a very clear problem or opportunity that will generate revenue or reduce costs. These programs take significant time and energy, and because of the investment and business penetration, are critical to do well.

Typically a transformative system would require integration with other applications over time. Initially, it may be in a stand-alone environment but becomes more integrated as the solution transforms the business, making it difficult to "unwind" from the organization once implemented.

A good example of an iterative transformation is an application core to the sales function, such as opportunity and pipeline management. Many companies will enable a stand-alone tool (sometimes integrated with a product catalog) to institute strong pipeline management rigor. As the pipeline becomes more accurate, they integrate it with revenue systems to show booked business versus sold business, resulting in a pipeline that provides a strong indicator of sales that can indicate realized revenue.

These four quadrants define a helpful model for thinking through the approach for any given project. In practice, there are two additional considerations to its use. When looking across a portfolio of projects, a company may have projects under development in each quadrant at the same time. For example, a company may be driving an agile transformation process while, at the same time, rolling out plug-and-play changes to the existing deployed pool and trialing new application exchange components. Additionally, a project may be in one quadrant at one point in time and then at a different stage, move to another, such as moving from trial to plug-and-play.

The point is, all four approaches are valid depending on the situation. Where companies go wrong is when they don't think through the approach or choose the wrong approach for their project. For example, many companies default to a trial approach because it doesn't require a business case, when, in reality, the tool must be more integrated into the business to add value. By not thinking through one's approach, a company runs the risk of integrating too much too soon, resulting in a less agile organization. We have also seen companies commit too quickly to a cloud license that, unfortunately, locks them into a solution that they cannot easily dispose of, leaving them no choice but to "just try to make it work."

Answering the following key questions increases the chances that the company takes the right approach for what it is trying to accomplish:

- How well defined, standardized, and adopted are our processes?
- How important is the need for having data from other systems to enable the processes? Can we enable the processes without access to large amounts of data?
- How confident are we that we think that the processes will help us achieve our business outcomes?
- How urgent is the need to enable the processes? Do we have time to hone them?

Many companies struggle with finding the optimum balance between business and IT for any given project. For example, they may be weighted so much on the application-centric areas for trial and plug-and-play that they are short-changing the process needs. Other companies spend endless time on process change and lose the ability to drive viral adoption or learn important feedback from the field.

All of the considerations of development method, implementation, and integration approach and balance between IT and business process can best be handled through a governance model that enables the company to cut through the issues and balance all of the competing needs.

Getting It Right: Critical Success Factors

There are certain factors that will increase the likelihood a company's investment in agile technology will produce positive business benefits. For any technology project to be successful, it should be led as a joint effort between the chief sales officer and the CIO, with everyone engaged and aligned to one common vision.

Governance is needed during the initial implementation of CRM and sales solutions. However, implementation is just the beginning. Governance postimplementation is even more critical as the organization continues to refine, optimize, and adapt the solution over time. After all, running and optimizing the infrastructure is different from deploying the infrastructure. This rigorous governance approach includes release management and standardized processes to implement the capabilities outlined in the program road map. Without clear, collaborative, rigorous governance after the solution is in production, there can be significant impacts, including a solution that does not evolve and support the organization effectively or a solution that includes "everything but the kitchen sink"—in other words, way too complex to use and manage.

Within the ongoing governance structure staffing, clearly established business and IT roles and responsibilities are critical; this includes effectively communicating business and IT resource time and effort required to implement requested changes. Active participation in meaningful, regular meetings between business and IT resources is also critical to resolving issues and making decisions efficiently. Such a staffing approach improves transparency and collaboration across business and IT resources by establishing the rules of engagement for the program. Joint planning between business and IT resources ensures that business processes and enabling technologies are tightly integrated.

Finally, cloud-based projects encounter the same risks as more traditional IT projects that can span years to develop and implement.

But a primary benefit of cloud technologies is the pace at which they can be delivered. Just as in multiyear projects, companies must put significant discipline and rigor around the critical project success factors (such as strong governance and sponsorship, clearly defined scope, and roles and responsibilities) to deliver on the promise of pace that cloud offers and reap the agility it can provide (Figure 17.2).

Success Factor	Decreases...					Increases...		
	Timeline	Delivery Cost	Support Cost	Solution Complexity	Defects in Production	Data Quality	Ability to Scale	Solution Adoption
Clearly Defined Scope	■	■						
Consistent Solution across LOBs and/or Geographies		■	■	■		■		
Complete "To Be" Vision			■	■			■	
Well-Defined Near, Mid-, and Long-Term Data Architecture						■	■	
Disciplined Environment Management	■					■		
Committed Sponsorship			■					■
Well-Defined Governance	■	■	■	■	■			
Clear Delivery Roles and Responsibilities		■	■	■	■	■		
Full Accountability within the Business			■					■
Ability to Course Correct	■	■						

FIGURE 17.2   IT Project Critical Success Factors Apply to Cloud-Based Solutions, Too

Conclusion

Cloud-based and agile tools can give companies the affordable means to be more collaborative, rapid, rigorous, and outcome-based in their decision making. However, the implementation approaches are non-trivial with several options available. That is why it's important to get the right balance from multiple dimensions and, hence, why a strong governance approach across business and IT is critical. If not designed, developed, and governed effectively, the result will likely be inflexible sales processes and systems that prevent companies from achieving the pace, agility, and financial benefits promised.

Agile tools, processes, and systems can have significant impact for the organization as stand-alone tools or single projects. But this evolution is not about any single project. It is about changing the institutional way that business and IT work together and are organized, and about changing the fabric of how decisions get made and work gets done. Getting it right can have significant rewards.

SECTION

V

Empowering Employees
for Selling Success

In the final section of our book, we devote our attention to the dimension that's arguably most critical to the success of the Agile Selling model: people.

For years, sales leaders have faced serious challenges when it comes to the sales workforce. They have trouble finding the right people, keeping them when they do, helping them build the right skills, and improving their performance. In fact, it's not a stretch to say that most sales leaders have a severe talent crisis—which is not an attractive scenario when the pressure is on to continually beat last quarter's numbers.

And it doesn't get any easier when selling through a new model that introduces more and more complex sales relationships and a whole new set of talent challenges companies must conquer.

In Section V, we take a look at what leading companies are doing to improve all aspects of the sales talent life cycle—from recruiting and hiring, to training and developing, to performance management, to retention. We discuss considerations for modifying talent strategies and operating models to accommodate Agile Selling, as well as creating a robust analytics competency and modifying learning programs to build the competencies and skills that can help the new approach succeed. We also review some of the key steps necessary to implement new talent initiatives in a coordinated approach that creates the genuine behavioral change across channel operations, sales operations, and the field sales organization that must happen for Agile Selling to take root and prosper.

18

Profiling and Shaping a High-Performance Sales Force

David Smith, Victoria Luby, PhD, and Patrick Mosher

Chapter Summary

- Improving the performance of the sales force remains a major challenge for most companies.
- CSOs clearly already have a sales talent crisis, and it will only get worse as the world in which companies are selling moves faster and becomes more complex.
- There are five building blocks for developing the kind of talent needed for the Agile Selling model to be successful.
- Rebuilding the talent model across the five building blocks requires a stepwise, coordinated approach aimed at creating real behavioral change across channels operations, sales operations, and the field sales organization.

Most CSOs, regardless of their industry or company size, share common challenges: finding good reps to bring in; getting them productive once in the door; helping them meet their numbers; and battling turnover, especially keeping the best reps on board. Recent CSO Insights research shows that the *average* annual turnover of sales reps is one in five (21 percent).[1]

Such high turnover is certainly frustrating. It could be that, because it's tough to find good sales talent, companies are bringing in people they shouldn't. Or, sales reps are getting frustrated and quitting because they aren't getting traction in their job fast enough. Whatever the cause in any one company, 47 percent of reps are not making quota and 38 percent of hired reps don't succeed. And the time to productivity is long: 73 percent of reps take six months or longer to reach competence.[2]

When it comes to building high-performance sales reps, sales executives' odds of success are long: 41 percent of them say they need help in identifying which reps need coaching. How can we help reps realize more of their potential, keep the great ones from walking out the door, and get new reps to full performance more quickly? And how do we do all of this while the existing workforce is struggling with the growing complexity of their selling environment?

There's no doubt CSOs have a talent crisis. But as the world in which companies are selling moves faster and becomes more complex, the talent battle takes on new levels of intensity. We are now asking sales reps to network, collaborate, influence, and sell in a world that is complicated, indirect, and often ambiguous. Sales executives can no longer increase sales by simply adding new reps. Gone are the days when a rep can sit at his kitchen table the night before a big call and pull together what he needs to have a successful customer visit the next day. Reps need input from multiple points within their organization, forcing them to navigate their own complex organization. Data is flying everywhere. Products are short-lived and constantly evolving. Influence on their customers comes from other customers, peers, other vendors, competitors, third parties, the Internet, and myriad other sources. The battle to build a high-performance sales team is hard and it's getting harder.

Success in the new world of selling requires new strategies and capabilities. Sales executives must create an environment that makes it easier for the seller to succeed in the marketplace—whether that is having all the content and insights the rep needs at her fingertips for that big call, reducing the time she spends on administrative tasks, or providing the right type of solution-selling and skills training.

This chapter focuses on the people-oriented actions that companies must take to make the shift to an Agile Selling model. Specifically, it profiles what leading sales organizations are doing to support their teams in the new selling environment and to create the agility they need to succeed.

Greater Complexity Requires New Sales Competencies

As CSOs know, selling is more complex than ever, and it isn't getting simpler. Customers now interact with and buy from companies in ways radically differently from in the past. With more information from which to draw insight about products and services, customers increasingly control their interactions with companies, picking and choosing among providers, searching for the best price and service, and bidding or bargaining for a better deal. The sales rep who can operate in this environment possesses excellent business and financial acumen and is market savvy, customer savvy, competitor savvy, partner savvy, and technology savvy (Figure 18.1).

Data is flowing everywhere—business partners, customers, field sales, social media, call centers—and from every direction, yet, getting information to the reps when they need it is difficult. As the consummate juggler, the sales rep has many balls in the air: gathering information on rapidly changing customer needs, navigating multifaceted customer relationship networks, and generating complex solution configurations, often by bundling product with third-party providers' solutions—and sometimes even competitors' solutions. As an extension of the company, channel partners also have to keep apace with the latest and greatest innovations in processes, technologies, analytics, and learning programs. Supporting the sales team and channel partners with data sourcing, analytics, and insight distribution takes a true analytics capability.

The sales managers' job is completely changing as well. In addition to managing quotas and pushing reps to make their numbers, sales

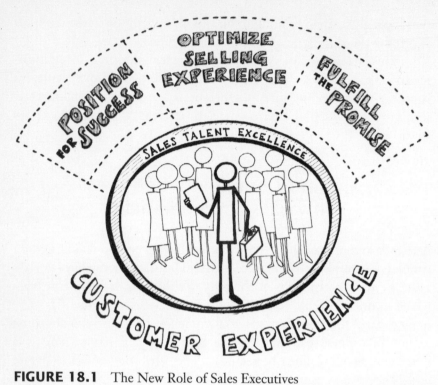

FIGURE 18.1   The New Role of Sales Executives

managers are tasked with motivating, coaching, and helping sales reps navigate the network in which they work, and building the capabilities and capacity of their sellers while keeping high performers engaged. The rapid changes taking place in sales, delivery, and service models are forcing sales managers to learn to lead in ambiguous situations. Great sales managers set and reset clear direction throughout the year and throughout the quarter rather than merely pushing quota attainment. They coach and help their sales reps navigate complex deal shaping as they also help them orchestrate their own organizations. This represents a fundamental shift in responsibility, positioning sales managers as connectors and influencers within a broad selling network.

In sum, creating a sales workforce for the new Agile Selling ecosystem involves building talent strategies, competencies, learning models, and analytics capabilities to create agility, speed, and stronger integration inside and outside the organization (Figure 18.2).

FIGURE 18.2 Sales Talent Excellence

What Has to Change: The Building Blocks for Creating Agile, High-Performance Sales Talent

Many sales organizations in B2B companies today are working to rebuild many aspects of their talent model to excel in B2B sales and shape their sales talent into strong performers. They typically make changes across five foundational areas:

1. **Talent strategy:** Said simply, performance leaders know what good looks like: They have profiles of high-performing sellers and sales managers, as well as straightforward strategies and tactics for their sales operations organization and channel operations. Their talent strategy isn't built on anecdotes and "conventional wisdom," but rather on analytical insights.

2. **Operating environment:** Performance leaders align increasingly complex operations to make it easy for sellers to navigate, maximize customer interaction value, and minimize low-value administrative burden.

3. **Analytics:** Performance leaders build a strong analytics capability that gets information where it is needed when it is needed most and derives insights from data that inform strategy and future decision making. They enable their staff to gain access to data and deep analytical understanding of the market trends, and they push this analytical capability deep into their organizations—not just through a distinct group of market researchers.

4. **Network, collaborate, and learn:** Performance leaders build up the skills of the sales organization to effectively and efficiently use insights to differentiate each and every customer interaction, from face-to-face meetings to tweets to even partner interactions where the company itself isn't present.

5. **Sales management:** Performance leaders build a sales management capability to orchestrate their team performance, navigate complex deal shaping, create a positive working environment that retains the best sellers, and coach sellers into high performance. This world is different than merely pushing sellers to barely exceed quotas.

Talent Strategy

Knowing what "good looks like" seems conceptually simple: Identify the best performers and bring in more like them. When asked what constitutes a high-performance seller, sales executives can easily provide opinions on the attributes of their best performers. But, the characteristics and behaviors for success are not necessarily intuitive. When Accenture presents a comprehensive list of sales competencies—established from our work in High-Performance Sales Force Analytics (HPSFA)—to sales executives and we ask them to choose five competencies that distinguish their high performers from core performers, they confidently choose their competencies. However, after we complete the analytic study, they find that they typically only picked 50 percent of the competencies that correlate with high performance in their sales organization.

By clearly profiling what "good looks like" for their organization, sales executives can build a talent strategy that aligns the necessary competency model, performance management, compensation, and culture to support and encourage the behaviors they are targeting.

When profiling what "good looks like," leading organizations employ analytics that correlate competencies, time/activity, and personality traits of their best-performing sellers. Such a model identifies the key target behaviors for sellers and provides detailed descriptions of the competencies that enable sellers to succeed in the environment.

In our experience, high-performance seller competencies are vastly different from one company to another. In other words, there is no single profile of the competency set for high-performance sellers. Each company's competency model is driven, in part, by the culture of the individual company, the solutions the company sells, its customers, and more. For instance, "team orchestration" may be a top competency of high-performance sellers in a decentralized organization where business units have much autonomy, but "team orchestration" may not play an important part for a high-performance seller in a centralized, hierarchical organization. And as shown in Table 18.1, in three examples of partner or channel account managers, different sets of competencies in each case are statistically related to high performance.

Understanding which competencies are required for high performance also influences the talent cycle, such as how to recruit sales reps and sales managers, which characteristics to look for in new hires, how to onboard them, and how to continually train them to be better at selling and managing in the complex world in which they operate.

Furthermore, the profile of what good looks like provides sales leadership with a blueprint for identifying, grooming, and developing the sales reps who demonstrate the competencies and traits for high performance. This "moving the middle" may include identifying those average-performance reps who, with the right development and support, have the greatest potential to evolve into high performers (Figure 18.3). Driving to high performance may require specific programs focused on performance coaching from sales managers, learning programs to develop targeted competencies, motivation systems

TABLE 18.1 Partner/Channel Account Managers: Competencies Statistically Related to High Performers

	Case 1	Case 2	Case 3
Build Rapport and Relationships		X	
Closing		X	X
Coaching		X	
Competitive Intelligence	X		
Decisiveness	X		
Develops the Solution			X
Drive to Achieve	X		
Partner Focus			X
Persuasion	X	X	
Strategic Thinking	X		
Uses Partner Network			X

Organizations need to shift the performance distribution curve, making the core perform like high performers

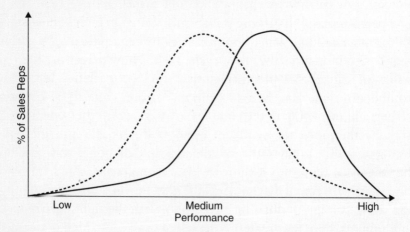

FIGURE 18.3 Moving the Middle

that drive the target behaviors, and sales processes and technology enablement that provide insight and drive high-performance behaviors. Fostering a strong sales culture helps a company retain the best performers and the potential high performers, while helping those who fail to demonstrate the competencies or capacity for agility in this new sales environment find other opportunities.

Operating Environment

Sales executives, channel operations executives, sales operations teams, and marketing teams all operate with good intentions toward improving the effectiveness and efficiency of how their company goes to market. However, for field salespeople, this often translates into 1,000 good intentions flowing down from various management teams, each requiring attention or change that distracts from their day jobs. Performance leaders create an operating environment that is easy for sellers to navigate and makes it easy for sellers to succeed.

By organizing carefully to govern the information, process changes and technology changes hitting the organization, and regulating what is released to sellers and customers, performance leaders create an operating environment that can actually increase a seller's capacity and capabilities rather than increasing administrative burden and making him or her feel grossly underskilled. An aligned operating environment positions sales reps for success, optimizes the selling/buying experience, fulfills the customer promise, and ultimately provides a differentiated customer experience.

Analytics

As discussed in numerous chapters of this book, today's B2B selling environment requires a strong analytics capability. There is no shortage of data: data to determine historical indicators of performance, but also data that is used as leading indicators of performance, new hot leads, new trends, competitor activity, and gaps to fill in sales operations. In leading sales organizations, analytics-driven insights are drawn farther and deeper into the sales organization. Information is available and widely used throughout the selling network, including sales management, sales leads, and selling partners. When fully used by the entire sales operation, the analytics capability can serve as a primary differentiator among sales organizations.

There are many ways to organize the sales analytics capability, but regardless of how it is structured organizationally, the key is that sales analytics are forward-oriented and designed to push insights deep into the overall sales organization so that everyone who needs access to this capability can take advantage of it as a competitive edge. Ultimately, sales analytics should drive high-value and differentiated customer interactions. For that to happen, sellers and their managers need an unprecedented level of new analytic capabilities.

Unfortunately, many companies choose to dabble in analytics instead of actually committing to building strong analytics capabilities. But dabbling won't enable companies to harness the analytical horsepower they need, nor to build the analytical competencies required to compete successfully in the long term. Sales organizations that want to fully equip their sales reps with the tools they need to succeed consistently over time develop analytical capabilities that address the most complex customer situation—one in which there are multiple channels and entry points, and customers who are rapidly switching. By developing an analytical capability that provides customer insights in the most complex environment, the sales organization can optimize to function smoothly when responding to the diversity of customer situations they may encounter. Quite simply, the right insights at the right time in the right hands drives a differentiated customer experience.

Network, Collaborate, and Learn

Whether walking with a customer down the hall, preparing for an important presentation, or negotiating a contract, sellers need the right information at precisely the time they need it. There is nothing new about this concept, but in today's world where customers have direct and real-time access to many channels of information, the seller needs to keep ahead of the game. The information burden is not solely borne by sales reps. The need for advanced networking, collaboration, and learning capabilities is no longer a "nice to have" but a "need to have" for all sales organizations.

The effective sales organization uses mobile technology and social media to not only push communication from management, but also gather key customer insights from their sellers and improve networking and collaboration. Innovative sales curricula can deliver "on the spot" learning at precisely the right time and in small bits that are easy to absorb. Collaboration capabilities such as Smart Monitoring, video-conferencing, and internal collaboration tools like Chatter allow sellers to pull the right information in real time and to receive immediate coaching from experts in their network.

Microsoft embodies this approach through its Academy Mobile, a nimble and effective learning capability that helps the company's salespeople learn about new products, solutions, and sales techniques so they can respond faster to customer opportunities. Academy Mobile is a social learning solution that Microsoft developed to serve as an internal platform for employees to share knowledge and learn about successful sales techniques used by other salespeople in the field. The content is provided by product experts and sales staffers, and is harvested from conference calls, presentations, and third-party vendors, and turned into short podcasts and vodcasts. Virtual meetings are captured, catalogued, indexed, and converted for sharing via Academy Mobile. Content is ranked by users, enabling the best ideas to rise to the top because of their practical value.

The platform has proven extremely popular, used by 22,000 people inside Microsoft as well as another 5,000 partners in its distribution network. Users generate more than 500 podcasts each month. Besides helping sales staff get up to speed on new products, the Academy also serves as a communications channel for field sales and is available on workers' mobile devices.[3]

Sales Management

Sales managers are the key to "moving the middle." An exceptional sales manager makes average sales reps perform in an above-average way. Performance-leading sales managers have enhanced their own comfort level with data, analytical skills, and strategic thinking. At the same time, they effectively manage by inspiring and motivating the sales workforce to higher agility and "turn on a dime" by governing the flow of change to their sellers.

When building sales manager competency plans, a company should be aware that, according to Accenture's HPSFA research, the competencies of high-performance sales *managers* are vastly different from those for high-performance *sellers*. In addition, the competencies of high-performance sales managers vary from company to company just as they do for sales reps. Thus, the first step is to understand what "good looks like" for sales managers within the organization, just as for sales reps.

As companies place greater emphasis on developing sales managers who are solution-focused and effective sales coaches, they necessarily must align the role descriptions, performance management programs, and incentive plans to support this emphasis. In particular, a company must make sure that sales reps see a clear connection between the sales team's goals, their effort, and their incentives. Otherwise, motivation will suffer and incentive ROI will erode significantly.

A Car Company Accelerates Sales Performance through Customized Coaching

A leading German premium automobile manufacturer faced a challenging market undergoing major changes due to increased competition and price pressure, high customer expectations, low margins and profitability, and decreasing customer loyalty from well-informed clients who demanded quality service.

The company recognized that its dealers were fundamental to achieving sustainable and superior performance for both the dealer network and the manufacturer. Thus, it launched a new dealer qualification and coaching process, initially in Germany, the United Kingdom, France, Italy, Spain, and Japan, and later rolled out in markets globally. Although the program started with a focus on new car sales, the program has expanded to all dealer business areas, including used car sales, service and parts, and business management.

The company identifies leading practices from the top-performing dealers and conducts workshops between coaches and dealer's headquarters to share these observations. It then executes individual coaching based on tailor-made action plans for each dealer.

The company relies on fact-based analytics throughout the retail performance process. It selects the dealers to be involved in the coaching program through a Key Performance Indicator (KPI) Cockpit. It also conducts root cause analysis with health checks of respective business areas to provide insights on how to improve performance. This enables coaches, dealers, and area managers to identify weaknesses and work closely together on sustainable solutions by balancing target achievement, profitability, and customer satisfaction.

Through this process, the manufacturer is experiencing increased sales performance, enhanced customer satisfaction and loyalty, and improved operating margins. In addition, products and services are marketed worldwide in a consistent brand- and customer-focused manner.

How to Change: Putting the Building Blocks into Action

Rebuilding the talent model across the five building blocks can require extensive effort and change. The key to success is to implement a stepwise, coordinated approach aimed at creating real behavioral change across channels operations, sales operations, and the field sales organization. Following are the pragmatic, concrete steps to take to put the building blocks for the new B2B sales talent model in action:

- Define your "secret sauce" in the marketplace.
- Define your data and information governance.

- Build analytic capabilities—deep skills in the organization and basic skills in sellers.
- Define your competency model and how to develop competencies.
- Build a sales academy that delivers real-time performance enhancements.
- Define and segment your performance management system.

Define Your "Secret Sauce" in the Marketplace

Defining your secret sauce means, in essence, defining the precise target behaviors for sellers that will drive a customer experience that is unique for your company. Once you define these target behaviors, building the sales culture and the talent strategy to deliver these target behaviors is a unifying effort for sales operations and human resource (HR) sales support teams. So often, this "secret sauce" is muddled with 1,001 initiatives. Keep it simple. Keep it consistent. For example, we observed the following coaching given to one organization's sellers: "If you are not talking to a billion-dollar company with a million-dollar opportunity on the table, you are talking to the wrong person in the wrong company with the wrong opportunity." This type of clear direction was critical in driving new behaviors for sellers in this company.

Define Your Data and Information Governance

Data and information governance enables the right information to be presented at the right time to the right place. There are several factors that contribute to excellent data governance design. The first is having a clear understanding of the sales ecosystem, or how the sales force maps to product and services, channels, geographies, and the customer. Second, the business must define how and where into the sales organization it should push the power to make specific decisions. Note that the more data and decisions are decentralized to the field, the more segmented and tailored the customer experience is. However, decentralized decision making can also drive an inconsistent customer experience. Getting the right decisions made in the right place may require modifying organization structures and job design of channel operations, sales operations, and field sales reps. The third factor of data and information governance is to define who needs access to what data and in what time frame.

A parallel effort is to determine the structure of the analytics capability—such as centers of excellence, a federated or partially centralized model, or a central shared service—and the analytics roles that most efficiently support effective data governance. Using these role designs, a company can create the competency requirements and learning and development plans to build the desired sales analytics capabilities.

Build Analytic Capabilities—Deep Skills in the Organization and Basic Skills in Sellers

Building an analytic capability is not about hiring a person with a doctorate in macroeconomics. It's not about hiring an amazing spreadsheet jockey. There are unique talent development strategies for key roles in the analytics team including analytics leadership, professional model builders, business analysts, business specialists, and IT specialists. Analytics leaders are corporate leaders who drive and sustain an analytics agenda. Professional model builders develop innovative and value-driving analytics models and algorithms. Business analysts apply analytics techniques to relevant and current business problems. Business specialists put analytic outputs to work—driving that differentiated customer experience. IT specialists ensure that the necessary data is available in the appropriate format. And the sellers must easily consume and translate all this great analytic insight into a meaningful customer interaction.

In one example of "things done right," a health-care solutions provider can create a comprehensive customer record for use by its sales team. Prior to meeting with a health-care professional, the seller uses a "golden record" from data that is legally acceptable to aggregate to understand more about the health care professional such as which conferences he or she has attended recently, and attitudinal and behavioral segmentation, as well as information about his or her product use in the past four years. Having this knowledge improves the seller's productivity during the meeting and enhances his overall performance.

Define Your Competency Model and How to Develop Competencies

Sales competencies are getting more and more complex to support more complex selling environments. For example, influencing and driving a more complex solution sale requires different skills to identify and address the customer's implied and explicit needs. This far surpasses the old product sale based on describing features and functions. To develop the necessary competencies, performance leaders define the career framework, competency model, and development map for their channel and sales resources, including analytics capability as well as skills for influencing others. Determining the competencies of high-performance sellers can serve as the foundation for building competency models for both sales reps and their leadership. As the environment in which sellers operate is dynamic, great organizations frequently reassess competencies for high-performance selling.

Developing partners' competencies is even trickier and the need for simple, elegant learning solutions is even more important. Sales executives must build up their partners' skills to ensure that their company's brand is not only adequately represented but also competitively positioned in the marketplace. How much should a sales executive invest in partner learning programs? What learning delivery mechanisms get the highest ROI? Certainly e-learning is efficient, but does it drive target behaviors? The key here goes back to the "secret sauce": identifying key target behaviors and key competencies for partners, and then building a blended learning program that includes e-learning, content, podcasts, vodcasts, and coaching/performance monitoring will yield the greatest results.

Build a Sales Academy That Delivers Real-Time Performance Enhancements

To help the sales team absorb information in real time and move toward strong influence-based selling approaches, performance leaders are modifying their learning strategy for their sales professionals—and many are adopting an "academy" approach to learning. An academy approach should include a comprehensive and consistent role-based curriculum made available to learners across the sales ecosystem. Using an academy approach, learning is targeted to jobs and roles, and designed to fill specific needs and skills gaps. There is rigor to the curriculum, but properly designed, this approach can also be a way to improve relevance. An academy, for example, can provide content tightly aligned to specific competency models and job frameworks so that learning is tailored to real, relevant, and real-time performance needs. A segmented curriculum allows sellers to select the knowledge they need when they need it. As input to the training, sales managers identify where it makes sense to cross-skill individuals on products, services, and solutions.

New skills development should include an opportunity for field staff to practice new influence skills. There are performance simulator technologies that objectively and accurately analyze participants' target selling behaviors based on vocal qualities. This brings a quantum leap in the effectiveness of role-playing as key drivers of high performance. Driving target behaviors into sustainable habits is like spinning gold from straw.

In designing curricula, a guiding principle to follow is to provide clear, succinct, and evidence-based learning content to the point of need. Sellers will tell you what is valuable to them by adopting the behaviors they learn from training, but they have to see that the learning content is authentic, proven, and of genuine value. Otherwise, the training will get the typical high ratings and nothing changes in the field. Sellers must see that the training will help them have differentiated customer interactions.

For new curricula, companies should select delivery channels that fit each of their specific learning needs. Social media technology best suits rapid communication for the workforce and allows companies to network internally and externally (i.e., Chatter, Yammer, Twitter). Information hubs where employees can get the latest thinking on product and service trends, competitors, channel partners, and so on, are also a great feature. Learning threads is a collaborative way for sellers to interact with their networks.

As explored in Chapter 13, internal collaboration tools like Chatter (Salesforce.com) and Office Communicator (Microsoft) allow immediate collaboration and learning for the salesperson. For instance, if the salesperson is meeting with a prospect and can't answer a question, he or she can put the question to the company's experts and receive an immediate answer. The result is that the seller is educated and the customer interaction is now a more informed and productive meeting.

When considering how to train others not employed by the company (channel partners such as value-added resellers, distributors, brokers, and independent agents), an organization may want to consider inviting partners to use its sales academy so that training is consistent with its direct channels and customer experiences are equivalent. Partners could even subscribe to the academy services for their employees and help convert your cost center into a revenue source. However, in general, the simpler the approach and the more adaptable the vendor is to the partner's processes, the better.

Companies also should take into consideration if the channel partner represents multiple—and possibly competing—products, that partner has multiple companies wanting to take its resources out of the field for training. From a technology standpoint, partners have multiple portals they must master to receive virtual training and product information, as well as to log opportunities and orders. The simplicity of the message and the method of delivery are key to driving a differentiated customer experience. Generally speaking, the more the training is integrated into the partner's selling methodology, the more it helps the partner's understanding of what the solution provides and how to sell it.

For example, one technology value-added reseller (VAR) conducted a study of its return on investment from its various vendors' training approaches. The reseller put one group of its salespeople through generic (nonvendor-specific) training on storage technology. A second group did the storage training and sales methodology training. A third group did storage and sales training and the team manager over those resources went through all the training, plus training on how to do quality sales coaching on the material.

Next, the company looked at the historical performance of each salesperson and measured results for six months after the training. For group one—those who had only storage training—there was no difference in results. For the second group, there was a slight increase in sales. For the third group, which had both training resources and whose manager was trained, there was a substantial increase (almost three times the other group's increase).

As a result of the study, the company learned several lessons. First, it clearly validated that the sales manager is influential in the performance of the company's sales team. Second, it showed that most effective sales force learning is wrapped around existing processes with consistent messaging and methods to make resources accountable along the way. Kudos to this organization for taking a scientific approach to its learning strategy—clearly measuring the effectiveness from real results rather than simply asking how "happy" learners were with the program.

Define and Segment Your Performance Management System

Companies that define and segment their performance management system and compensation models encourage the target behaviors that are most critical to achieving a differentiated customer experience and attaining business goals.

In the "old world," performance management was all about quota attainment. In this "new world," sellers require motivation more like sales executives. It's still appropriate to provide a quota system with significant pay at risk based on attainment of the sales target. But they should also have a performance rating that has a number of components attached to it, such as:

- Adoption of new tools and driving value from new tools, processes, methodologies, and analytics/insights.
- Effective collaboration and networking, both internally and externally.
- Strategic objectives achieved, such as customer retention, or loyalty.

This does not mean that companies should create a complex motivation/incentive structure that confuses sellers or demotivates them. When significant pay is at risk, sellers will always figure out what directly correlates to maximum pay.

Conclusion

Sales organizations today are confronted with an increasingly complex and fast-evolving selling environment in which customers choose their preferred channel and desired customer experience. To succeed, sellers and their managers must demonstrate their agility in navigating this increasingly complex environment, and their ability to generate unique experiences that influence customers in a more complex and competitive landscape.

Companies that build new competencies, embrace analytics, develop new approaches to learning and information sharing, and increase collaboration with channel partners and customers, will likely reach their financial and strategic objectives. And they will also create a productive and fulfilling environment for their sales teams that helps them win in the never-ending battle for high-performance sales talent.

Notes

Chapter 1

1. Marketing executive research, Accenture, 2012.
2. "Unraveling Complexity in Products and Services," Knowledge@ Wharton and George Group, 2006. http://knowledge.wharton.upenn .edu/special_section.cfm?specialID=45
3. Ibid.
4. Thad Rueter, "Most Shoppers Go Online to Research Products Before Buying in Stores," *Internet Retailer*, March 30, 2012, www.internet retailer.com/2012/03/30/most-shoppers-go-online-research-products.
5. "The Value, Role and Performance of the Physical Retail Channel for Communications Service Companies," Accenture, 2010, www .accenture.com/us-en/Pages/insight-communications-retail-north-america-summary.aspx.
6. Target Corporation 2011 Annual Report, http://investors.target.com/ phoenix.zhtml?c=65828&p=irol-homeprofile.
7. Ann Zimmerman, "Showdown Over 'Showrooming,'" *Wall Street Journal*, January 23, 2012, http://online.wsj.com/article/SB100014240529702 04624204577177242516227440.html.
8. "The New Realities of 'Dating' in the Digital Age—Accenture Global Consumer Research Study," Accenture, 2012. www.accenture.com/Site CollectionDocuments/PDF/Accenture-Global-Consumer-Research-New-Realities.pdf
9. Ibid.
10. "Connecting the Dots on Sales Performance: Leveraging the 2012 Sales Performance Optimization Study to Inform Sales Effectiveness Initiatives," Accenture, 2012.

Chapter 2

1. Michael Lewis, *Moneyball: The Art of Winning an Unfair Game* (New York: W. W. Norton & Company, May 10, 2003).
2. Accenture Global Consumer Pulse Research, 2012.
3. "Fast Forward to Growth: Seizing Opportunities in High-Growth Markets," Accenture research report, 2012, www.accenture.com/us-en/Pages/insight-fast-forward-growth-seizing-opportunities-high-growth-markets.aspx.
4. Anthony O'Donnell, "Nationwide Offers Policyholders Free iPhone Claims App," *Insurance & Technology*, April 23, 2009, www.insurancetech.com/claims/217100056.
5. www.marketingmagazine.co.uk/news/1134857.
6. Chris Murphy, "Why P&G CIO Is Quadrupling Analytics Expertise," *Informationweek*, February 16, 2012, www.informationweek.com/global-cio/interviews/why-pg-cio-is-quadrupling-analytics-expe/232601003.
7. Ibid.
8. IDC, Worldwide SMB Update on IT Spending: Looking to the Rest of 2012 and Beyond, Doc #236576, Aug 2012.
9. "Fast Forward to Growth."
10. Ibid.
11. Ibid.
12. Ibid.
13. Ibid.
14. Ibid.

Chapter 3

1. "Connecting the Dots on Sales Performance: Leveraging the 2012 Sales Performance Optimization Study to Inform Sales Effectiveness Initiatives," Accenture, 2012.

Chapter 5

1. "Digital Channels—Reaching Doctors in China," Accenture research report, 2011, www.accenture.com/SiteCollectionDocuments/PDF/Accenture-Digital-Channels-Reaching-Doctors-in-China.pdf.

2. http://carinsurance.arrivealive.co.za/what-is-an-insurance-aggregator.php.

3. "Holism: Enabling High Performance Insurance Distribution," Accenture, 2011, www.accenture.com/us-en/Pages/insight-holism-enabling-high-performance-insurance-summary.aspx.

4. "Succeeding at Microinsurance through Differentiation, Innovation and Partnership," Accenture, 2012, www.accenture.com/SiteCollectionDocuments/PDF/Accenture-Microinsurance-PoV-01-12.pdf.

5. Ibid.

6. "Next Generation Partner Relationship Management (PRM)," Accenture, 2010. www.accenture.com/SiteCollectionDocuments/PDF/Accenture-Next-Generation-Partner-Management.pdf

7. www.sap.com/corporate-en/press.epx?pressID=7860.

Chapter 6

1. Lewis Carroll, *Through the Looking-Glass* (New York: Random House Special Edition, 1946; originally published 1871).

2. "Televerde B2B Marketing Study Highlights Automation Technology Adoption, Lead Generation Trends," *DemandGen Report*, March 23, 2012, www.demandgenreport.com/industry-topics/industry-news/1201-televerde-b2b-marketing-study-highlights-automation-technology-adoption-lead-generation-trends.html#.UA7OSHAXXyk.

Chapter 7

1. Business-to-Business Customer Experience Management Benchmarking Study, ClearAction LLC, © 2010.

2. "The Accenture Global Customer Preferences Study for Chemicals— The Call to Become Customer Smart," Accenture, 2010.

3. Business-to-Business Customer Experience Management Benchmarking Study, © 2010 by ClearAction LLC.

4. "Connecting the Dots on Sales Performance: Leveraging the 2012 Sales Performance Optimization Study to Inform Sales Effectiveness Initiatives," Accenture, 2012.

5. Naveen Jain and Varun Ratta, "Making Your Organization Customer Smart: Practical Strategies to Initiate Transformation," Accenture, 2012.

Chapter 8

1. Bob Okon, "New Center Promises to Keep Navistar Trucks Moving," *Herald News*, June 11, 2012, http://heraldnews.suntimes.com/photos/galleries/13122879–417/new-center-promises-to-keep-navistar-trucks-moving.html.

2. Patrick Dunne, "Dynamic Pricing Trend Sweeps Across Major League Baseball," *TicketNews*, February 22, 2012, www.ticketnews.com/news/Dynamic-pricing-trend-sweeps-across-Major-League-Baseball021 222303.

3. http://ge.com/products_services/finance_consumer.html.

4. http://en.wikipedia.org/wiki/Power_by_the_Hour.

5. Eric Savitz, "Netflix: Was the Subscription Price Change a Giant Mistake?" *Forbes*, September 15, 2011, www.forbes.com/sites/ericsavitz/2011/09/15/netflix-was-the-subscription-price-change-a-giant-mistake.

6. John Bacon, "From Netflix: Changes, An Apology but No Price Break," *USA Today*, September 19, 2011, http://content.usatoday.com/communities/ondeadline/post/2011/09/more-changes-at-netflix----and-an-apology/1.

Chapter 9

1. "Connecting the Dots on Sales Performance: Leveraging the 2012 Sales Performance Optimization Study to Inform Sales Effectiveness Initiatives," Accenture, 2012.

2. Eamon Javers, "New Big Brother: Market Moving Satellite Images'" CNBC, www.cnbc.com/id/38722872/, August 16, 2010.

3. Ibid.

4. Eamon Javers, "From Russia with Profits: Spy Pictures of Crops'" CNBC, www.cnbc.com/id/38738523/, August 17, 2010.

5. Ibid.

Chapter 10

1. "Boosting the Effectiveness of Sales Compensation," Accenture, 2012.

2. "Charting Your Course to Trade Promotion Optimization," Accenture and Promotion Optimization Institute survey, 2011.

3. "Connecting the Dots on Sales Performance: Leveraging the 2012 Sales Performance Optimization Study to Inform Sales Effectiveness Initiatives," Accenture, 2012.

4. "Charting Your Course to Trade Promotion Optimization," Accenture and Promotion Optimization Institute survey, 2011.

5. "Connecting the Dots on Sales Performance: Leveraging the 2012 Sales Performance Optimization Study to Inform Sales Effectiveness Initiatives," Accenture, 2012.

6. Ibid.

7. Ibid.

8. "Charting Your Course to Trade Promotion Optimization," Accenture and Promotion Optimization Institute survey, 2011.

Chapter 12

1. U.S. Census Data, 2007, www.census.gov/econ/smallbus.html, and Small Business Association, 2011, www.sba.gov/sites/default/files/sbfaq.pdf.

2. "IDC, Worldwide SMB Update on IT Spending: Looking to the Rest of 2012 and Beyond," Doc #236576, August, 2012.

3. Ohio State University and GE Capital research program, 2012, "National Center for Middle Market Research," www.bloomberg.com/apps/news?pid=conewsstory&tkr=GE:SW&sid=a83lfrCB6fOA.

4. www-03.ibm.com/innovation/us/engines/?ca=agus_splemmhom-20090701&me=print&met=engines&re=engines&S_TACT=USMMP606&cm_mmc=agus_splemmhom-20090701-USMMP606-_-p-_-engines-_-engines

5. http://news.xerox.com/pr/xerox/pagedoc/nr_XeroxSMBMarket_Fast Facts.pdf.

6. Ohio State University and GE Capital research program, 2012, "National Center for Middle Market Research," www.bloomberg.com/apps/news?pid=conewsstory&tkr=GE:SW&sid=a83lfrCB6fOA.

Chapter 13

1. "Connecting the Dots on Sales Performance: Leveraging the 2012 Sales Performance Optimization Study to Inform Sales Effectiveness Initiatives," Accenture, 2012.

2. Ibid.

3. Ibid.

4. Jason Falls, "Why Dell Is Still a Great Case Study," *Social Media Explorer*, December 13, 2011, www.socialmediaexplorer.com/social-media-marketing/why-dell-is-a-great-case-study.

5. Robert Wollan, et al., *The Social Media Management Handbook: Everything You Need To Know To Get Social Media Working In Your Business* (Hoboken, NJ: John Wiley & Sons, 2011).

6. www.highbeam.com/doc/1G1-207142496.html.

Chapter 14

1. http://worldpopulationreview.com/population-of-china-2012

2. "Urban–Rural Income Gap Narrowing in China," China Economic Net, October, 20, 2011 http://english.peopledaily.com.cn/90882/7622194.html.

3. Christian Requena, "The Art of Winning the Chinese Consumer: New Battlegrounds, Different Strategies," Accenture, 2012.

4. "Commerce Department and P&G Reach Agreement on the 'Village Market Project,'" China.com.cn, April 26, 2007.

5. "Masters of Rural Markets: The Hallmarks of High Performance," Accenture, 2010.

6. Christian Requena, "The Art of Winning the Chinese Consumer: New Battlegrounds, Different Strategies," "The Art of Winning Rural Consumers in China," Accenture, 2012.

7. Ibid.

8. "Rural Mobile Phone Penetration Rate of 90 Percent," research in China, June 2, 2011.

9. Christian Requena, "The Art of Winning the Chinese Consumer: New Battlegrounds, Different Strategies," "The Art of Winning Rural Consumers in China," Accenture, 2012.

10. "Consumer Products Trends in Emerging Markets," Accenture, 2011.

11. S. Mitram, "Nokia Expands After-Sales Reach," *Telegraph*, August 3, 2009.

12. Nasreen Seria, "Africa Boom Lures Investors as Growth Set to Double," *Bloomberg*, May 2010.

13. Ed Cropley, "Davos Special Report: Africa Rising," *Reuters*, January 2010.

14. Jerry Guo, "How Africa Is Becoming the New Asia," *Newsweek*, February 2010.

15. Johanna Mcgeary, "Africa Rising," *Time*, January 2010.

16. Worldbank Africa Development Indicators, 2010, as referenced in "The Dynamic African Consumer Market," by Grant Hatch, Pieter Becker, and Michelle van Zyl, Accenture, 2011, www.accenture.com/SiteCollection

Documents/Local_South_Africa/PDF/Accenture-The-Dynamic-African-Consumer-Market-Exploring-Growth-Opportunities-in-Sub-Saharan-Africa.pdf.

17. Standard Bank Group–Kenya SME Pilot, www.hks.harvard.edu/var/ezp_site/storage/fckeditor/file/pdfs/centers-programs/centers/cid/el/gem-2010/presentations/Standard_Bank_Group_SME_Pilot.pdf.

18. Jasson Nissa, "No Whitewash: Unilever's Drive to Dominate Africa," The UK Independent, August 31, 2003.

19. Grant Hatch, Pieter Becker, and Michelle van Zyl, "The Dynamic African Consumer Market," by Accenture, 2011.

20. Mats Thoren, "Distribution Is the Name of the Game," *Ericson Business Review*, February 2007.

21. EABL Annual Report, 2010.

22. Poplulation Reference Bureau, UN.org, 2010.

Chapter 15

1. "IT Operating Model Keeps Things Nimble: Creating a Global IT Operating Model that Fosters Agility and Innovation," Accenture, 2012; "Mind the Gap: Insights from Accenture's Third Global IT Performance Research," Accenture, 2010.

2. Drew Fitzgerald and Kristin Jones, "Salesforce to Acquire Buddy Media for as Much as $745 Million," *Wall Street Journal*, June 4, 2012. http://online.wsj.com/article/SB10001424052702303830204577446183312832146.html.

Chapter 16

1. GSMA, "Nilson Report, United Nation Department of Economic and Social Affairs," Accenture analysis, 2012.

2. *BusinessWeek* archives, "The Technology Payoff," posted on June 13, 1993.

3. "Connecting the Dots on Sales Performance: Leveraging the 2012 Sales Performance Optimization Study to Inform Sales Effectiveness Initiatives," Accenture, 2012.

4. "Always On. Always Connected. Keeping Up with Mobility," Accenture CIO Mobility Survey 2012, 7. www.accenture.com/us-en/Pages/insight-acn-cio-mobility-survey-2012-always-on-always-connected.aspx.

5. "Making Social Media Pay: Rethinking Social Media's Potential to Bolster B2B Interactions, Customer Loyalty, Revenues and Brand Reputation," Accenture, 2011.
6. Tammy Erickson, February 16, 2012, http://blogs.hbr.org/erickson/2012/02/why_we_use_social_media_in_our.html.

Chapter 17

1. http://newsroom.accenture.com/article_display.cfm?article_id=4935.

Chapter 18

1. "Connecting the Dots on Sales Performance: Leveraging the 2012 Sales Performance Optimization Study to Inform Sales Effectiveness Initiatives," Accenture, 2012.
2. Ibid.
3. "The Learning Enterprise," *Outlook Journal*, June 2012; "Creating an Agile Organization," *Outlook Journal*, October 2009.

Index

365